THIS FOR
REMEMBRANCE

THIS FOR REMEMBRANCE

The Autobiography of
ROSEMARY CLOONEY
An Irish-American Singer

by Rosemary Clooney
with Raymond Strait

ϙ⅋P
A Playboy Press Book

Playboy and Rabbit Head design are trademarks of Playboy, 919 North Michi-
gan Avenue, Chicago, Illinois 60611 (U.S.A.), reg. U.S. Pat., marca registrada,
marque déposée.

Trade distribution by Simon and Schuster
A Division of Gulf + Western Corporation
New York, New York 10020

Designed by Tere LoPrete

Library of Congress Cataloging in Publication Data

Clooney, Rosemary.
    This for remembrance.

    1. Clooney, Rosemary. 2. Singers—United States—
Biography. I. Strait, Raymond, joint author. II. Title.
ML420.C58A3   784'.092'4 [B]   77-13490
ISBN 0-671-16976-9

For my sister Betty, who lived all these days by my side— except for the last year, when she was in my heart.

Contents

Contents

OPHELIA: There's rosemary, that's for remembrance . . .
William Shakespeare, *Hamlet*, Act IV, Scene V.

Foreword

To me, Rosemary Clooney is a unique lady in many respects. She combines the ability to deliver a song with an unquenchable sense of humor.

Rosemary has never changed since the first day she came along. She sings any kind of a song—blues, rhythm, comedy, ballad, torch, soul—it doesn't matter. And she does them all well, with a wonderful tone.

But you always have the feeling that underneath whatever she's singing, she is amused and entertained by what she's doing.

More than that—to work with, and tour with, she's the most congenial person imaginable. I've never seen her out of sorts, temperamental, carping or in any way the kind of a performer who creates problems for other performers.

I guess she's what we, in the trade, generally call "a trouper." Her attitude is "Let's get to work. Let's get it done. Let's have some fun—and make it as good as we can."

Kathryn and I and the children are very close to Rosie and her children. It's a relationship that's very rewarding to both families, I feel. We get along well together. We have a lot of fun together.

I think her children are the nicest young people I know. Bright, cheerful, talented, agreeable, and very fond of their mother—as they should be.

Looking back over our long relationship, I have to smile. I'm reminded of all the good times we had together, the fun we had working with the musicians; the kidding, the needling, the ribbing, the laughs—in pictures, radio and television.

She's a great lady.

BING CROSBY
September 1977

THIS FOR
REMEMBRANCE

CHAPTER I

The Twilight

When a man walks out on a woman, it's sad. When the man is twenty-five and the woman is approaching her fortieth birthday, that's a disaster. I was that woman in 1968. My lover of two years was fifteen years my junior and his goodbye lit the fuse to a powder keg. I was also that powder keg. Like an atomic bomb, there had been so much compressed into my brain since childhood, I was ready to explode. Jay's exit was the catalyst that soon shoved me over the brink into mental chaos.

All the little neutrons and protons of life were out of control. Rosemary, who had always been told she was the strongest, was at the door of total collapse. By July I was in the psychiatric ward of Mount Sinai Hospital, so unable to cope I was reduced to scrubbing floors as therapy.

My long marriage to Jose Ferrer had ended, not once but twice. The two-year affair with Jay had been something I could hang on to. Something that was mine personally, not to be shared with anyone. Not even my five children. It wasn't out of shame that I was so selfish—I was never ashamed of our relationship. It was just that all my life I had been expected to share everything with everybody. This was a very personal love that belonged only to me.

It didn't matter that he was newly married when we met. His wife wasn't involved in my life, and from my point of view I was not involved in hers. I didn't want to hurt anybody, it was just a situation I wanted to perpetuate. But we weren't going anywhere. I didn't want to marry him. I couldn't see a twenty-five-year-old heading up a household that consisted of five children, three of them boys approaching their teens. It didn't fit into the scheme I had figured out for myself.

Nevertheless, if it couldn't go on forever, I didn't want to hear about it.

I was booked for a tour of the Far East beginning in early February. Jay would go with me, of course, because he was the drummer in my band. He lived in San Diego and we usually met at the Beach and Tennis Club in La Jolla. I would reserve an apartment for the night—rarely a weekend because of my responsibilities at home—and drive down to meet him.

It was the last week in January. From the moment I drove the car out of my driveway I had an ominous feeling that I couldn't explain to myself. In La Jolla I met Jay, and there was something about his kiss, his manner—he was so quiet. Something was wrong. We took a walk on the beach before dinner. I'd brought groceries along so I wouldn't spend precious time at the market when I could be with him. I fixed some kind of stew, something easy that I wouldn't have to watch very carefully. I put the burner on low simmer and we took a walk along the beach. The setting was gorgeous—sunset on a late winter afternoon. We walked, hand in hand, like young lovers, but his touch wasn't the same. There were butterflies in my stomach because I sensed the calm change in him.

Very little was said by either of us on the beach. I walked along, looking up at him from time to time, marveling at his handsome features, dark hair tousled by the ocean breeze. He was very tall, several inches over six feet. I thought of our times together. His tenderness. He was a combination of so many things, all the qualities of a true American musician: warm, compassionate, sensitive, very kind. And something which appealed to me greatly, that I'd never had enough of: He was marvelously verbal. He talked to me about love and wrote me long love letters, which I carried around and read and reread. Zsa Zsa Gabor once said that women fall in love with their ears because of the things that men say. How true that was and is of me.

And there was something terrifically exciting about having a twenty-five-year-old lover. Someone to look at you in your fortieth year and say, "Wow! I like you." That possibly is one of the great ego trips of the world, because it comes at a time when a woman needs it the most.

There was a feeling of warmth between us. The sense of security I felt in being wiser than this young man who made me feel so good—being able to introduce him to things. The great restaurants in New York where everybody looked and wondered who this handsome man was with Rosemary Clooney. Trips to the museum in Boston or being invited to colonial homes. I often sensed his wide-eyed gratitude and appreciation.

But there had been another side to our affair—the age difference. It was a troublesome thing. Not to him, to me. We often talked about it, and it was always I who brought up the subject. Not too long ago I'd asked him, "Doesn't it ever bother you that I'm so much older than you?"

"It's not that much," he smiled. "If I love you, what difference can it make?"

"A lot."

"Then why don't you think of me as thirty-five instead of twenty-five. Would that make you feel better—if you think thirty-five?"

"But the truth—the facts. How can I act like that doesn't exist?"

"Well, don't I talk thirty-five?"

"Yes."

"Don't I act thirty-five?"

"Yes, but you're not."

"Don't I make you happy in bed?"

"Oh, yes. Always."

"As though I had the experience of ten more years."

"Yes, but . . ."

It was my hang-up. Something that was always on my mind —especially when I was around my friends. I would watch very carefully for some hint that they noticed something was going on. I tried hard not to show it, which probably meant that everybody suspected something anyway.

When it came to money he had always been very considerate. He was not some gigolo that I was supporting, nothing like many of the men I saw with other Hollywood women who were my age and older trying to stay young with a kept stud. It was that consideration which so contrasted with the rest of my life. I had always been taken for granted by my family, both emotionally and financially. Rosemary will pick up the tab. I was the oldest. I could do it. I was strong. I could do all those things. Jay handled that differently. He took some of the responsibility off my shoulders, and I loved him for that.

As we walked along the beach I realized, but wouldn't accept, that I wanted to control Jay. I'd fantasized for so long about life. There was no reason not to keep on doing it.

During dinner Jay and I talked about small things—music, shows. I wouldn't allow the conversation to get too close to a serious subject. I didn't want to talk about our upcoming trip to the Far East because I was afraid.

We finished dinner while it was still light outside, and I can remember the last rays of sunshine striking the window, playing rainbow with the panes of glass. For a few seconds there was dead silence. Then he spoke: "I'm not going." Just like that. He didn't have to say going where. I knew what he was talking about.

Funny the tricks your mind plays on you at times of crisis. Before I said a word, the thought flashed through my mind, "My mother will be delighted." She had openly disapproved of our relationship, always reminding me that I was an Irish Catholic, as if the guilt wasn't just below the surface anyway.

"But the plans," I said, stung by his words. "It's the Far East, then home for a week, and then it's Germany, it's Spain, it's England, it's Brazil, Canada. Think of all the things to see and do. You can't just throw that all out the window that easily." I tried with all my being to sway him, even resorting desperately to the attractions of such an international tour.

He shook his head. "No, Rosie, it's no good. I'm not getting anywhere and neither are you." This was the thirty-five-year-old talking.

I appealed from another direction. "You know how much I need you." I knew he was terribly worried that I would overdose on barbiturates. The first year we had been together I hadn't taken many pills. But slowly I was taking more and more.

"You're strong, Rosie. You'll be all right. Besides, I'm going into therapy. I've got to get over this, and I can't do it alone. Whatever has to be done, I'll do it, but I've got to get my life going somewhere."

My reply must have hurt him. I said, "Anybody who needs that—that kind of help—who can't get things together in his own mind with his own self-will is weak."

Realizing I'd almost gone too far, I backed off. I had to think. To reason things out. We'd talk about it later. There was a sense of purpose on his part that was different, and gave me the feeling it was all over. The end. He wasn't argumentative. Just firm. I'm sure now that it was just as painful for him.

I had one of what would be a string of irrational ideas. I decided to seduce him. It had worked before. Why not now? Everybody knew you could get a man to promise anything in bed. It was woman's ultimate weapon.

We slept together. It was a tempestuous, stormy night. I tried to create hurricanes and earthquakes—to shake him back to his senses.

I awoke alone. He had left early. Alone in the apartment, shock insulating my real feelings, the feelings of total rejection, I began to get into my Scarlett O'Hara characterization. I spoke to myself as I faced the bathroom mirror: "I'll think about this tomorrow. I can't handle it right this very minute. But I can fix it. I'll take care of it tomorrow."

Certain that he would call me, I drove back to Beverly Hills. In less than a week I would be leaving for Tokyo. After two days and no call, I began to panic. I decided to pull out what I considered my "big guns." It wouldn't be proper, I told myself, to call him direct. But there was nothing wrong in having my manager contact him to find out what time he was getting into Los Angeles to leave for the trip. I handled it all as if I had nothing to do with his absence.

My manager called me later in the day and said, "Rosemary, did you know that he's not going?"

I acted surprised. "Of course not. Did he say why?"

"He said it was for personal reasons."

I thanked him and hung up.

I started a program of psyching myself up for the trip on which only my secretary, Ingrid, would accompany me. Of necessity she was aware of my romance. Secretaries have to know those things in order to protect you. She became the focal point of my babblings about the trip.

"We'll have fun," I told her. "It will be an exciting trip. It's going to be something special. We'll shop, see the sights, go to parties. Who needs a man? We'll be too busy for that."

Now I was in a hurry to leave, but before the time came I went on a wild shopping spree in Beverly Hills that continued for weeks through the Far East, Europe and South America.

Ingrid and I drove to the airport in a rented limo, got on the plane and looked toward the Land of the Rising Sun.

The entrepreneur, Tats Nagashima, met me at the airport and made me welcome in the fashion that only Orientals are capable of. I was treated like visiting royalty. Tats had lined up all my concerts. He was really a good friend and I'd worked for him before when I was in Japan. Educated in the United States, he spoke beautiful English, and was strikingly handsome.

From the beginning I complained. Room service was never quick enough. The makeup girl brought the wrong shade of makeup—nothing really to be upset about—and I blew up at her. I was fighting and bickering about work conditions—something I had never done throughout my career. I complained to Ingrid. "I'm not being paid proper attention when I'm onstage. All they do is talk when I sing."

It was a totally illegitimate gripe. In Japan it is the custom of the land to have hostesses who come and sit with the Japanese men in nightclubs. There's nothing wrong with it; it's an accepted practice. After sitting through the first show they're not especially interested in seeing it over and over again, so they become very talky. That's what they're supposed to do—sit and talk and entertain the gentlemen. But rejected (and every day becoming more self-centered) little Rosie felt slighted.

Every comfort was made available to me, but nothing was satisfactory. The hairstyle was all wrong. I picked on Suji, a darling little girl who did everything possible to be of help. If I had been all right, none of it would have bothered me.

I was also upset because I couldn't go to Vietnam to entertain as originally planned. It was the year of the Tet Offensive, and that began to aggravate the paranoia I was starting to exhibit. In my mind the Tet Offensive was partly designed to persecute me.

I know I was not as popular with the people at the club in Tokyo as I had been previously and when I arrived. My behavior was erratic at times, and nobody knew why. What Tats and the others did not know was that I was strung out on pills most of the time. I only took them at night, but the effects of barbiturates are long-lasting. Six Seconal capsules a night—a dose that would O.D. someone not accustomed to it—was normal for me. Also, in Japan it was easy to get other things, so I was taking tranquilizers along with my sleeping pills, which did not make me sleep.

Downers had a reverse effect on me. I didn't sleep—all I did was go, go, go. I went around jacked up all the time and I'm sure the fatigue and chemical changes had something to do with my surly attitude.

Alcohol was no problem. Never has been with me. I've been drunk several times in my life, but never a drinker. I might have a martini before dinner, or scotch on the rocks, but I wasn't interested in alcohol.

My wardrobe was not neglected, however. I found an original designer and added several thousand dollars' worth of dresses to my already bulging clothes closets. Not being able to sleep I spent my days in the shops—always looking for "things" but never sure what it was I wanted. When in doubt, spend. That was my motto, and I practiced it religiously.

One night after the show I was alone in my suite at the Hilton Hotel in Tokyo. It had not been an unhappy evening; I had been well received throughout the engagement. But I was bugged. Ingrid was avoiding my presence and my outbursts as much as she could. I rarely write handwritten letters. That night I sat down and wrote an eleven-pager to Tats, delineating all my imaginary slights and affronts.

Immediately upon receiving it, he came up to my suite, bewilderment etched into his honest and sincere face. "What is the matter, Rosemary? Have I offended you? If I have, I apologize. Please tell me what I have done and I will correct it."

"You've done nothing Tats. I think that's the problem. You've been avoiding me. I must have done something to you. Don't you like me? You know I wouldn't deliberately offend you."

No, I'd done nothing to him. But if I would just explain to him my complaints he would quickly remedy them. I couldn't give him any logical answers. My ramblings were unintelligible to him and he left my suite as mystified as he had been when he received my written diatribe.

How could I explain to him that I was feeling invisible? Feeling that nobody could hear me, that nobody saw me—except when I was onstage singing? I was like Robert Sterling from the old *Topper* series. I was dead. Just walking around among all these people and frustrated because I could see them and they couldn't see me. I related to them, but I felt they only related to me when I was onstage. I didn't want attention if that was the only place I could have it. I was tired of putting all my life and energy into singing time. If you cram too much energy into a space that small, it takes very little to detonate an explosion. I didn't know that then. That bit of enlightenment came later.

From time to time I would focus on my children, which was always a worry for me anyway. In Tokyo it became an obsession. Who had a right to deprive me of my children? I would call them on the phone, and the calls usually left me feeling even more alone. They assured me they were all right. In my mind it meant they didn't need me, they didn't care, I didn't matter to them.

My mother was at home with the kids and she would get on the phone with me. If I said I felt tired, or wasn't sleeping, or that working conditions were not good, I got her stock answer to everything. "Rosemary, you're strong. You're the oldest. You'll be all right." Even when she didn't say it in those words, I sensed that was what she meant. The irony of it all was that she wasn't strong either. I had to be strong for her, too. I had to be very careful about what I said to my mother because she would find in anything I said reason to accuse me of taking too many pills; I was afraid she might find some way to stop me from taking them. I always denied the truth, of course, but while she may have been wrong about a lot of things, she was right about that. I certainly didn't need the hundreds and thousands of downers that passed through my system over that span of troubled years.

Poor Ingrid. How I made that girl suffer. She had her own problems, her own ghosts to cope with. Born in Germany during World War II, she was the daughter of a man on Von Braun's rocket research team and was smuggled from the Russian-occupied sector of Germany to the American sector and then to America. Being manic-depressive I had to always be on the go, day and night, and Ingrid, of course, had to accompany me. I was dragging her around everywhere with me, and it was obvious that she was worn out. An unmarried girl who was devoting all her time to me when she should have been dating and having a good time. She was a good secretary, had been with me three years and was loyal beyond question, but she could take only so much of my bizarre nocturnal adventures. She was constantly having to explain my strange behavior, especially to people who had known me before when I was sane and rational.

Irritated when I couldn't find her, I upbraided her more and more without any real reason except my own personal hell that no one could have straightened out. I'd explain her to myself, as I did everybody else: "Well, of course. She's just like all the rest. Everybody else goes home to their own things and I'm left alone in a lousy hotel room. She's avoiding me."

And she was, but not for the reasons I had conjured up. Poor little "Blue Rose." Nobody loves me. Nobody wants me. I developed an attitude that projected like a giant billboard, saying, "Who do you think you're mistreating, buster? Do you know who *I* am?" My meaning was always more than just implied. I vacillated between being terribly sorry for myself and then terribly cross and demanding with people.

The one thing I never complained about was the bands. My backing was always good. Of course, onstage, by getting the attention I needed I felt accepted. The band was part of that.

Bangkok was the exact opposite to me of Tokyo. I thought it the most exciting, most intriguing, most gorgeous of any place I had ever visited in my life. It was a fairyland. Everything that a fantasy could give you for a sensual existence. I remember small boys, like cherubs, going ahead of me down the hotel hallways spraying perfume in my path; silk pillows scattered about the floors; exotic fruits that were prepared before I went to bed and put on a table for me. It was the other end of the spectrum for my famished and dehydrated ego.

With all that great attention I again didn't sleep and had an excuse for not sleeping. I was having a good time. I was happy, I told myself. I kept telling Ingrid, "This is the kind of treatment I should get. I'm a star." My ego was being saturated with this enormous fantasy trip. It was like giving candy to a diabetic.

Bangkok was and is known throughout the world for great beauty on the one hand and abject poverty on the other. People later asked me about my reaction to the poverty—what I thought of it in contrast to the opulence I had been exposed to. With a straight face I told them, "I wasn't aware of any poverty." And I wasn't. It wasn't bothering me, so I didn't see it.

I hadn't really thought about Jay, nor had I dated since I'd left America. In Bangkok I met a charming English newspaperman who took me out to dinner a few times. Nothing romantic really, just paying attention to me. We had great talks, or rather he talked great. I was gradually starting to lose touch with reality. It was the first time in my life that my conversation wasn't sprinkled—every other sentence—with anecdotes about my children. I was suddenly talking about great philosophical things. The injustice of the Vietnam War, for instance. If I could find something big enough to make me angry or concerned, then I wouldn't have to deal with myself. I needed a problem bigger than my own.

My spending spree continued in Bangkok. I bought dresses

in Tokyo, silk and diamonds in Bangkok. Just one more diamond would make everything all right. It would fix things. I would fix things. I was losing ground rapidly.

But time moves on, and so did Rosemary. I left Bangkok and its majesty by commercial airlines, landed in Manila and was taken by military aircraft north to Clark Field, where the hospital for Vietnam War casualties was located. I was met by a nurse—a major—and on the steps of the hospital she asked me, "How much can you take?"

I said, "I don't know." It had never occurred to me. "I don't know what I can take."

"All right," she answered, "we'll start off with ambulatory patients and work our way up. When you say you can't take any more, we'll end it there."

Ingrid had already backed off. She couldn't handle it. Too many bad memories from childhood. So I was facing it alone with the nurse. I never, during the tour of the wards, asked to stop, but I felt like it. I was overcome with a feeling of inadequacy, of not being able to do something more tangible. All I could think of was to take down addresses and telephone numbers of people to call when I got home. Mothers, wives, sweethearts—I filled little notebooks with those numbers. It was the only thing I could hook onto. And I kept my word. When I got home I contacted every single one of them, still feeling inadequate. How could I tell them anything? How could I convey the boy's real feelings.

I felt revulsion at Clark, but I swallowed it. Arms and legs missing I could handle all right, but there's no getting away from somebody without a face. You can't cover that up with a sheet. The shock of it brought reality into sharp focus for me and I remember thinking—or maybe I even said it to the nurse—"If they could see this back home, the war would be over tomorrow."

I almost got away completely from my personal involvement because of the wounded soldiers, so acute was the realism of what I was seeing. And I think that's something very strange

for somebody who is heading for the kind of breakdown I had.
My total objectivity of the moment involved hating the war
very much. These were not names in a newspaper, they were
human beings. I thought of the young people I knew: Jay—
and especially my three sons. A flash hit me. When I get home
I'll take the boys away somewhere. It doesn't matter where.
Just away.

What a contrast from Bangkok. I recall a young man who
seemed in terrible pain. I tried to talk to him, but he just seemed
to stare and glower as if wondering what the hell I was doing
there all in one piece. I couldn't wait to get out of the hospital
and away from anything that reminded me of it. I didn't even
wait for a plane back to Manila; I asked for a car and driver.
On the way into Manila I became quite fearful. It was the
paranoia of being in a strange place and expecting some nocturnal people to come out of the night and slash us up. I'd
heard stories of guerrilla activity in the hills. The driver didn't
help; he was the original maniac of the highways.

I had a couple of concerts to do in Manila and was popping
downers like crazy, trying to calm myself down. I imagined I
was running out of sleeping pills, so there was nothing to do
but load up on more of the same. And getting tranquilizers in
Manila was as easy as asking. You never really run out; you
just develop a sort of inner system that alerts you when you're
down to a six-months supply. You can always find a way to
get them. During the last few years of my pill-popping days,
when I was really into them strongly and they were taking
over my life, I'd go to a dinner party and couldn't wait to get
to the hostess's medicine cabinet. If there were any pills there,
I'd steal them.

My analyst later would tell me how I hurt myself with un-
necessary worry. Worry, he explained, was a total waste of
time. If you can do something about it, then you do it. If you
can't, then this niggling at your subconscious all the time is
totally destructive.

But that was later. Right now I was committing myself

to avoiding reality. Procrastination became a full-time occupation.

The Clark experience must have set me up because in Manila the bitchy, paranoid side of Rosemary popped out of my subconscious. I felt uncomfortable without some personal musician with me so I had asked for Paul Moer, a pianist, to join me. I needed someone to rehearse the band and someone I could work with who understood my arrangements. Paul was fantastic. He was dependable and one hell of a musician.

I was happy about that, so I resented the audience. I found superficial reasons. The orchestra was too far away from me in this beautiful club because I was spotted in the exact middle of the room and the orchestra was half a nightclub away from me on a bandstand. Having to complain about something, I griped because I was separated from the orchestra.

"I'm too far from the band," I told the promoter. "I'm used to having the band behind me." That had nothing to do with it. I could sing with the band in the next room if I could hear the music. This one, however, was a bit more legitimate than the excuses I usually had.

Buying up beaded dresses, pills and complaining took up most of my time offstage. I was losing weight, not eating, not sleeping and pretending to be very happy in front of the audience I was growing more and more to hate.

From Manila it was home for a week and then off to Germany. I did a very strange thing while in Los Angeles that week. Strange for me anyway. One day I got in my car and drove to San Diego. I didn't try to call Jay, just drove around the San Diego streets looking, hoping to find him somewhere, without success.

Ingrid, although so tired she was merely going through the motions, accompanied me to Germany. We went the polar route and landed in Frankfurt, but I wanted to stay in Weisbaden at the Naserhof Hotel, a lovely old establishment I was particularly fond of. I was carrying on this odyssey that I had

planned for the two of us—Jay and me—by myself. I was determined to have a good time.

My delusions of happiness were marred by the assassination
of Martin Luther King. I heard the news on Armed Forces Network at one of the bases. It was either just before or just after a
performance, because I would have otherwise been somewhere
else. I can vividly recall my feelings as I walked down the
streets of Weisbaden on one of my daily shopping sprees. Certain that everyone was blaming me specifically, because I was
an American, for Martin Luther King's death, I reacted to this
fantasy by putting them down in my own mind. How dare
they accuse me after they had murdered six million Jews during World War II without feeling one bit sorry for what they
had done? Can you imagine that line of reasoning? The anger
inside me had to find a way to surface, so I found myself a
whipping boy—the German people.

My attention span was becoming shorter and shorter. I was
becoming more and more isolated—no communication with
Jay, no communication with Joe. I began to feel that my children were avoiding communication with me. My immediate
past became something that happened in another lifetime.

I barely remember spending three days in Spain. I remember only the seven days I had off before my concerts in Brazil.
My commitments were all being filled. I was never late for a
performance, but it was like a treadmill, and I couldn't get off.
More and more things were beginning to fall in on top of me.

Spending my week off in London, I checked into Claridge's
where I'd lived with Joe when Miguel was a baby—where I'd
been pregnant with Gabriel. Yet I don't recall any nostalgia. I
did see old friends, though—Irene and Arthur Howard, Leslie
Howard's brother and sister. She had worked as an assistant
on one of Joe's pictures. Both of them perfectly marvelous
people. I had tea with them and I believe dinner one evening.
My manic state was taking over again. Everything was in high
gear . . . couldn't slow down. I was going so fast I'd have

eight or ten appointments in one day and be late for half of them, trying to keep up. My excuses were ridiculous when I wasn't on time.

My weeping spells were increasing. I wept over Martin Luther King. My conversation was filled with non sequiturs. I could see the bewilderment on people's faces but couldn't understand their problem. I made sense to me. It was a particularly bad time for me in London because there would be large spans of time when I wouldn't be able to remember what I'd done or where I'd been. I was very vocal, I know, about the war in Vietnam, but my part in discussions often made very little sense.

Fortunately the English accept eccentricities a little more easily than most people. As a matter of fact I had to do something really outlandish to get the attention I thought I needed and wasn't getting.

There was a publican I had met on the first trip I made to London with Joe. His name was Paddy Kennedy and he had a pub in Belgravia where all the Irish used to hang out. It was called The Star, and was open on Sunday mornings. Joe and I had visited there often when we were in London together. So I had to go see Paddy and all the expatriates, all the Irish actors who gathered there to drink and bemoan the fate of the auld sod.

I insisted that Paddy close up and take me to dinner. Paddy never left the club, but he made an exception, locking up the place and allowing the Irish to sit and stew on his doorstep until Rosemary decided it was time to come back. And we were late. The disgruntled Irish were furious with him and gave me long accusing glances. I couldn't have cared less what they thought.

Paddy had a men's pub upstairs where women really didn't go. But I went there and took a seat in the corner of the room all by myself, proceeding to get rip-roaring drunk. I started to cry. The more I cried, the angrier I got. Finally I said to myself, "What would really cause an uproar in this pub?" I decided to try something and see if I could do it.

With all the lustiness of my Irish lungs, I roared at the top of my voice: "Fuck the Irish!"

Well, my life wasn't worth two cents in that place. Those angry faces began to rise up from their places, reddened and massed like an ocean wave hitting the beach, starting in my direction. Out of nowhere Paddy's voiced boomed out, "The first person that lays a hand on 'er answers to me!"

The sea of angry faces was still there, but the tide ebbed. It was out of respect for—and fear of—Paddy, not Rosemary Clooney. I know Paddy was happy when, satisfied with my accomplishment, I called out, "Get me a cab, Paddy."

The following day I couldn't even remember the incident. It was much later when I was in analysis that I remembered this little bit of mayhem.

Ingrid couldn't take this craziness any longer and begged off from Rio. She was going home. I had a new reason for being angry. She was justified, though. She saw the crash coming and was tired of being dragged around by someone who was so damned manic. Although berating her for deserting me, I had no choice but to let her go.

Claridge's had sent up a young English girl to help me with some correspondence, so I asked her how she'd like to make the trip to South America with me. She was delighted. I don't think she had any idea what she was letting herself in for. My letter writing was increasing. I was sending letters to everybody, filled with unjustified complaints. I remember we went tourist class because I cashed in my first-class tickets and put more money with it so we both had tickets. On the one hand I was buying everything in sight, and on the other skimping on plane fares to save money. Totally illogical and erratic behavior for me.

As I started packing for Rio it suddenly occurred to me that I had shopped so much and collected so many things that I didn't have enough bags. The morning I left I remember gathering up all the stuff that wasn't packed and piling it into the top of a dress box. It was at my feet in the car that took us to the airport, besides which I must have had fifteen of those little Air France handbags cluttered about me.

That's the way I boarded the flight for Rio. The stewardesses stared at me in wonderment and I gave them hostile looks, waiting for them to dare to challenge me. They didn't. Nevertheless, as soon as we were airborne I wrote a bitingly critical letter to the president of Air France, a letter that rambled on without really pinpointing any specific complaint. Rosie was at her best, finding fault where none existed.

Instead of staying on the plane to São Paulo, which was my destination, I insisted on getting off at Rio. More anger. More frustration. And more criticism—until somebody discovered my error and arranged for us to be whisked over to São Paulo.

Then in São Paulo I hit a new high. The pendulum swung 180 degrees. Mania set in. Rosemary was very happy and excited—and not sleeping. Too much to do. São Paulo was exotically exciting, and Brazil was gorgeous, fantastically beautiful. I loved it. The concerts were great, and I was enthralled with all the beautiful nightclubs, where good music was always playing. I went to some fantastic parties where the press and photographers had a field day with me. I was witty. The quotes were sensational and I got a lot of press coverage. I look at the pictures now and am amazed that I looked so good when my mental condition was so bad.

But paranoia crept in, as always. The pills saw to that. I started questioning the promoters. I thought they were cheating me. I wanted to know how much money they were taking in, how many seats were available at the concerts and how many were sold. I got so upset about it that I called the American consul general, a marvelous man who helped me through that siege of insecurity. He was a poet and gave me a book of his poems. He was kindly and talked in a soft voice, always reassuring me.

He became a sort of temporary messiah to me. I was sure he had been sent by God and had all the answers to my problems; all I had to do was study his book of poetry. I began to find hidden messages in his poetry. I was finding directions that I should take, which I now realize was one of the terrible breaks in my personality. It was all very bizarre. I remember being awake quite early in the morning in São Paulo and seeing a strange light over the city. I'd seen something like that in Australia. The whole city was lavender. Shades of blue and lavender. I still don't know if that was caused by atmospherics or if it was a product of my own imagination, something I wanted to see, something that reflected my state of mind.

I shopped at Ipanema Beach, picking up things for the kids. I remember going to Copacabana Beach in front of my hotel and finding the man who sold cloth kites. I bought five— one for each of my children, all in different colors. These kites, along with an Irish Republic flag an expatriate had given me in London, became very important items to me. They had some meaning in my twisted mind.

Brazil ended for me in a swirl of parties, extreme highs and bottomless lows. The dark pages of insanity were being written on my mind, and I was so lost in the abyss that I couldn't have stopped the coming event with a locomotive's brakes.

Rosie was touching her last base in the game of sanity. Twilight was fading into night.

CHAPTER II

Black Night Descends

Arriving in New York from Brazil on Mother's Day, I first called my children. I wanted to talk to them. It never occurred to me to be concerned about my own mother. It was only being a mother myself, away from her children, that concerned me. The call left me in tears and depressed, I was so far away from them. I couldn't take this alone, so I called Godfrey Cambridge.

Godfrey had become very dear to me. In London I had appeared on the British equivalent of Johnny Carson's "Tonight Show," and Godfrey had been the only other American on the program. A very famous cricket player from the West Indies was on the show and used Martin Luther King's death as a reason to be anti-American. He talked heatedly of the way blacks are treated in America. I took it personally and started to cry; my sense of guilt had grown daily since leaving Germany.

Godfrey took this man's conversation and turned it around, making it a funny incident.

"You remember that English picture, *Zulu*?" he asked. "Not only were the Africans—the blacks—butchered, but they were so dumb they stood right in back of each other so that one spear could kill two of them at a time." He dealt with it in a manner that turned an ugly inference into a humorous affair. I felt better because he had in reality said, "Hey, the Americans aren't the only ones."

I wanted him to be my close friend, and he was. He sensed what was happening to me because he was a very sensitive man. After the breakdown and long road back, he and I talked and he told me he had seen what was happening.

In New York we had dinner together and he said, over our meal, "Rosie, you've been working too hard. This has been an uncommonly bad year for you. You've really got to have some time off."

The thought that someone gave a damn what happened to me brought me to tears.

"You see," he said, soothingly, "you're just awfully tired. Please get some rest—for me."

I'll never forget that dinner in the Oak Room of the Plaza.

I was supposed to catch a plane the following morning. I had concerts in Canada. I deliberately missed the plane. I purposely "overslept" and missed it. In my own time I phoned my lawyer, Lewis Boies, in Los Angeles. I was distraught and erratic. Pills had so completely taken over my life that I was having hangovers from the pills like any alcoholic does with booze. I was not only hung over, but genuinely pissed off because my youngest child was taking first communion and I was 3000 miles away on business.

Lewis flew into New York and hired a Lear Jet to fly me to Edmonton in time for the concert. He, too, knew something was wrong, but he wrote it off as fatigue, not mental disarrangement. His presence and the hired jet boosted my ego. I loved the flight because of the attention I was getting. Loved

somebody taking care of me. Loved getting where I was going
—and so fast. As a result of this stroking of my ego, my Cana-
dian concerts were supergood. At least the ones in Edmonton
pleased me.

But then I had a date in Calgary and was there for five days,
doing two shows a night. It was a huge hall and had no seats.
People just milled about, and when the show was on they'd
drift over to the bandstand and listen. Some of them. Others
talked right through my songs. That agitated me, but what
could I expect? It was a convention.

I met a doctor while I was there, and in our conversation
told him I was concerned about not having a yellow fever
inoculation. I'd just come from Brazil and was worried about
having to get a shot. The whole thing was so silly, but I wanted
some reassurance.

"You really needn't worry about it," he said. "I'm sure there
will be no problems." He was very nice to me and reassuring,
but I'd traveled so much that I hated being five days in one
place. It felt almost like inertia. I had to keep going. So I decided not to stay in Calgary. I'd been to Banff National Park
before and found it beautiful and peaceful. It was only 75 miles
from Calgary. That's where I'd spend my few days, where the
mountains were 12,000 feet high, where they still had snow in
May and where the season hadn't officially started, so there
were few people around.

The Banff Springs Hotel hadn't opened up for guests yet,
so I took rooms at The Rimrock, hiring a car to drive me to
Calgary every day—a 150-mile round trip every single day I
was there—just to be away from where I was working. An
enormous amount of money was spent just to appease that
thing inside me which kept moving, never sleeping.

My shows were not good because I was almost free-associating. If anyone looked at me in what I considered a strange
way, I'd cut the show short. I was singing all right—I think. I
never read any of the reviews so I don't know what they said
about me. Being busy and feeling very energetic, I assumed
everything was okay. If I was doing my job, then there should

be no problem. More important, nobody would say, "Hey, Rosemary—you're cracking up. You're turning into a loony." The most I ever got was, "You look tired. You need a rest." People on the outside must have been looking at me and thinking I was something out of an old silent movie. Running too fast. Jerking and lurching along at a totally unpredictable pace.

Someone touched me emotionally in Canada. There was a young man, a boy actually, who drove me back and forth between my work and my quarters. He gave me a small plaster buffalo one day and very tenderly and seriously said, "We're taking care of things that are unique and that can become extinct, so you've got to take care of yourself, just the way we've got to take care of and protect these animals. You are unique and you're destroying yourself."

This very simple and sweet boy was the only one who saw me objectively. He cushioned his words in loving and caring tones. I don't think the impact of what he said ever reached me, but the gesture did touch me. During the meal on the plane to Los Angeles I clutched the small buffalo in my hand, using only one hand to eat with. If people looked at me strangely, and I'm sure they did, they were wrong. And that became another object for my anger. It didn't matter what they thought. Who were they? Nobodies, that's who. I needed that buffalo next to me. It was tangible proof that somebody cared for me off the stage.

Arriving back in Los Angeles in time for my birthday (May 23), I started unpacking and giving the kids all the things I had collected for them along the way. There was no party for me. My party was seeing the excited expressions on their happy faces. I knew they loved having me home and having me with them. They were wonderful to me, and those moments were quite sane. It was a lot like Christmas, being in familiar surroundings with dear and loving faces that meant so much to me.

But such bliss did not hold my attention any longer than anything else. My timing mechanism speeded up. I had to do something to keep busy. That started me thinking about my career. "I'll have to deal with these people I work with," I told myself. "My manager, the record company, my lawyer. . . ." I got on the phone and requested their presence at my home on the night of my fortieth birthday.

In the meantime I had sent a cable to Bobby Kennedy who was a dear friend from the days of the 1960 presidential campaign of his brother, and said I would like to help out in the California primary which was coming up in June. He had been delighted, so I was looking forward to being involved in that, too.

Time seems to telescope because I did so much. I spent the afternoon of that day collecting photographs of myself from albums, drawers and folders. It was almost as if I had to have tangible evidence that I existed. I had them all around the living room—sad ones, happy ones, moody and bright ones. Just photographs everywhere of myself. I was losing touch so fast that I had to be reminded who I was. I'd look at those pictures as an artist appraises a painting from a respectable distance, saying, "That's me. Or is that me? Or is that really me over there?" I wasn't sure any more.

I looked about the room. It is a massive living room, the room in which George Gershwin composed "A Foggy Day in London Town," and his last song, "Our Love Is Here to Stay." I tried to figure out how I fit into George Gershwin's life. It was all so crazy, with no sense of timing or logic.

The professional men in my life arrived. Some sat on a couch on one side of the large rectangular low table, the others on a comparable couch on the other side. I paced nervously, appraising them, looking for flaws in them, seeking reasons to criticize them. I think there were five or six men there, but I can remember only Bill Loeb (my manager), Lewis Boies (my attorney), and Dick Pierce, head of Dot Records, where I enjoyed a very short relationship.

Standing there in the middle of the room I told myself, "With all these brains together in one place, they ought to be able to come up with something to make me happy." I wanted somebody to say, "Rosemary, it doesn't matter if you ever sing again. I like you anyway as a person." I wanted somebody to say, "It's okay. You've done an extraordinary job just to get from place to place."

But nobody said any of these things. Finally, the conversation turned to the amount of money I had spent on my most recent worldwide jaunt. Lewis, who has always been very understanding of me, said, "You've gone through thousands of dollars in a very short time, Rosie, and you have nothing to show for it. That's extraordinary. You just can't do that."

To myself I said, "That's what you think. I can do anything I want to do." But that started my shower of tears that went on throughout the night, intermittently, like midsummer rains on a hot muggy night in my hometown of Maysville, Kentucky. Just when it looked like things would clear up, another cloud would open up and dump its moist burden on the earth. I was duplicating that scene in my own way.

If they thought I was going off the deep end, they never said so. Looking around, I saw those same bewildered looks I'd been seeing on people's faces for months. I thought the whole world was about to jump off its axis.

In the middle of this totally unproductive assemblage the doorbell rang. It was one of the men from the Robert Kennedy campaign. He arrived with some tickets for the big gala that was to be held the next night in Los Angeles. I remember asking how the campaign was going and that he replied, "Very well."

Suddenly I was aware of being away from myself—out of my body actually—watching myself as I talked to this man about Bobby and the campaign. At the same time I was fantasizing about the men in the living room, telling myself how powerful I was to be able to command their presence and make them wait for me while I indulged myself in something very important like a presidential campaign. Why couldn't they see me as I really was? Why weren't they proud of the fact that I was bright and intelligent and interested in things other than singing.

All fantasy, of course. I had no idea what they were thinking, but the swings of the pendulum were getting closer and closer together. Within minutes I would alternate between euphoria and total depression. If I'd known anything at all about psychiatry or mental illness at the time, I'd have known something very wild was happening to me. But I didn't.

I don't think we resolved anything that night about my career, but I immediately threw myself into the closing days of the Bobby Kennedy campaign. Bobby asked me to hostess a rally for him in Oakland until he arrived, and I liked that idea. After all the traveling I'd just finished doing I said to myself, "What a good thing to do, I'll go to Oakland, do this thing and then fly to Hawaii to see my sister Gail."

In Oakland everything went beautifully. There was an aura of excitement about Bobby's campaign, and I was caught up in it. I remember once, though, questioning my being in Oakland. It was a very liberal-oriented community and I momentarily asked myself, "What am I doing here? This is not an easy place for my particular thing, my middle-of-the-road music. It would be better if they had two or three rock groups to keep everybody going. More in keeping with the times."

Nevertheless, I had no real apprehensions. I could not be touched by such mundane things. I was Rosemary the Great. I could not be hurt. I could not be stopped. I was flying. As a result of this attitude, everything went along great. I sang, introduced people and generally had a good time.

Bobby finally arrived with an awful lot of people. He came up on stage and the crowd roarded its approval. He leaned over and whispered in my ear, "Thank you for being here."

He made his speech, and then somebody screamed from the audience, "Sing a song!" Bobby couldn't sing at all. He was absolutely tone-deaf. He asked me to help him, and I remember John Glenn, Bobby and I sang "When Irish Eyes Are Smiling." Bobby was singing in my ear and it was absolutely monotonic, not one tone varied from the other. I got hysterical and started laughing. Bobby never knew why. He thought he was doing just fine. I had great love and affection for that man. I had great hope. . . .

When he left the stage I had a moment of fear—for him. He couldn't find a way through the curtain, and people had started swarming toward the stage. There was security, but not much. It frightened me that these people were coming so close and he was unable to get off stage. My conductor and his wife were there with me—Bobby and Paula Thompson—and Paula finally found a hole in the curtain and said, "Senator! This way." And she pulled it open so he could get through.

I went to San Francisco and the Fairmont Hotel where I'd worked just a year before with Jay when things were lovely. There were some haunting memories, and I sat down and wrote him a letter, just on impulse, and sent it to the musician's union. I don't know if he ever got it, but it was never returned to me.

In Hawaii I was absolutely excited. Still popping pills to the point where I no longer kept count. If I felt I needed them, then I took some. There was no shortage. I still had quite a stash from my trips abroad, where I'd loaded up on tranquilizers that could be bought across the counter. Celebrities are seldom if ever questioned about their medications at customs, and I was very clever. I had them spaced in small quantities throughout my luggage. You get to be very smart about such things. People who are really going insane are very shrewd and calculating.

Kennedy had become my cause—the cause bigger than myself. In Hawaii Bobby's campaign headquarters was practically nonexistent, and the people there questioned me about my interest in the campaign and the candidate since he wasn't there. In his absence they didn't feel there was a lot I could do. I was furious about that. My anger had a legitimate channel, and I became very vocal in expressing it.

But I went out with my sister and some friends and phoned

a disk jockey who was an old friend, and oddly enough, later at night I was listening to his program and he said, "I have a friend at the Royal Hawaiian Hotel and I wonder what she's doing in town." Then he played, for me, "Mrs. Robinson," and that hit me smack between the eyes. He was totally unaware of what he had done, but paranoia still had its tentacles around me. I wondered what he did know and how he found out. Who had told him about Jay?

Three days of the islands and I flew back to Los Angeles for the primary windup. I had loads of messages from the Kennedy people. They wanted to include me in a large group of celebrities joining Bobby's one-day whirlwind tour of San Diego, and his giant wind-up rally at the Ambassador Hotel in Los Angeles on election day.

The Kennedy people chartered two jets out of Los Angeles the day we went to San Diego. I did not go down on the same plane Bobby and Ethel went on. I think Andy Williams was in their party. It's hard to remember some of the others—Rosie Grier and Rafer Johnson were there. They had been with Bobby all along the way. Pat Morita, the comic, was with us, too. Pat, a brilliant performer, was adored by everybody. We talked on the plane. I think he sensed my problems, but certainly not the extent of them.

In any event we did the show in San Diego and waited for the candidate to arrive. He had shows going on all over town, and I was handling this particular one in an old Spanish Hotel whose name slips my mind. Before I ever got off the ground at the Burbank Airport I was acting like Rosie the nut. I had an El Dorado Cadillac which I drove over to Burbank to catch the plane. I was still spinning from the trip to Hawaii and charged up from three or four Seconals which I'd taken to slow me down. As you know by now, they had the exact opposite effect, so that by the time I got to the airport I was as high as any of the planes likely to take off that day.

Due at the airport at four o'clock, I left my home in Beverly Hills, just off Benedict Canyon, at 3:45 P.M. Not only was

I flying, but my Cadillac could have belonged to Batman that afternoon. I took back ways, short ways and roads that almost didn't exist. At precisely four o'clock I pulled up in front of the Burbank Terminal, parked the car, left the keys in it and the motor running, grabbed my little bag and bolted for the front entrance.

The porter yelled, "Hey, you can't leave your car here!"

"I just did," I said.

"But what am I supposed to do with it?"

I called over my shoulder just before the door closed behind me, "So sell it!"

Bobby Thompson was my conductor again in San Diego so my activities were well handled musically. I'd worn a red, white and blue outfit down on the plane and changed into an evening gown before the show. I was singing when Bobby and the troops came in, including Andy, Rosie and Rafer. When Bobby started speaking I was still on the stage with him. Just me and him alone up there. I don't know why, but I was. Maybe he asked me to stay, or maybe I insinuated myself on stage. That part of the scene is a total blur to me.

Someone had given Bobby a flower and he was holding it in his hand as he spoke—the thing he always said about some daring to dream and asking why, and ". . . I dare to dream and ask why not." His hand caught my attention because it was shaking while all of this was going on and I couldn't understand that. It's strange because when you lose touch with reality it's like looking through everything from the wrong end of a telescope—you concentrate almost on instinct, and instinctively you know what people are feeling in a strange, eerie sort of way. Your intuition seems to get sharper because reasoning power is not in the way. There's no sense of logic; you're operating from a totally subconscious control room with no manual control at all—and no governor to tell you, "That's silly. Don't be ridiculous. He's just tired, that's all." Consequently I read whatever I wanted into the things I saw or heard.

He finally finished his speech. My eyes zeroed in on the

shaking hand and flower. Security moved in and started getting things together. Bobby came over and grabbed my hand and said, "You come on my plane with me."

"But I've got to get Maria." (My daughter standing right in front of me.) We left the hotel in an open car. Bobby sat in the front seat between two men, Maria and I sat in the back seat, and Ethel was perched on the tonneau of the car, waving to people along the way to the airport. Rosie Grier and Rafer Johnson were riding on the front fenders as kind of outriders.

Ethel leaned over and said to me, "Bobby isn't feeling well, so he isn't going to sit up here." I had the feeling Bobby probably wouldn't carry San Diego, a natural Republican stronghold. That was confirmed in my mind when two burly motorcycle policemen pulled up alongside us and in a disapproving tone of voice one of them said to Ethel, "Get down off there and sit in the car. It's against the law to sit on the back of a car." They were very rude and it angered me. Ethel, lady that she is, thanked them and slipped down beside me in the seat. I realized then that she was very pregnant and was doing all of this with the car in motion. I'm sure she was worrying about Bobby, but all she'd said was that he didn't feel well.

We had a lot of press and celebrities on the plane back to Los Angeles. There were four seats in the forward part of the plane, just by the door, and the four of us—Bobby, Ethel, Maria and I—sat down in them. Freckles, Bobby's dog, was there and Maria was patting him. Bobby, who had a wonderful way with children, smiled at her and said, "Will you hang on to my coat for me?" I recall that she held on to his coat like it was a person—sort of hugging it. Bobby was tired and excused himself to take a nap. A section where you usually hang coats had been converted into a berth with curtains. Bobby climbed into it, pulled the curtains together and catnapped the short distance to Los Angeles.

The plane landed in the area reserved for charter planes at Los Angeles International Airport and everybody quickly scattered. I came down the steps of the plane with Maria, Ethel and Bobby, and I was saying something to Ethel when I felt somebody kiss me on the neck. I turned and it was Bobby with his infectious grin.

"Thanks, Rosemary. I'll see you tomorrow night. Right now I'm going to get some sleep."

Faced with a no-car, no-cab situation, I hopped a ride with the press people on their bus which was going to the Ambassador Hotel. It seemed like a good idea at the time. We walked into the Coconut Grove so Maria could have a bite to eat. I wasn't hungry. I was never hungry any more; those little pills certainly went a long way. Afterward we took a cab home, and somebody from the Democratic Committee brought my car home from Burbank.

The following day, June 4, was a Tuesday, and Election Day. I voted early and everything was fine. The air tingled with excitement. That night when I went down to the big Kennedy rally at the Ambassador, I took with me the people I knew who had worked so hard for Bobby—Bobby Thompson and Paula, Pat Morita and my children Miguel and Maria. I was sure it was a big night for the Irish, and to prove it I wore a new kelly green suit with green shoes. I had the insides of the coat covered with Kennedy buttons, so that I was flashing my credentials. I also had the little green voting stub pinned on my lapel and had made up my mind not to talk to anybody who hadn't voted.

It was quite late, past 10:30, when we arrived, and everybody was in a jubilant mood. Things were happening. A kid on a natural high from the momentum of the campaign was singing "This Land Is My Land," and somebody asked me to sing, too. I did, even though I had no music. I was caught up in the sense of purpose and the possibility that it was all going to happen right there that night. Bobby's winning was going to make Rosemary feel secure. Miguel found a friend about his age, and they were all over the hall having the time of their lives. Maria stayed near me because she was younger.

Somebody with a camera wanted a picture of Rosie Grier

and me together—the two Rosies that worked in the campaign. I thought, isn't that nice. Word came down that the candidate would be joining us soon, that he was going to win and would be making his victory speech.

Time gets a little fuzzy here. I mean there is a gap. I don't remember too much about his entrance into the hall and his speech. Yet, I recall telling someone what a good speech he made. Then the applause.

Stage right, off the stage, I was waiting with his sister Jean. Her husband, Steve Smith, was on the podium with Bobby. Bobby was supposed to come toward us, a path had been opened for him. But he took a different route, turning on his heel and going directly back from the podium. Seeing this, the crowd began to close the aisle and there was a tremendous crush. I remember being concerned about my children. I was perhaps two feet from the pantry door—with Maria, Miguel and Jean Smith—when I heard what I thought were flashbulbs popping. There was instant commotion ahead of me.

Things then dissolved into slow motion for me. It was all happening faster than my mind could comprehend. We were ground together by the mass of people around us, like spices in a grinder, trying to get with the rest of the Kennedy party. I clung to Miguel and Maria, trying to protect them from the crowd. I saw a woman come out of the pantry with her bloodied hands over her face. My mind kept saying, "No, you didn't see blood. It's your imagination." But the woman was totally hysterical. To my right, Jean Smith had managed to climb up on a chair, trying to get a better view of the inside of the pantry. Then the awful words, which swept through the Ambassador like a prairie fire on a windy day: "He's been shot! He's been shot!" Just a voice in the crowd, an anguished voice crying in the wind and the storm.

My hand flew to my mouth as I said, "Oh, my God! Not again! Not again!" Maternal instinct supersedes all else in times of crisis. I was blindly reaching to touch my two children. There was a television set to my left sitting on top of a table. I shoved Miguel and Maria under it, dropped to my knees beside them and began to say the rosary. I thought, "If I can keep them busy saying prayers they won't hear, won't see, won't know. . . ."

"Hail Mary, full of grace . . ."

Steve Smith's voice drowned my words with grimly realistic words of his own: "Is there a doctor in the house? Is there a doctor in the house?"

How many times had I heard comedians use that line in their routines? But this was no comedy. No joke.

Someone gripped my shoulder. I turned to find Bobby Thompson, his face ashen and filled with concern. "Rosemary, we've got to get out of here."

Mechanically I shook my head. "We can't leave while there's somebody running around with a gun. My kids . . ."

He was bending over, trying to get me up, and all he could say was, "We've got to leave. Got to get out."

I must have heeded his urging, because I next remember following him to an exit. The police later said that the hotel was sealed off, but that just wasn't true. I got out. We got out. Bob Thompson, his wife, my kids and I. So any number of people could have done the same thing.

On the outside I lost my sense of direction. I couldn't find the front of the Ambassador Hotel, and there were people screaming and people running in every direction like a crazy-quilt pattern. Sirens were wailing, all kinds of sirens. Police, ambulance. I couldn't understand why the policeman had smiled at me at the door. He was standing by the exit and I ran right past him on the way out, but he made no effort to stop me. He just smiled. Maybe he recognized me, I don't know. A celebrity can walk through things like that if they recognize you. If I had been the one who shot Bobby, I could have walked away into the night and nobody would have known the difference. But it made me wonder how many people got out of that "sealed" building.

I remember watching them put Bobby into the ambulance,

but I couldn't go where he was. My feet wouldn't move. I saw Ethel there at the ambulance. I heard somebody yell out, somebody close to the ambulance, "How was the security, Sam Yorty?" I thought that was odd. Mr. Yorty was the mayor of Los Angeles and he wasn't even there. I kept thinking, "People should be able to handle themselves better. What an insane thing to say."

Somehow Bobby Thompson got us all into his car, and in the midst of what can only be described as slow-motion bedlam, Bobby had the presence of mind to go in the opposite direction, where there was little traffic, and got off Wilshire Boulevard as quickly as he could.

"Turn on the radio," I said. "Turn on the news." Maria's head was on my shoulder. I put my arm around her as she cried softly. I remember there were white spots on my green suit from the salt in her tears that had dried there. Miguel was just terrified. He kept repeating, "I'm all right if you're all right, mama."

I said, "I'm all right, honey."

I made a deal with God in the car: If he would let Bobby live, I'd go to confession and take communion and go back to church. It was quite a concession on my part, because I hadn't been close to the church in a long time. It was a stupid thing for me to suggest. You don't make deals like that with God. Who was I to believe I was so important that I could religiously blackmail God?

Well, I'd call Father O'Reilly at Good Shepherd Church when I got home. Get back in touch with God—that was the thing I had to do. That would fix everything. God would make Bobby all right again. Things were going to be okay. I would put things back in their proper order.

I would do nothing of the sort.

CHAPTER III

Insanity

"Father O'Reilly," I said into the mouthpiece of the phone, "Robert Kennedy was shot tonight. I know it's late, but I had to call. I've got to see you in the morning. I must go to confession." It was after one in the morning, and I slept very little afterward, but at six o'clock I was through with my confession, attended mass and took communion. I'd propped myself up in front of the television all night, getting all the news about Bobby and catnapping during commercial breaks.

I hadn't seen or talked to Ethel Kennedy. She was at the hospital. My communication had been limited to Father O'Reilly and my immediate family. The television set became my constant companion for the next eighteen hours. Long, dreary, tiring hours of hope, despair and prayer. November of 1963 kept flashing in my mind as if they were showing a rerun on television of the assassination of John F. Kennedy. Seeing all of this imagined programming, I began to believe the networks were screening all of this exclusively for my benefit, to tell me something that nobody else knew. It was television one more time, looking in on my private life.

Then, in my mind, something happened. My mental processes did a complete, twisted flip-flop. Probably to protect myself from what had become impossible to live with, I said to my mother, who was watching television with me, "I know what's happening now. This is nothing more than a giant plot, and it's being perpetrated by the government of the United States to show us how little we appreciate what these great people do for us. It's nothing at all. Just an object lesson."

Mother looked at me strangely but said nothing, which only infuriated me.

"Don't you understand anything? Bobby Kennedy is not dead. It's a hoax. So none of this is true."

Bobby died shortly after 1:30 on the morning of June 6. Bobby died, and I laughed. When the news came on I said to anyone who might have been in my bedroom with me—and I honestly can't remember just who was there—"It's going over. Look at them." Well, I thought to myself, this will sure as hell shake up the apathetic people. This will make them appreciate something good in their lives. No more Vietnam War. No more young men getting killed. None of these horrible things that go on in the world. It takes this kind of object lesson to make people understand.

When Frank Mankiewicz made the death announcement I thought, How wonderful! Just wonderful! I remember my Aunt Chris was visiting us from Washington, and so she must have been with me along with my mother and children. My mother, I recall, always talking of my being strong, began to sob softly, "He's dead. He's dead."

All the time I kept saying, "No! No! You just don't see the truth. There are things you just don't know about." My family was staring at me with blank expressions on their faces. Oh, well, I thought, what the hell do they know about politics?

Carol Burnett, I decided, ought to turn on her television and watch this crap. She was a good friend of Bobby's. She'd certainly see what I was talking about. So I found her private number and called.

"Hello."

"Carol?"

"Yes. Who's this?"

"Rosemary."

"Oh, hi, Rosie."

"Are you watching television?"

"No, feeding the baby."

"Well," I said, punctuating each syllable for emphasis, "you better turn it on. It's the goddamnedest farce you've ever seen in your life."

"What do you mean?" she asked with puzzlement in her voice. She didn't know what I was talking about.

I had assumed she would know exactly what I was talking about. Her obvious bewilderment was disappointing, and I hung up without any further explanation, sure she would call me back later and agree with my analysis. But she didn't.

Then I heard that a young Jordanian had shot Bobby. Now I was absolutely sure that it was a plot, and that it was almost concocted for me personally. I don't know how I linked the two incidents, but I remembered several years before, when I had been playing at the Waldorf in New York, King Hussein had been a regular visitor to hear me sing. It got to be a joke with the waiters and the maître d' who would come up to me and ask, "Is your friend the king coming in tonight?"

The king and I became quite friendly from those visits—on which he was always accompanied by an older man who I'm sure must have been someone from the diplomatic corps or the State Department. Hussein had once written me a lovely letter and, remembering that, I immediately went rummaging through old papers and souvenirs in search of my private "evidence" that there was a hoax afoot.

My next stop was an urgent appointment to see Father O'Reilly. Arriving at the church with my letter clutched tightly to me, I confronted Father O'Reilly almost indignantly. "Look at this," I said, trembling with anger, "and tell me I'm imagining things."

He took the letter and slowly read it. I waited, impatient, until he finished. "You see," I said, not waiting for him to say anything at all, "this is not happening. It's not true. He's not dead. And I'll tell you why. This is the king of Jordan that wrote me this letter, and Sirhan is a Jordanian subject. King Hussein would not do a thing like that to me. So it's all a plot."

Dr. Monke, my psychiatrist, would eventually explain to me what was happening to cause my erratic behavior. I was like a mouse going through a maze, looking for an exit and taking all the wrong turns. My brain was short-circuited. The lights were going out.

Father O'Reilly, gentle man that he was, treated me with tenderness, but the facts were the facts. "Rosemary, what you think just isn't true. It isn't the real situation. Senator Kennedy is dead. You must understand that. I know he was your friend, and we all hate to lose those we love, but he has gone to be with God."

"Are you a part of it, too?" I asked. But of course, I thought. Why shouldn't he be? If everybody else was in on the farce, why not the Catholic Church? It figured.

When I got back home I was an impossible person, expressing my anger with curt remarks and slamming things around. For the first time I noticed my mother sort of flinched when I yelled something at her. That afternoon my doctor, Edwin Butler, showed up and suggested that I go into Saint John's Hospital for a rest. I knew my mother had called him. Everybody wanted to get Rosemary out of the way so she wouldn't be able to tell the world what was going on. I think at the time I felt somewhat triumphant that my mother feared me enough to want me out of the house. She had been staying out of my way ever since the night Bobby had been shot. She couldn't cope with me anymore. Nothing the doctors gave me would knock me out, and I was getting Demerol shots in doses you wouldn't believe. The problem was I was just too far gone. My system just wasn't accepting sedation anymore.

I had never, up until now, felt patronized by the people around me or by those I came in contact with. At Saint John's all of that changed. I felt patronized there. I felt I was being humored just to keep me quiet. I could have walked out anytime I wanted—I was in a private room, not the psychiatric ward—and to me it was foolish to be there. Visitors were prohibited—"Doctor's orders," the nurse said. "You're here for rest and you can't get rest with a room full of visitors." If my doctor knew what was wrong with me he never gave me any hints. I figured he was just going along with everybody else.

Hospitals were not part of my plans, so I was home in a couple of days watching the Bobby Kennedy funeral on television. Watching the funeral train I kept thinking this must be footage from the John F. Kennedy funeral. It never occurred to me that he had been flown to Washington. After it was all over I decided to call Ethel Kennedy in McLean, Virginia. All during our conversation I couldn't stop crying.

She sounded very courageous and strong. Very together. But then, she's a very together woman. Watching the funeral and talking to Ethel was the closest I came to believing that Bobby was dead. This lovely lady said to me, ignoring her own grief, "Rosie, you've got to remember that he was really happy because he got to spend the day before he died with you."

Her words hit me in a strange way. I was so touched that she said it—and then my head took over. I started talking to myself. I was doing a lot of that now. "Who are you to think that? To believe that? To believe that Bobby enjoyed being with you?" I told myself that Ethel was only saying that to spare my feelings. She was my friend. Therefore I just dismissed anything she said about Bobby not being with us anymore. I was operating on several levels, making up alternatives as though they were truths. I was rationalizing everything and closing my eyes to reality.

I had to get away. Maybe if I left Los Angeles I'd meet somebody who knew what was going on. Somebody who would say to me, "Rosemary, I'm going to take you to meet Bobby. He's all right. You'll see. He'll explain it all to you."

Work had escaped my frame of reference until Bill Loeb called to remind me that I was opening at Harold's Club in Reno on July 4. I couldn't even remember signing myself out of the hospital. How could I be expected to remember anything so trivial as work? It is only with a sense of vagueness that I remember packing for the trip. My bedroom was strewn with notes, long letters and bits of paper on which I had scrawled my irrational feelings. Just bits and pieces of paper. All the senseless scribblings of an irate fringe-area lunatic.

That would all be behind me. I had a mission to accomplish in Reno. In Reno everything would be all right.

Deciding to take my own car, I had to have company, so my Aunt Jean, to whom I was very close, went along with me. I also took my son Rafael and one of the children's teachers from the Catholic school, Rae Burnson, who was an excellent driver. The trip, as I remember it, was uneventful. I'd made up my mind not to mention my true feelings about Robert Kennedy's situation because people wouldn't allow me to speak the truth. I was now more sure than ever that it was some kind of punishment that I must endure. I must have done something terrible, and I'd just have to work it out. Better not to say anything, though, because people would only worry unnecessarily. They might even put me back in the hospital, and I didn't want that. Yet it remained in my mind. Like the tides, the situation would become acute, and then recede and I'd reach out toward normalcy. Each time the wave came in, it came closer.

Sherry Harrah, Bill Harrah's wife, recommended a place for me to live. It was a nice hotel with huge rooms opening out onto a large swimming pool. Once everyone was settled in I went over to the casino to my rehearsal. Something happened during rehearsal; my brain snapped and I began barking orders to everyone and making impossible demands. In the middle of one of my fanatical tirades, singer Jerry Vale came into the room, and that seemed to calm me down. I don't know where he was working, but he had the cover of a magazine with Robert Kennedy silhouetted against a sea of faces. He'd brought it, I think, to show me because I was Bobby's friend. I looked at it, and then at Jerry, and laughed what must have seemed to him a maniacal snigger. I said, "Isn't that the most foolish thing you've ever heard in your life?"

He looked at me in utter bewilderment and just walked away. What I'd meant was, "It isn't true." Somebody must know what I knew. Somebody must know he was alive besides me.

My opening went all right, I think. Nobody told me otherwise. "My people" were there—although I am not certain if they were there at the same time—Bill Loeb, my manager; and Lewis Boies, my attorney. I had my big guns just in case anything went wrong.

I recall a very hurtful incident. There was a group of young people who were opening the show, and I'd certainly not endeared myself to them. My temper had been vented on them as well as everybody else within earshot, and their reaction was to not like me very much. There was both an elevator and escalator in Harold's. One night coming out of the elevator, I heard one of the girls in the group comment about a picture of me encased in glass in the lobby to advertise my appearance. Several of them were gathered around the picture and one of them said, quite audibly, "That must have been taken about ten years ago."

They didn't know I was right behind them until I spoke up and said, "No, it was taken in February of this year." I'd caught them totally off guard, it was obvious to me they were embarrassed, and I enjoyed their embarrassment. How dare they demean me? I was the star of the show!

Time escapes me somewhat here again. I was behaving so weirdly. Nights I would roam about the building. I always seemed to find ways to get into the kitchen, where I poked around, into everything. I couldn't sit still. I was looking for something, but I wasn't sure what it was. Maybe I connected the kitchen with the pantry at the Hotel Ambassador in Los Angeles.

At times I would be so perfectly normal in my behavior and so lucid that people would hardly know they were talking to the same person. Some must have thought there were two Rosemary Clooneys. There *were* two—and several others that would pop up out of nowhere like jack-in-the-boxes.

Never a gambler, I was now gambling. I'm sure people often thought I was drunk at the tables because I looked and acted like a drunk. But alcohol wasn't doing it. It was the pills. Good old pills. Not drinking is probably the reason I'm here today. If I'd been chasing all that dope with booze, I would probably have been a stand-up DOA because I sure as hell wasn't getting any sleep.

In Reno I thought about suicide. It was the only time in my life that I ever entertained the idea that I could tempt the fates.

Things moved into high gear, and I remember them fuzzily. My scenes changed. People came and went. At one point Rafi returned to Los Angeles and my other son, Miguel, who was at the time, thirteen, was there with me. Aunt Jean had to go home to take care of her five children. God bless her, she put up with a lot because she loved me. I loved her too, and I still do. She has always been my second mother.

Miguel had a friend with him, Blaise Bellew, and I was reminded of Saint Blaise who was the Patron Saint of Throats. Throat blessed. My associations were wild.

These events were spread over a two-week engagement, and somewhere along the line I became paranoid about living in Reno. I decided I didn't like Reno anymore. I did my shows and went to the casino, where I gambled like a madwoman, which, of course, I was. As I said, I was never a gambler, but now I was gambling intensely—and winning. It was as if I had a touch of Midas in my soul. I was raking in enormous amounts of money. Ironically, this only strengthened my paranoia about

Reno. I thought, "If they're letting me win, it just shows that I am right about all this. They know I'm being persecuted, and they're giving me money to let me know I'm right. How stupid they are. Do they think they can buy me off?" Such was my thinking.

I had a friend who worked for Bill Harrah. I'd met him when I'd played Harold's Club in Tahoe. His name was Hans, and he had a motel in Tahoe, plus three or four houses behind the motel which were located right on the lake. When I decided to move out of Reno it was in one of Hans's houses that I took up residence, commuting daily back and forth to do my show in Reno, never missing a show but constantly being a bitch about everything because I had no sense of stability or security. Funny thing is, while I have a memory of living in Tahoe, I never really moved out of my hotel in Reno, and consequently was paying for accommodations both places. I was still spending money like an Arab on an oil junket—the difference being that I wasn't Arabian and couldn't afford expensive junkets. But I was Rosemary the Great and I defied anyone to challenge me. All I had to hear was "No, Rosemary" and I would overindulge myself with whatever the "no-no" was just for the sake of saying, "Go fuck yourself, buster. I can do anything I damned well want to."

I do remember that I had some of my things in both places. What I had done, from what bits and pieces of information I've been able to gather from people around me, was pile a lot of things into my car and take them to Tahoe. If I was missing anything, I would either go out and buy it new or drive back to Reno after it. Just anything to keep from lighting in one place for any length of time. Rosie had to be movin' on, and that's the way it was.

Two nights from that engagement are quite memorable.

It was my daily habit to make up a list of faults and complaints to submit to my manager, Bill Loeb, while we were in Reno. I was really going crazy. If he didn't make everything right, then I would write him little memos expressing my instant dislike for him. More than one time I told him I no longer needed his services. Five minutes later I wouldn't remember a damn thing about it.

After a particularly bad evening, when in my mind people weren't paying attention to me, I decided to lay it all on the line. Rosie was going to tell the world all about the Bobby Kennedy Hoax and all about her persecution at the hands of dozens of imaginary villains—including Bill Loeb and Harold Smith, who owned the casino.

On this particular night I'd taken my usual half-dozen Seconals after the show and, as anybody who has ever been a downer freak can tell you, I was flying higher than Ben Franklin's electrical kite, thanks to the reverse action I got and my total resistance to sleep. Well, Clooney wasn't going to let the world rest. She especially wasn't going to let Bill Loeb sleep when, in her mind, she was paying him to be at her beck and call twenty-four hours around the clock. How dare he sleep on her time?

You see, I was completely capable of stepping outside of myself and referring to myself in a minimum of two dimensions —often three or four. I got Bill on the telephone and our conversation went something like this:

"May I ask why you didn't answer on the first ring?"

The startled man's reply was, "Because it is after three o'clock in the morning and I was asleep."

"On whose orders?" I asked belligerently.

"On what?"

"Don't bullshit me, Bill. I want you on the job at all times." His bewilderment only incensed me further. If he didn't understand what I was talking about, then he must not be paying attention to what I was saying. "I want to call a press conference," I said in dictatorial tones.

"Fine. Call me in the morning and we'll set it up. Is there anything in particular you want to announce?"

He shouldn't have asked that.

"You're goddamned right there's something in particular I

want to announce, and I want you to get on the phone and get some people up here."

"Can't we do that in the morning, Rosemary?"

"We cannot. I want a press conference at six a.m. on the dot. Not one minute later. Do you understand me clearly?"

"I understand you, Rosemary, but I don't think you're going to get people out of bed on three hours' notice unless you've got something really devastating to say."

"Would you consider it devastating if I told you you were fired for inefficiency?"

By now he was fully awake and obviously trying to cope with the maniac on the other end of the line.

"What you should do, Rosemary, is take something so you can sleep."

My screech could be heard in San Francisco. "You are some kind of not so funny guy," I screamed into the phone. "Now you listen to me and you hear me good. I want a press conference at six in the morning and I want Frank Sinatra in attendance. You got that?"

"But, Rosemary, you know I can't get them—"

I'd heard all I wanted to hear. I had issued my ultimatum and I expected it to be carried out. I hung up without so much as a goodbye.

Bill, of course, ignored my erratic tirade, and by daylight had completely forgotten about any press conference. But I hadn't. I called the press conference. The woman who was handling publicity for Harold's Club suggested I hold the conference in one of the rooms in the club. I said, "No. This can't be associated with my work. It can't have any commercialized aspect to it." I wanted someplace completely away from Harold's.

There was a country club where everybody met about lunchtime. There were a lot of people there—a lot of press. Bill had gone on back to Los Angeles, so I was handling it on my own. The publicity girl tried to be helpful, but it was my show.

I was asked by one of the reporters what my message was. I said, "It's simply that I am retiring."

"You're kind of young to retire, aren't you, Miss Clooney?"

"I feel as though I've given as much as I can," I said. I kept myself to short sentences, hoping that someone would slip up and let me know that they knew about this hoax going on about Robert Kennedy. I looked for that slip so I could pounce on that and say, "This is the real reason I am retiring." Then people would have to realize what kind of man Bobby Kennedy was. They would have to come to their senses and realize that Robert Kennedy had to be the next president of the United States. I saw it all coming out at the press conference, vindicating my thinking. I thought how smart they all were not to be tripped up by me, because I was a clever lady with all the *real* answers.

Most of them asked some obligatory questions, took notes and started to leave. One man came up to me. He was the stringer for *Time* magazine.

I thought, "Aha! Another connection." *Time* had been nice to me always. I'd been on the cover of their magazine. So once again I made an immediate judgment, trying to reconnect my short circuits. *Time* was something I could identify with. Perhaps he wanted to tell me he knew the truth about Bobby.

He said, "You seem very unhappy. Is there something that is bothering you?"

I said, "It's Robert Kennedy's death."

"Oh, that's right. You are very close to the Kennedy family...."

For just a moment I sort of grasped the reality that Bobby was dead, and the whole interview ended in a shambles. I sobbed woefully, my mind leaving the scene ahead of me. I could no longer be understood, and he graciously said, "I'm sorry." The meeting—the press conference—was over, as was my short encounter with reality.

That night I was flying again. Demons lurked everywhere

—in corners, in the windows, in the audience. Particularly in the audience. I don't remember going on stage for the first show. The first thing I have any memory of was saying to the audience, "Why are you here? This is so unimportant, what I'm doing. You don't care about me. I'm not a monkey in a cage. I'm a person." About that time someone, hoping, I'm sure, to get me off whatever kick I was on, shouted out, "Hey, Rosemary, how about 'Come On-a My House'?"

"You see how stupid you all are? You ask a dumb question about a silly song."

The audience was stunned. My language may have been even more abusive. I don't know everything I said to them. But I had a few more words before my departure. "Come On-a My House" was my finale, and so I put my hands on my hips and said, "You want to hear the way 'Come On-a My House' really sounds without my voice on it?" I turned to the band and said, "Play it, gentlemen," and walked off stage. And they played without Rosemary Clooney.

In my dressing room I sat and I fumed. Nobody could approach me. I was like a hand grenade with the pin pulled. Nobody could tell whether it was a dud or the real thing, because one minute I could be completely sweet and kind, the next a raving monster. Or I could be on a super high, laughing and having fun, only to do a flip into total tearjerking depression. There were seldom any happy mediums.

The owner's son always sat in the front row of the club wearing some sort of white satin guru jacket. He was the last person in the world I needed to see backstage, although I guess he really was trying to be helpful. Anyway, he came back to my dressing room and brought a man with him.

"Rosemary," he said, "I think you better see a doctor, and I've brought a doctor from the audience to talk to you." From the tone of his voice I assumed he was implying that I was drunk. As I've said before, I didn't drink, but I acted like I did. I acted like I was on all kinds of drugs, but the only things

I was taking were the sleeping pills and tranquilizers. What I had was a chemical imbalance in my system, coupled with the ever-obvious fact that I was losing my mind—and rapidly.

The man represented to me as a doctor was as drunk as a lord—I could smell the booze across the room. It could only be a plot, I thought, and here I was, away from my home and people I knew. What would I do if he tried to get physical with me? Who would look after Rosemary? So I did the only think I knew to do—something I'd been doing for a long time.

I darted out of the dressing room like a streak of lightning before anybody could grab me. I was barefoot and wearing a simple little zip-up shift. It was between shows, but I couldn't have cared less about the second show. This man could have been Frankenstein as far as I was concerned.

I ran down the up escalator in my bare feet, trying to get downstairs on a treadmill that was going in the opposite direction. The whole thing was like a drug-induced dream, but I finally reached the street. Wearing nothing but the skimpy dress, with no purse, no identification of any kind—nothing—I grabbed the first cab and went to the hotel in Reno where I still had a suite. I have no idea who, if anybody, paid the cabdriver, but once in my bedroom, where there were still a lot of my things, my rage took over completely. I tore the room apart. I threw things. Broke things. Ripped expensive dresses to shreds.

I have a faint recollection that Miguel was still in Reno with me, but no idea at all where he was while I was on this rampage —I just know he was not with me. The poor kid would have been frightened to death seeing his mother turn into a raving lunatic. How any of my children coped with me is a credit to something either their father or I (in my saner days) had instilled in them. God bless them, they were wonderful to me.

My car was there and so were the keys. Alone, I got into the car and decided I'd take the old Mount Rose Road to Lake Tahoe. That road isn't used often because there is a much more direct newer one, but Mount Rose—a winding, twisting, two-lane highway—suited my mood. As I drove along toward the mountainous highway I said out loud to the open countryside, "If I'm supposed to live, I'm going to test myself. I'm going to test God and find out if he really loves me. If it is in the stars that I'm to live, then God will let me drive on the wrong side of the road all the way up to Lake Tahoe and I won't die. If God really loves me, I won't die."

Thus I began my Russian-roulette, death-wish drive up the mountain I had set out to conquer or be conquered by. I stayed on the wrong side of the road all the way. I remember seeing headlights ahead, like shooting stars heading right toward me and then veering away in a swoosh at the last second. I recall grinning crazily and saying, "That's one for you, God." It was like saying the little verse we used to say when we picked the petals off a daisy when I was a little girl—"He loves me, he loves me not. . . ."

How long the ride over the mountain took, I have no idea. Did anybody miss me? Probably. I didn't care. There wasn't anybody in the world but me. God was out there somewhere tuning in on one of his little lost sheep. As I pulled into Tahoe, I remember thinking, "If God loves me so much, then how can so many people be against me?" I felt invincible. Not once did I ever think of innocent people in the oncoming cars. That wasn't my problem—it was theirs. The only thing I could think of was God's plan for me to live or to die. It was the closest I ever came to suicide.

Rafi, my smallest son, was at Tahoe at the house I rented from Hans. I remember that Shecky Greene, that great comedian, was playing at the Lake, and he came over to the house to see me. I was in bed, exhausted, exhilarated and wide awake. Somebody must have told him what had happened in Reno, because he promised to go do my show for me. I'm sure he saw the state I was in, because he took Rafael back with him to his hotel. I remember Rafi telling me later that they watched a football game together on television.

I will never forget Shecky for that. He's a remarkably kind, gentle man—in fact one of the few comics I've ever known who is truly a kind man. Ironically, there is usually another side to comedians—a streak of cruelty offstage. This never applied to Shecky, a rare human being.

My brink of despair was rushing up to meet me like the end of the runway for a plane lumbering in vain to get off the ground. The time sequence of the events that followed is uncertain. It may have been the same day, that night or another day, because time was slipping rapidly away. Day and night ceased to register with me; there was nothing but right this instant. I remember an ambulance coming to the house for me. The only person with me was Rae Burnson, who never left me for a moment. I appreciate that from the bottom my heart. I was certainly in no shape to be alone.

I have a vivid recollection of being quite paranoid about the ambulance, thinking that it had to do with the doctor whom Harold, Jr., had brought to examine me. The attendants brought the stretcher into my bedroom, and I seemed willing to do as they said, but I began to panic when they put restraining straps on me. I had my purse, so timewise it must have been at least the next day because I had left it at the club in Reno. I begged them not to put the straps on me, and I kept telling myself, "They don't hear me. They just can't hear me. Maybe I've lost my voice."

I felt I was being forced to go, and when I was placed in the ambulance and the doors shut me into that small space, I freaked out. I kept saying I couldn't breathe, and one of the attendants opened a sliding window panel above my head. I think the restraining straps were right at my elbows so I was able to move my lower arms. I had my purse clutched on my stomach in both hands, and with the window opened I managed to get my wallet out of the purse and toss it out the window, hoping somebody would find it and know I was being kidnapped and taken to God only knew where.

"God-only-knows-where" was a small hospital on the south shore of the lake. It was in a beautiful setting of trees—groves of trees—and very pretty, but I still felt I was being held prisoner. Once inside I was given a tremendous shot—the needle looked like they'd borrowed it from the horse veterinarian. I slept right away, but not for long—probably no longer than an hour. I woke up in a strange room alone without any restraints. I guess nobody expected me to wake up so soon.

I got out of bed and started to wander around; finally I found myself in front of the baby nursery, just staring blankly at the little babies in their cribs. I saw a door which I thought was to the baby nursery, but when I opened it and went in I found myself in a stock room where they kept diapers and little baby things. My mind said, "You've been tricked!" I went into another rage and started throwing everything I could lay my hands on out into the halls. Don't ask why —I don't know. I do know that it took several people to subdue me and I was given another shot, which didn't work. I just fought so hard against it.

My next memory is of being in a waiting room. Just sitting there, numb. Miss Burnson was there, and my lawyer was on his way up to Reno with an air ambulance. Everybody was there except Rosemary. My body was there but my mind had long since gone away by itself.

The medication finally caught up with me. I had exhausted whatever strength I had left in the nursery linen closet. I fell asleep in the waiting room. Events took place without my knowledge. I vaguely remember being put aboard the hospital plane, but numbness again overtook me and I slept.

When I woke up I was in Saint John's hospital in Santa Monica—again. This time I was in a part of the hospital I'd never seen before. I'd given birth to five babies in that hospital, but I had never seen this section, not even when I was in for "rest." It was somewhere away from anybody else, where they had double locks for violent cases. I was a violent case in a violent ward.

But I slept. All those months and years of not being able to sleep came crashing down on me and I slept.

The first thing I noticed when consciousness finally returned was that I had never been in a room at Saint John's that didn't have a crucifix in it, but back here, where you really needed it, there wasn't one. Isolated away from the world, I needed and wanted God.

Dr. Butler had called in a psychiatrist for me. I can't remember his name but he was a man that Howard Hughes had retained for a certain amount of money who later sued Mr. Hughes for nonpayment. Funny how you remember gossip.

He might have been a good doctor for Howard Hughes, but I don't think he was a good doctor for me. He came to see me in "crazy flats," and it was just that! All the scabs on the face of society were hidden away there. People were screaming and moaning throughout the ward. You could hear vomiting and retching and angry, violently foul language that would make a sailor squirm.

There were things going on I'd never seen or heard before, and having a stranger as my doctor only added to my total confusion. I was alone, pretty well out of it, too. One of the big injections I'd been given at Lake Tahoe had left a terrible bruise on my arm. That splotch on my arm became kind of a stigmata. I couldn't remember how it got there, I just recall looking down and thinking that God must have given that to me as some kind of sign.

I kept on looking at the colors of the bruise, which was really big—about five inches across. There were greens and yellows and blues—very dark blues. All of a sudden it started taking on a substance of its own like a relief map. Yes, it turned into a kind of relief map in my sick mind, and the dark splotches took on the character of rugged mountains. The world of mental collapse is a strangely disconnected place. I didn't recognize my craziness. It seemed logical enough to me. When you're that far into the world of the damned, you have no more judgment. That's all gone. Life is really quite simple when you're relieved of the mental processes.

Remember, I spoke of the shrewdness that comes with this

kind of mental illness. Sometimes it cuts through all the extra baggage and lets you get right to what's going on, what's going to work for you. You develop a sense of what people want you to say, and you say it.

While I was on that ward they had restraints on me, and I begged the male nurse on the ward to please take them off because I couldn't stand the confinement. He was really nice to me, and I convinced him I wasn't going to become violent. Being tied down gave me a feeling of claustrophobia. I had called out for somebody to come and help me so many times that I had lost my voice. I was mouthing the words, but nothing came out. There was no sound. I'm sure that guy was happy when I lost my voice. It was the first time I'd let him have any rest.

Getting rid of those restraints gave me an idea. If I could talk my way out of those straps, then I could talk my way out of my confinement. In order to get out of the locked ward in Saint John's I would have to say what they wanted to hear—right or wrong, true or false. That's where a certain sensitivity, a feeling for what people wanted from me, began to come into play. It's like a prisoner going before the parole board. He knows that to get out he's got to say what they want to hear, and so that's what he says.

Rosemary was picking up some "stir lingo." It worked. I got out of my cage and was not sleeping in a room with a lock on it, although there was that double door with the double lock that kept us all separated from sane society. I could wander about the entire ward, though, and I did. The rooms were very nice, very pretty. There was an occupational-therapy room, but nobody insisted that you go. I liked to look in and see what the other inmates were doing, but I didn't partake of anything myself. I had ambivalent feelings about the other patients. On the one hand I felt very close to them, and yet I could not associate them with anything that had any meaning to me. I was still harboring the idea that I was a prisoner of the Bobby Kennedy Hoax.

It wasn't very much like your usual nut house. They didn't take everything away from you, only things you might hurt yourself with. As a matter of fact it was more like a country club for the wealthy wacky, if you could ignore the fact that you were in a locked ward with attendants guarding you.

I was moved into a pleasant room that reminded me of a nice motel room. It never occurred to me that the purple, green and blue colors that decorated the place were there for the purpose of subduing the more aggressive patients. I made that discovery after I reentered the world of *sane* society.

The doctor finally took enough time with me so that I could pull my best con job on him. We had a nice conversation—actually I talked and he listened. He would ask questions and I would answer the way I thought he wanted me to answer. I wanted out.

"Doctor," I finally said, with all the humility of a dispossessed tenant begging not to be set out on the streets, "I've got to go home. My children need me and there's nothing you can do for me here that can't be done at home."

I was given, and I assume passed, a Rorschach test. I remember saying to the psychologist who gave it to me, "In the movies they always have these in black and white, and now they're in color. Isn't that amazing?" He nodded, and I wondered if I'd said the wrong thing. Obviously not, because the doctor assented to my going home.

"You'll have to have an around-the-clock nurse with you, Rosemary—for a while anyway."

I didn't care if I had a ward full of nurses as long as I could go home. I was getting depressed again, and my depressions led to violent reactions. Later I found out that my mother had insisted on a nurse. She feared I might become violent when there was nobody at home except the two of us, and she was afraid she couldn't handle me. I sensed her fear when I got home. I gloried in that. Of course I did. I loved it. I really loved the fear in her eyes, because for the first time in my life I had some power over her. It was strange, that feeling of power, because my mother was possibly the most successfully manipulative person I've ever known. She had always done it with me, both as a kid and as an adult. Never was she loud, and never insisting, but it always ended up the way mother wanted it. Not this time, though. I was really busting out. I was cutting the cord whether she wanted it or not. I was cutting loose and letting my mother drift in her own direction. I would go my own way—I thought.

My nurse was sympathetic and understanding and didn't really get in my way. But she never left me alone. I tried to pick up some of my old routines, like walking. I've always enjoyed a nice walk in the afternoon, so nurse and I would go out for walks. I wasn't violent anymore. Nurse, dressed in her white, starchy outfit, took me for my walks like somebody giving their pet poodle its daily exercise. I'm sure everybody in the neighborhood was peeping out from behind their curtains and thinking, There goes crazy Clooney and her keeper.

But none of that bothered me then. I didn't know. I was like a little baby. I had accepted the nurse as my keeper, although my explanation to myself for her being around was the same as always. Paranoia had so completely taken over that I thought this was all a plot against me and I would overcome it; I would discover the real reasons for my being a prisoner, and was certain that one of those reasons was the fact that I was one of the very few people who knew that Bobby Kennedy was still alive.

Whereupon I made a pact with myself. I'd go along with all the nonsense in order not to be locked up again. If they locked me up, then I couldn't prove to anybody that I was right and the rest of the world was full of it.

I have a cousin Phyllis, my Aunt Rose's daughter, with whom I have always been very close. She is married to Dr. Sherman Holvey, a brilliant doctor and a brilliant man. Sherm was probably the first person in my family who really was aware that something was not normal about me. That I was not just "tired." I had seen him before I went on the European tour, after the South Pacific and Far Eastern nightmare. He had sensed something then, but he and Phyllis had gone away for a vacation so they weren't around when my mental faculties began to tilt radically. After they returned they came to see me, and I know he must have been appalled at what he saw in my behavior. He came up to my bedroom and talked to me for a long time, but I have no memory even today of his visit.

The impact on him was so great that he called my mother and rest of my family together to discuss what he knew must ultimately be the confinement of a badly deranged Rosemary. My mother had no idea what to do. She had trouble just trying to stay out of my way. I think Sherm more or less took over and did what he knew he had to do.

He said to my mother, "There's only one doctor I know of who can help her. That's Dr. J. Victor Monke. She's got to see him now. We'll get him on the phone. There is no time to waste because she's already living in the twilight zone. It's got to be done now because she's not benefiting at all from the treatment she's currently getting."

My Aunt Jean was also there, and together the family had to make the judgment. Should I be locked up in order to help me—and to protect my family from me? Sherm was very wise in his explanations to the children, telling them of my condition in terms they could understand.

Dr. Monke, based upon Sherman's appraisal of my condition, refused to come to my house to see me, and he didn't think I was in any condition to visit him at his office. There was only one way he would accommodate me and that was if I signed myself into the psychiatric ward at Mount Sinai Hospital. I don't think Dr. Monke would have even bothered with me if Sherm hadn't interceded, because his patients were few and he was totally involved in lecturing and teaching. He was not at all the sort whose ego would be boosted by having a celebrity on the ward. He was a man dedicated to the service of the mentally ill. He had founded the psychiatric facility at

Mount Sinai, which is one of the best in the country if not the world.

Sherman came up to my room and put it bluntly on the line to me. "Rosemary, you need help and you need it badly."

"Everybody needs help. I'm not going to be locked up again, so forget it."

I resisted with all there was within me to do so, even though he made it plain that I was just a step away from total insanity. To me he was a messenger from "them."

What finally persuaded me to take his advice was a visit by Father O'Reilly. Nothing planned—he had just stopped by to see how I was doing—but I remember his exact words when I asked him, "Father, just give me one good reason why I should listen to what the doctors want me to do."

After blessing me, which I had asked him to do, he took one of my hands and placed his free hand on my head as he spoke. "Rosemary, you should go because God wants you to go."

That made sense where all else had failed. I don't know how he knew what to say unless God was speaking to me through him, but there was no argument from me after that. In my heart I was giving myself over to God's care because I was convinced that only God understood me, only God could lift this great burden from my mind. Jesus had said, "Suffer the little children to come unto me."

I went as a child. Maybe I would learn again to be an adult. Nobody really knew for sure.

CHAPTER IV

The Psychiatric Ward

Aunt Jean drove me to the hospital. I took the nurse with me, too, which was not necessary, but I wanted somebody on *my* side. I liked her all right. She wasn't hurting me and she was there and always sympathetic to my complaints. I can't even remember her name now, but I thank her for being kind to me.

I remember I wasn't worried about being away from the children and leaving them alone because they had gone to Florida to be with my sister Betty and her family. I do think I had a little bit of a change in my attitude at the hospital because of what happened when they asked me to sign in at the desk.

The nurse pushed a paper across the counter to me and said, "Sign this, please."

"What's that?"

"You're committing yourself," she said, eyeing me somewhat warily.

"Fuck that!" I snapped. "I ain't committing myself."

"Well, then just sign it."

"I can't write." I picked up the pen and made a gigantic "X" across the page. I guess somebody witnessed my signature —maybe Aunt Jean and the nurse—but I certainly wasn't worrying about it. Maybe they just took Dr. Monke's word that I was to be admitted.

I hugged and kissed Aunt Jean, and the doors of the psychiatric ward at Mount Sinai closed and locked behind me. I was now a patient, feeling more like a convict—if I was feeling anything logical at all. I was searched, of course, and they took my purse. Everybody gets shaken down for contraband.

Somehow I have the memory of being on the eighth floor, but I'm not really sure—only that it was up high. I had a room where I could see out the window, and the first thing that caught my eye was a large billboard advertising Patti Page at the Fremont Hotel in Las Vegas. Well, that was the final indignity to me, because Patti and I had at one time been quite friendly but our relationship had been strained and cold for a long time. Right away I was convinced she was also part of the plot. Not the best way to begin my stay in the hospital.

I was allowed to keep my civilian clothes, but I was very restless. Maybe the Patti Page thing set me off. I wasn't doing anything that I was supposed to do. I became erratic, loud, and disturbing to the other patients. Not that there was anything tranquil about the ward. It was simply that there were rules and I wasn't abiding by them. Dr. Monke had seen me a couple of hours after I was admitted, and my hostile behavior took place after he left. They didn't fool around with me; I was put in isolation. However, I was only in isolation about six hours. In time I cooled down. Nobody, sane or otherwise, wants to be locked up in isolation, and I was no exception.

As a patient "on the ward"—which meant I had free access to the facilities on the ward—I met a very famous comedian whose name was a household word. It would be unfair to use his name, so I won't. But seeing him in that setting was sort of unbalancing for me because he had been a friend for a long time and was in show business, so I kept wondering what he was doing there. Men and women were mixed on the same floor, and seeing him walk up and down the hallway would throw me out of any kind of acceptance that this was a hospital. I kept thinking maybe it was Las Vegas or a party someplace. It was very difficult for me to get hold of the total situation.

While I was there he and I had long conversations—or rather I had conversations with him. He didn't talk much because he was a very depressed man. He would pace the halls almost like a zombie, and I developed an inner fear that maybe he had been given a lobotomy. There again, the short circuit in my mind was trying to reach out and connect with something that could be related to the present. Lobotomy sounded reasonable to me because in my disorganized state it made sense. Over and over I told myself, "If this is a hospital, then what is he doing here?" Then I thought, Maybe he knows Kennedy is not dead. Maybe that's why he's locked up here. Maybe he would be my confidante.

One of the first things I was acquainted with at the hospital was the treatment rooms. There were maybe four of them, with little slots on the doors where the doctor could slide his nameplate in so you would know he was in there with a patient. To me they were like interrogation rooms I'd seen in jails on television and in movies. Very, very small cubicles, just room enough for two people. There were no windows, and I can't even remember the color of the walls.

On my first visit to a treatment room I remember facing Dr. Monke and saying, "I want out. I don't want to be here."

He listened to me, but needless to say, I stayed. He did suggest that I didn't need my personal nurse. He said the treatment would probably go better if I didn't have her with me. He was taking away my current crutch, but because there was such a sense of calm and of security in him, I didn't object. He looked like a college professor, very warm, but firm, and he wore horn-rimmed glasses. I remember thinking how right they looked on his face.

All I know is I had a sense of someone taking charge without screaming, without force, yet with authority underlying everything he did. He never said, "You *will* stay here," or "You *will* do this." Nothing like that at all. He always seemed to suggest, but in a very positive way. Not once did he say, "Rosemary, that isn't true. What you're thinking isn't true." He listened to me. He picked up what I was thinking and feeling. I think I probably started to see him as a father later on, but at the time I just realized there was someone in authority who was listening to me, that if there maybe *was* a plot, this was the one person who would be on my side and believe in me.

With my back against the wall, I opted for the one person who could really help me. I rejected everybody else, but strangely enough I accepted him. It must have been his expertise in handling mental illness, because later on I found out he didn't handle all patients the same way. One patient on the ward told me, and I had no reason to doubt it, that she was going to leave and he put his foot against the door and said, "Don't you try it!"

I can see the way he reacts in a group today and I see the way he handles different people. All of the people in our group have been analyzed by him, so it is kind of an advanced group and we have all been through the same program. We all know a lot more about ourselves than we did. He seems to know exactly the kind of treatment each patient needs. From the beginning I felt he understood me totally, and I believed in him and his methods. He made no pie-in-the-sky promises.

When your condition is acute enough to require hospitalization, your attention span is not going to be a fifty-minute hour, and mine certainly wasn't. So our sessions together would last for twenty minutes, more or less. I think I enjoyed my meetings with the doctor more because there was none of the usual sterile, medical approach. He always dressed in street clothes, as did the nurses on the ward. That may well be one reason why he didn't want me to have my own nurse with her starched stiff white uniform.

The one big difference, outside our mental status, between the patients and the nurses was that people in authority all wore chains around their necks with keys on them. Keys. Keys became like the thing people had when they were well enough to walk out the door. A symbol of locked doors being opened. Being cured. Being free. Those were the people who said good-night to you. Keys became a status symbol to me. I took to wearing my keys around my neck.

Dr. Monke was very smart. During our conversation one day he asked, "Do you have a car?"

"Yes."

"Why don't you have it brought here and we'll put it on the lot so that when you feel better you can drive somewhere?"

This was during my first week in the hospital, and he couldn't have said anything that would have made me feel more secure. I knew I couldn't get out, but the car being there gave me a feeling of freedom just around the corner. It was brought and placed in the parking lot where I could see it from my window.

The car was the white El Dorado that I had taken my dare-devil drive in over the mountain from Reno to Tahoe. You couldn't miss it because in one of my wilder moments I had taken flower decals and placed them all over the car. It was an attention grabber, my white El Dorado looking like a General Motors flower garden. It seemed right to me. I was a part of the hippie generation; I couldn't have cared less what anybody thought about it, it made me happy. I relished the idea of driving through Beverly Hills with those goddamned flowers pasted all over the place. I was getting attention, and I loved getting the attention. People would give me that. People would stare at me as I drove by their big homes with the gardeners ministering to their well-groomed lawns. You could see the questioning looks in their faces: "What is *that*?" or "Who the hell is *that*?" I loved every minute of it.

Anyway, there was my white, flower-decalled Cadillac in the parking lot, and I could look out the window and see it, with my status-symbol chain and keys around my neck. I had authority, if only in my own mind. I wore my authority proudly.

The rooms in the ward were large and comfortable. Mine was a four-bed room, divided by planters with a lot of foliage, so that you were really in close contact with the person on your side of the room. I believe the girl on my side of the room was named Sue, but I can't be sure. On the other side we had one bed that became kind of a transient situation—people coming and going all of the time. But the other bed was occupied by an older lady who evidently reminded Sue of her mother. They used to have terrible fights. They argued constantly about one thing or another. Sue didn't like her at all, and after a while I understood it, too. The old lady could be a pain in the neck. Once she tried to cut her wrists with the metal pop-top off a soft-drink can. That annoyed everybody because it meant the doors had to be left open at night.

In our transient bed we had a suicide-attempt patient come in, which really upset the room. There was a rule that said you couldn't close the door to your room if you had an attempted suicide in the room. It particularly upset Sue.

"Goddammit!" she sputtered. "We have to have a suicide in here and that means we're going to have that fucking light shining in our eyes all night. How come we get all the suicides?"

I laugh in retrospect, but I wasn't laughing then. My sense of humor had not returned yet. But I agreed with Sue. What a drag, the door open all night long. Of course the young girl who had attempted suicide was instantly disliked by all three of us. I remember her unhappiness. She was a young mother with kids at home, and I recall feeling sorry for her. We didn't talk much, it was just a wave of sadness I felt at the idea of a mother with small children feeling life wasn't worth living.

In order to avoid your own problems in a mental ward, you find whatever you can to bitch about. I remember we weren't allowed to have razors, so we couldn't shave our legs unless there was someone in authority with us. Sue didn't like that; she always bitched about that. But those were the rules of the place and we all suffered equally.

I found it wonderful, however, not to have to bear the burden of responsibility for the whole thing. It was like being a kid again, with both good parents in your doctor. I certainly felt that about Dr. Monke. I enjoyed living within the bounds of what I was supposed to do and was not supposed to do.

We had a kitchenette and whoever had the duty of fixing snacks had to clean up, which involved scrubbing the floor. It was not a big area, but easily became something to gripe about. I didn't really mind it all that much. I'm sure it was therapeutic because it gave me a little bit of responsibility, but not more than I could handle at the time.

I wasn't allowed visitors except my cousin Phyllis and Sherm. When Sherm made his rounds at Mount Sinai he always stopped in to see me after he'd seen his patients. Always encouraging me, always very positive about my progress and my future. I became very fond of him during that time. I love him and Phyllis very much.

Under the guidance and treatment of Dr. Monke a very beautiful thing happened to me. I am today able to show my emotions, which I never could before. I can cry over sentimental things. That has become something very precious to me. Tears will wash away a lot of problems. I remember as a young teen-ager I was unable to cry when my grandmother died, and everybody thought that was very strange. It's a terrible thing not to be able to cry when someone you love dies.

You know you're making progress and are on the road to recovery when your sense of humor returns. I have a very vivid recollection of the first thing that made me laugh. We were allowed to watch television only in the evening—which was not at all like Saint John's, where they had the television going all day long and if you wanted to sit in front of it like a catatonic fool, it was all right. At Mount Sinai you had to earn it, and everybody had to agree to the shows. We were like children who had to learn how to behave in society, and we were rewarded for being socially acceptable in our small community and punished when we were not. If you can imagine all the nuts in a ward—there were twelve or fourteen of us— trying to decide on the same show, then you must already be laughing. It was majority rule, and often somebody didn't like the majority's choice and would stalk out cursing our dumb selection of shows.

I remember this one night we were watching a pretty far-fetched drama about people in a mental institution. We were like people in jail watching a prison film, laughing and gibing when the "keepers" were on the short end of the stick, and applauding any points made by the patients. We watched it intently, but it was so far away from the truth that all of us started laughing. It got to be like a rolling thing. Somebody giggled. Then our attention went back to the screen and we saw the way the nurses were acting and there were curses throughout the room. Honest to God, we were like characters right out of *Cuckoo's Nest*.

That was the first time I really laughed, so hard that my sides ached. I was falling-down hysterical, because it occurred to me, here were all the crazies watching a TV show about more crazies and it was nothing like the truth and the comments we made along the way were just uproariously funny.

After my laughter finally subsided I realized how long it had been since I'd laughed. I broke down and cried because I suddenly knew how far away from reality I had been for so long. This was my first step back to reality and normalcy.

I thought a lot about that film afterward because I didn't know if it was exaggerated or not. It had dealt with a public facility, and I knew that public mental hospitals weren't anything like Mount Sinai. Mount Sinai was really run like a commune. We had psychodrama—with a therapist who turned out to be Betsy Drake, who had been married to Cary Grant. Interestingly, when I saw that face I realized it was a familiar one, but I was so much better by that time that I realized it was right for her to come there, that she was not another one being locked up. I was getting back into synchronization; my shorted-out circuits were being repaired one by one.

I must say that Betsy was a very good therapist. She had that gentle way of speaking—a very soft southern accent—and a softness about her that was most attractive, and psychodrama with her was very interesting.

We had a lot of young people on the ward—I think because of so many bad drug trips. Drugs were rampant among kids in the Sixties. One boy I took a liking to was there when I went in and I suppose was going to be there a long time after I was gone. He was about fourteen, and I sort of took over with him. He was my friend, and though I'm sure I treated him like a son in a lot of ways, first of all I treated him like a friend. He loved the breakfast drink Tang, and ate it right from the jar with a spoon. He was very possessive about his bottle of Tang and the first time he ever made a move toward anybody was when he offered to share his Tang with me. I accepted his offer although I hated the stuff. I did it for him and I felt very honored that he asked me to share something of his. The nurses all thought that was good.

What it boils down to is that you are reduced to basics. You are working within that microcosm of society, working out those contacts before you have to apply it on the outside.

We had our therapy sessions—the group together—on the ward with a therapist. I think he was the doctor in charge of the facility then. Dr. Monke no longer headed up the unit; he only came to treat private patients. At any rate, I should point out that a group in a hospital like that is quite different from a group that you come to weekly. While plenty of hostility gets aired in any group, hospital groups can and do get pretty rough. There is no social give and take, no couching things in terms that will not raise the hostile feelings of another person. So it got to be kind of rowdy at times.

I got involved in that rowdiness and loved it. It was an opportunity to tell somebody just exactly what I thought about them without worrying about any social recriminations. I remember the unique feeling of telling someone flat out what I was thinking, which I had never done before. From the time I was a tiny girl I had always edited my thoughts. I lived with so many relatives that I had to toe the line, had to make sure that I never offended anyone. I strove to please, otherwise I wouldn't get anyplace.

Now I discovered there's a tremendous feeling of freedom in being able to say what you feel. My God, it was like a rush. My heart would pound, I would get so excited about it. Strange, the very simple things you lose sight of once you start spiraling off into society's ways of doing things. You lose sight of the things that make you happy, even the smallest things—like clean sheets and being able to tell somebody the truth, whether you loved them or hated them. Like appreciating flowers and gardening and walking someplace. And touching—oh, yes, mostly that.

I had never been in the habit of actually saying what was on my mind—not to my mother, not to anybody. I do now, though. Always and immediately. I do it with my children, and I think they do it with me, too. But it is not a hostile thing with us now. We respect one another and accept each other's right to personal feelings.

I now have a better relationship with my children, which makes me a better mother. I did all the functional things before, but now I get to the deep-seated things that are what motherhood is really about. I believe that parents who complain about their kids not communicating with them are communicating all one-way—toward the kids. When they go through the motions of listening, they never stop what they're doing. They never sit down and really listen. You have to allow your children their opinions, if only to give them a sense of being right sometimes. Too many parents seem only to point out when their children are wrong.

I think my stay in the hospital really brought that home to me. Of course, it was not all "say exactly what you think." There was a routine. A nurse or therapist—always a person, never a bell or alarm—got us up about 7:30 in the morning and we got dressed and then went to breakfast. We ate in a place that was kind of like a cafeteria. You selected what you wanted, and hot food was sent up from the hospital kitchen. After breakfast we had medication call, which meant everybody lined up at the window where the medicine was dispensed—and you had to down your pills or whatever you were getting right in front of the nurse; there was no hoarding or secretly not taking your medication.

Medication came every four hours. We always got it right after breakfast and always before nap time. Everybody was required to take a nap whether they needed it or not. I was getting Thorazine, which was later discontinued, and a mood elevator which takes some time to work. It is cumulative, so I didn't begin to feel very much better until after the first three or four days. My mood did come up as time went on.

Occupational therapy was also on our daily agenda. I went, but I really wasn't too interested in it. I drew some dumb things and I tried to make something out of a kind of plastic material, but I couldn't really get with that sort of thing. Many of the others were heavily into projects, though. I particularly remember one young girl who painted. She didn't want anybody to see it until she was ready to show it. I was intrigued by her diligence, and I'm sure it was excellent therapy for her because it was something that really held her interest. I got impatient watching her going over and over it again and again. Very meticulous. My curiosity got the better of me and I said, "I'd really like to see your painting. Show me what you've done."

Finally, she turned it around. It was a painting of a huge medicine bottle filled with Tuinal. She had painted one capsule beside the bottle on the table as if all she had to do was reach out and take it. Tuinals, of course, are sleeping pills—downers —and users know them as "rainbows." Everybody got a big charge out of her humor.

Our group sessions were enlightening at times and often quite helpful to the community as a whole. They gave us a common purpose, because, as I've said, we were, however small, a society unto ourselves.

I remember quite vividly my famous comedian friend bringing one of his problems to the group. He had received an offer for a major motion picture and he didn't think he could do it. We all talked to him and gave him encouragement.

"Of course you can do it," I told him.

"No. No," he sort of mumbled, totally depressed, "I don't think so. I don't believe I can be funny." And he slumped back into his depression.

We all felt a closeness to him, and I felt good at being able to tell him something positive about himself, even if he didn't heed the advice. It was a plus for me. I was thinking about somebody besides myself—a sure sign of progress in my recovery. It was totally different from my negative attitude when I entered the hospital.

But it didn't just happen for me. I had my own moments of obstinacy. For example, they always had calisthenics in the dayroom. One morning when I sat down to breakfast, one of the nurses, the keys jangling around her neck, came over to me and said, "Rosemary, I want you to go down to the day-room and do your calisthenics—*now!*"

Something in her authoritative manner rankled me; without batting an eyelash I said, "Fuck you!" and kept right on eating. I was surprised at my own outburst. It was an emotion I felt and I just let it out. I felt good about it. However, I wasn't too thrilled later on because due to my display of temperament I was grounded for a couple of days. We used to take walks on the streets of Beverly Hills from time to time, but no walks for Rosemary for a while. That was my punishment for that particular outburst.

I think I did enjoy those outings. It was during one of our walks that I realized more of my faculties were returning. I was coming around a little more every day. Coming around enough to fear being recognized by somebody I knew, which was not altogether impossible since our walks took us down Beverly Boulevard and past Chasen's, where any number of my friends wandering in or out might see me. Consequently I walked on the other side of the street and turned my head toward the store windows when I passed Chasen's.

The hospital was careful not to let anyone who might create a big scene go on those walks. My comedian friend never went. Not because of any scene he might make, but simply because he never felt up to leaving the ward.

There was one incident during one of our walks, however, that was both funny and dangerous. On one corner there was a large drugstore and we were allowed by our chaperons to go in and buy a candy bar or gum. I remember this one because having been so heavily into downers I can appreciate the humor in it. One of our young men—he was about twenty—went into the drugstore with us, and somehow—nobody knows how because he never told—he scored some Seconals. We were very closely supervised and the only thing I can imagine is that he either knew someone in the drugstore or had somebody there to meet him.

Anyway, he got them, and about an hour after we got back to the hospital he was bouncing off the walls, he was so loaded. He was promptly taken down and had his stomach pumped. So much for fun and games on our daily constitutional.

One thing I've always enjoyed is reading. On an average I read three or four books a week. Nevertheless, I had one book with me that entire four- or five-week period and I never did get through it. I just couldn't concentrate that much on any one thing. That was one of the last things that came back to me, my ability to concentrate and enjoy books.

I wasn't totally forgotten by my friends while I was in the hospital. Although I wasn't allowed to have flowers, Dr. Monke must have authorized an exception because during my first week there I received a tremendous bunch of flowers from Bob Hope. He did a marvelous thing—he sent along a card that said, "I hope it's a boy!" I remember that well and remember knowing it was from him and intended to be funny. That was one of my first pluses, because not much of anything was funny to me in the early days of my hospital stay.

Bing Crosby had been on safari and when he got back to London he wrote me a three-page letter, which really touched me. I was moved by the fact that he knew so much about me and that he took the trouble to do it. Those feelings were also an indication that some repairs were taking place in my mental works.

Came the day I asked Dr. Monke if I could go for a drive in my car. I think that took some courage on my part because I was safe, protected and had a sense of security there at the hospital. I didn't think a lot about it. It just came out in one of my sessions with the doctor.

"Dr. Monke, I'd like to go for a drive in my own car. What do you think?"

"I think that would be all right. How long would you like to go for?"

I didn't think about that either. It just came out. "An hour?"

"All right," he said, without any embellishments. "I'll leave a slip at the desk with the nurse."

I had it. I had permission to go outside. The one thing everybody looks forward to. I had the permission I needed—and now I was scared. I wasn't worrying about being in touch with reality—I now had that—but I didn't know if I would slip out again. I didn't dwell long on that negative thought, though, but quickly got myself together after the session and went out and got into my car. I must have sat there in the car for about fifteen minutes of my hour. Oh, the freedom of choice—you don't really value it until it is parceled out to you in small quantities.

I didn't know where to go. I could go anywhere I wanted to if I could do it in an hour. I didn't want to go home. My kids weren't there. They were in Florida with my sister. My mother was there, but I didn't want to see her. Not just yet. So I drove around the block four times, smiling within, happy to have those precious moments of freedom and wondering to myself about the people on the streets who took for granted their freedom to come and go.

I completed my last lap around the block, drove into the hospital parking lot and parked the car, pleased with my ability to handle a normal function that millions of people accomplished without thought every single day of their lives. I now knew I would be back on the streets again before long. Just how long, I wasn't sure. But I was sure I would.

When I came back on the ward the nurse said, "Let's see the purse." I think Dr. Monke was there, too. I was so elated with myself. There were no pills in the purse, which was essentially what they were looking for. But I must have picked up a book of matches in the car when I smoked a cigarette, and they took those away from me. We were allowed a lighter, but no matches.

Nevertheless, I went back to my room feeling good and enjoying a certain status with my roommates. I had been on the *outside*.

Not long afterward I was allowed my second trip outside. This time I had two or three hours and I decided to go home. Neighbors, I am sure, raised their eyebrows as my floral-decalled Cadillac pulled into the driveway, but I don't think I even thought about that. I was curious to see how my mother would react, because nobody had told her I was coming home. I'll never forget the look on her face when I walked in on her. Fear froze her features, and I felt sad, sad that she had any reason to fear me. I didn't say anything to her about it, but I felt sad.

I said, "Hello, mother."

She tried to laugh and said, "How did you get out?" It didn't come out in a laughing way. I could almost feel the panic in her voice.

"I got a pass from Dr. Monke to leave the hospital for a while."

"That's wonderful." She said it, but she didn't look like she thought it was wonderful. She looked skeptical that they would let this madwoman out on the streets with a car so soon.

I had brought some dirty clothes home to wash. Mother didn't come down to the laundry room with me; she never left her room all the time I was there. I put the clothes in the washer, went back up to my room and fell asleep on the bed.

I woke up about half an hour later with a start, wondering if I'd overslept my pass. My clothes weren't completely dry, but I didn't want to be late. I gathered them up in a bag, went up to my mother's room, said goodbye and left.

I think Dr. Monke was proud of me. I was proud of the confidence he had in me. Thanks to him, I was now dealing with life on a more rational level again. I was even dealing with the matter of Robert Kennedy. I had, of course, discussed Bobby with Dr. Monke at great length. It's funny, when you start getting back in touch, to realize the things you were thinking. But one day, gradually, I just realized that Bobby was dead. The paranoia had subsided. When I first entered the hospital the drugs they were giving me probably perpetuated my feelings about Bobby Kennedy. Now the drugs were down to a bare minimum. Of course it was all part of Dr. Monke's treatment; the medication dosage worked in a proper relationship to the other therapy I was getting.

It began to dawn on me that all the things I'd seen as plots against me, traps, persecution, were not. The first feelings I got about those things were feelings of terrible shame at what I'd done. Humiliation. That was very hard for me to get past, and from my group sessions I've found that it was the same for others. That's something very difficult to discuss even with your doctor during those early stages of recovery. I don't think I went into any detail about those feelings until I was out of the hospital and into analysis.

Something happened toward the end of my hospital stay, something that probably happens to a lot of people who are hospitalized for mental problems. I didn't want to leave the hospital. Not that I was in love with hospitals, it was simply that it had become my haven. Dr. Monke was kind but firm about it. He did not want the hospital to become my crutch.

He said a marvelous thing to me just before I was released. "Rosemary, this has been something that has happened in your life. A breakdown. And it may never happen again. What we've done, however, is put a Band-Aid on something that needs more help. But this is your decision."

He did not say, "Rosemary you must go through analysis." There was no pressure. He just said, "This is your decision. If you go into analysis it is going to be painful, it will be long and it will be expensive. But I really think you should do it if you can—for your sake."

I had such implicit trust in him that I didn't think about it for a second. I said yes. I didn't want to lose touch with this man who had brought me so far back from so far away. Somehow, some way, I would manage the pain, the time and the money. I would go the whole route. I would be a whole person—perhaps for the first time in my life.

CHAPTER V

First Things First

My children came home from Florida, and I came home from Mount Sinai. They had their fall terms at school ahead of them, and I had my first sessions of what would be three years of intensive analysis, three days a week, with Dr. Monke.

I got home first, and after I'd had an opportunity to collect my thoughts about my future I was ready to sit down and lay it all out for the kids. What they could expect of me and what I expected of them. Family conferences were nothing new in our household. I've always treated my children as I treat all children—as people. I've never talked down to a child. There was never a place in our home where the kids "hung out," as opposed to where I lived. Our home is a house where all of us live together, and we each have a place where we can go to be by ourselves. They are never excluded from conversations that my friends and I have, and my friends accept that. As a result, my friends are my children's friends; there's never been an age difference.

Consequently, it was not difficult for me to tell my children the prognosis for our immediate future together. I sat down with them, and although I did not set out to make a big speech or anything like that, to an outsider it may have sounded like a speech.

"I'm going to be in analysis for a long time and I want to let you know my feelings. What we've got here is a household and I've got to work out a lot of personal things. I think we'll exist most comfortably with mutual consideration, and that's the way it's going to be. Don't expect that I will give up all my feelings for myself in order to do something for you. It's imperative that you get your priorities straight, and so will I. We will compare and see what is most important for both of us in a given situation. If it works out for you—solid. If not, you're going to have to understand it."

And that's the way we survived. I feel very fortunate. We've had a very, very good relationship all the way.

I had no idea the effect analysis would have on me, on my personality. I can tell you up front that it eventually did change my personality. What it almost changed to was what I was in the beginning before things started taking their toll, before conflicting roles I thought were important for me to play wedged their way into my life—like being a proper wife for Joe, a proper mother for my children. I remember the first year and a half of my success as a singer. Life was such a lovely thing then. It was like a merry-go-round, and I was having such fun. But I got to be like the girl who "stayed too long at the fair."

My first visit to Dr. Monke's office is worth describing, especially to someone who has never had that experience. I sat down in a chair, though I noticed that there was a couch in the office. I felt very foolish: I knew all the rules but didn't know the reasons for them. And I felt uncomfortable about lying down on the couch. I told Dr. Monke how I felt.

He said, "Well, that's not unusual."

That made me feel better.

"But," he went on, "let me tell you why we have a couch, so you won't feel there's anything about it to cause you any worry or concern. On the couch your body is relaxed, or can be—or needn't be. At least you are in a position where you can rest a little bit and you are looking at nothing to distract you. The doctor is in back of you so that you don't even have to look at him for an expression of approval or disapproval of anything. You're not shading the conversation for an expression in his face."

He was right, of course, but in that first session I told him I'd rather sit in the chair, and, as always, he did not insist. So we just sat and talked. I wanted to know how long he thought my analysis would take.

"I have no idea, Rosemary. It depends on many things. It's not something we can pinpoint so early."

That was not very encouraging to me. I didn't know if I'd ever be able to go back to work. I felt very far away from work. I shrank from the memory of my bizarre behavior over the past year and wondered if that would make going back to work difficult. I mean, would they even want me again?

Later on I discovered that my fears were well founded—club owners were very cautious about booking me. I'd had a good reputation over a twenty-year period, never doing anything outlandish or away from the "norm," but one time it had happened was enough to send it all crashing around my head. Reno had been the only onstage incident. Granted, there were difficulties working with me that last year, but I was always on time and always knew my songs.

I grew worried about how I would handle the financial end of things, because seeing Dr. Monke three times a week was going to be a really expensive proposition. But I was committed to the treatment and I would find a way.

Our first session sort of laid the groundwork for things to come. I was much like a child on the first day of school after being promoted to a higher grade. You know the school, but the curriculum is higher-echelon and tougher.

Still, I left Dr. Monke's office feeling better. I knew I was doing something positive.

I had never asked Joe for any alimony when we divorced— only $1 a year, which in California used to be standard procedure with women who didn't need alimony. It was originally designed as a sort of "rainy day clause." It left open the possibility of a raise in payments later on if the woman really got into desperate straits. Some women also used it as a handy device for keeping their fingers on the pulse of their ex-husbands' financial situation—just in case he discovered gold.

My situation was a practical one. I had five children, I was facing very high medical costs for an undetermined period of time and I couldn't work. I did the one thing I knew was right. I went back into court and asked for more than token alimony, and it was granted. Joe was very helpful. He never protested. He understood what was happening with me. I don't think his lawyers were too happy about it, but then lawyers aren't always the last word, much as they'd like to think they are. You must remember that throughout our marriage I was the one who paid all the bills that came into our home; paid them out of my income—not Joe's.

Actually it turned out to be a better deal for Joe in the long haul. Alimony was taxable for me, so in the tax situation I think he probably did better. But Joe would have gone along with it regardless of any tax considerations. He's that kind of man, very much concerned about his children and their welfare, and I think he was also concerned about me. Joe is a good human being.

My sessions with Dr. Monke were pleasant, usually, because he never pressured me for answers or tried to force my dialog into any channels. It was free expression on my part, and once you get into the habit of free-associating it's like being a totally inhibited person who one day finds a way to become just as totally uninhibited. You free yourself from a cage and become your own person without worrying what others may think of you. What you think of yourself is what becomes important. It is the only way you can ever look at yourself honestly and decide what you like and don't like about that person with your name.

Although we never began with, "Let's start at the beginning," for the sake of continuity in this narrative there must be some chronological order to my telling of it. For instance, I would begin a session by telling Dr. Monke about something that was bothering me or had me upset. I recall one time when I began with, "Today on the phone my brother sounded very curt with me. I realize he was busy, but so am I, and this hurt my feelings very badly."

Dr. Monke asked, "What did he say? What was his tone of voice?"

From that expression of my feelings we were able then to go back in time to a place where I could relate those feelings to something that had happened perhaps years before. A time when I remembered feeling the same way. It is simply amazing how that sort of pairing up of the same feelings at different times can help bring into focus the reasons you feel the way you do about certain things, or the reasons why you react in a given manner to certain situations.

That's the way we did it, and essentially over the three years of analysis my life story was unraveled and I was able to put everything in its proper place, like stringing clay beads, one bead at a time.

My very first memory is of lying with my face to the wall in a small bed. It was in an apartment my mother and father had during one of the few periods they were together, and my father had just come home from work. I was angry with him because he had promised me something and hadn't kept the promise. I remember he came into the room and was being very sweet to me.

He said, "Come on now, turn around. Why are you unhappy? I'm sorry. Turn around and see this present that I found for you on the street today."

Childish curiosity won out and I turned to face him and see

what wonderful gift he had brought me. It was an oversize crystal marble—possibly three inches in diameter. Not one you could really play marbles with, but I was fascinated with it. It had no color at all and it was a little roughed up on the surface, probably from bouncing on the asphalt street. I cherished it, and I remember with a sense of wonder that this grown-up man could say, "I'm sorry that I didn't keep my promise."

That was the earliest time I can remember that happening, too. I remember warmly the sense of pleasure I got out of making up with him and being with him. This was before my sister Betty was born, so I was probably between two and three at the time.

And I remember my Grandmother Clooney's apartment and living there with her. It was in the same building where my grandfather had his jewelry store, which was on the first floor, facing Market Street in Maysville, Kentucky. It was my fourth or fifth birthday and there was a party for me. I was in the bathroom and my grandmother was dressing me and getting me ready when an early arrival came with a gift. I poked my head out and she handed me a present through a crack in the bathroom door and I thought how marvelous to be in the bathroom getting dressed and opening up a birthday present.

One time, when I was about five and my sister Betty was barely two, we were up in the attic of that building. I remember it so well because it was in the winter and very cold. My father's sister, Olivette, was a piano player and had her own band, and she stored her trunks on that upper floor. Betty and I got into one of those trunks and found all those marvelous things that Aunt Olivette wore on the bandstand, and of course nothing would do but to get dressed up in Aunt Olivette's beautiful show gowns. Somehow or other Betty and I managed to get down the stairs and out on the street without being caught by my grandfather who had a rather alert eye as to who came and went up and down those stairs.

Maysville is situated on the Ohio River, and the Ohio can

be treacherous, so we were forbidden at all times to go near it. Nevertheless, I took Betty by the hand and we made our way to the river. We were making believe that we were going on a trip and a boat was coming to take us away.

There was a concrete grade, and Betty and I were standing right on the end of it at the edge of the icy cold water. Suddenly—I don't know how it happened—Betty stepped off the side of the grade and fell in. Instantly the water was over her head and I was grappling for her hand which I managed to clasp just before it disappeared beneath the surface. How I did it I'll never know, but I pulled her out, drenched and as heavy as lead with Aunt Olivette's soaking-wet long dress on. Somehow or other we made it all the way back to our attic. She was sputtering and cold, but she let me take care of her and get her back into her own clothes. She never told on me, and until now nobody ever knew about it but my sister and me.

Betty and I loved to sing; and to get us to sing, all you had to do was ask. My Grandfather Clooney often had friends come into the jewelry store, and Betty and I always cooperated when they asked us to sing a song for them.

There was no dearth of music in our family on either side. Although my mother's father, my Grandfather Guilfoyle, died when I was only two weeks old, I heard all the hand-me-down stories about him. I'm told he was a very lively man, well built, and loved dancing. He had a real love of music. Aunt Olivette, on my father's side, was the pianist and instrumentally probably the most accomplished member of the family. There was also my Aunt Ann, my mother's sister, who was a nightclub singer and one of my early idols—someone who actually sang for audiences and got paid for it. It was a long time from my early performances for Grandfather Clooney until my first paycheck as a singer.

Grandfather Clooney was politically inclined and served quite some time as mayor of Maysville. He was also an excellent watchmaker and jeweler and always interested in everything. A self-educated man, he was bright, intelligent and in many ways ahead of his time, and I loved him very much. His mother and father had immigrated to Maysville from Ireland so he was a first-generation American. He was only twenty-two when he passed the State Bar and got his license to practice law.

Mother and father were like a soap opera—and a bad one at that. Daddy was a drinker, and when he drank he was in a world all by himself. When the drinking became a problem, my mother would go home to live with her mother, my Grandmother Guilfoyle. I spent most of my early childhood with my Grandmother Clooney, but when mother and daddy split, often as not mother would take me with her to her mother's house, so that my life was the same as my mother and father's—like moves on a checkerboard. Betty and I spent very little time actually living with mother or daddy. We were almost always with one of our grandmothers.

I think a lot of daddy's problems stemmed from his mother. She adored him and indulged him to the point of making him into a somewhat spoiled mama's boy. His natural instincts as a male were to escape that kind of maternal domination, and he found the easiest way to do that was the bottle.

She tried the same thing on Betty and me, really spoiling us the same way. We were indulged the same as my father had been, and if you contrast that to the simple life with little of anything material that was my Grandmother Guilfoyle's mode of living, it is easy to see how confusing life was for young, impressionable girls like Betty and myself. I soon got the wrong idea that all the good things came from Grandmother Clooney. When she wasn't around, there wasn't much worthwhile. That was a very bad set of ideas for me to be presented with.

Betty was born in Lewisburg, Kentucky, where my Grandmother Guilfoyle was living at the time. Mother, I guess, was separated from daddy and living there with her. I was at Grandmother Clooney's. I remember the first time I ever saw Betty. Someone had taken me out to Lewisburg to see my new sister. I was three years old and have a vivid memory of my first glimpse of her in a dresser drawer because there was no crib. A crib would have been a luxury to my grandmother who, as a widow with nine children, had difficulty making ends meet.

Grandmother Guilfoyle had been a tireless worker all her life. At that time she was doing practical nursing at night and caring for her own family during the day. It was an exhausting schedule, but necessary in order to support the nine children she was burdened with bringing up alone. I think relatives pitched in from time to time, because it was that kind of family, but there never seemed to be quite enough. Certainly not enough to let her quit work and be at home all the time with her own family.

Grandmother Guilfoyle had other attributes that more than compensated for her lack of financial wealth. She was a sensational cook, great seamstress and could put a stick in the ground and come up with a garden. She had good old-fashioned know-how. All the things I enjoy doing right now I really believe come down to appreciating my Grandmother Guilfoyle a lot more after I was grown and had a family of my own.

In 1928, the year of my own birth, Maysville was a lazy little river community that, like the Ohio River, had its moments of beehive activity—usually in the spring. The economy of the country was generally in excellent condition and nobody had any way of knowing that within another year and a half a worldwide depression would create bread lines and soup kitchens and massive unemployment.

People who live by rivers are different. They are survivors, and so we survived. Daddy was a painter—when he worked. Mother worked too. She seemed to always enjoy work and being out among people. I was not a particularly happy child, but I had some happy times. Never as outspoken as my sister Betty, I was more quiet and loved to read, which I still do. If I liked something I was good at it, so I was quite good at English.

We were a devoutly Catholic family, so religion was an integral part of my early childhood. Sometimes I enjoyed that, and at other times it became too dogmatic for my way of reasoning things out for myself. I never liked learning by rote prayers and verses that made no sense to me. I would ask questions. I wanted explanations and I was never satisfied with the answers. "You must have faith" doesn't mean a lot to a child who is inquisitive about life and the unknown. The church, at that time, was not as modernized as it is today. Yet, in spite of all the Gothic rhetoric that bores a child, there was a lot of mystery attached to it. Holy Week particularly fascinated me. The Crucifixion. The passion play always held my attention. Even then I thought it was a terrible crime, but with all my wide-eyed fascination about it, I still didn't understand why. I believed it, though, because everybody said it was so.

One of the greatest times of my early life was part of one summer when mother, daddy, Betty, Nicky and I all lived together in the same house on the east side of Maysville. We kids called it "The Kool-Aid House" because mother fixed us Kool-Aid while we lived there. It was the only time I can remember my mother actually being in the kitchen fixing meals for the whole family when I was growing up. My brother Nicky was only about two, I think.

I believe my mother and father really loved each other very deeply. I know that after they finally broke up and each of them remarried, they wrote letters to one another all the time, all those years. They never broke contact. I don't think either of them was very stable, and maybe that was the problem. Daddy was certainly more down to earth in his ways of expressing himself and he had a brilliant sense of humor. Mother, on the other hand, was more secretive and terribly manipulative. When daddy was sober he was marvelous fun to be with, more than anyone else I've ever known. Mother always seemed to be preoccupied.

Not counting my sister, I had one really good girl friend while I was growing up, and she is still my dear friend. She was a black girl, Blanchie Mae Chambers. A lot of people who were not born and brought up in the South just don't understand the genuine love and affection that a black and white often have for each other. Somehow the publicity about atrocities and injustices that have been visited on black people by whites in the South has obliterated the really good relationships. People elsewhere never seem to realize the sort of close association that you can have with somebody of a different race.

Blanchie Mae's mother worked at the New Central Hotel which was just across the street from my grandfather's jewelry store. I spent most of my playtime as a little girl on the street in front of my grandfather's store. When it got too hot on the streets, Blanchie Mae and I would often follow grandfather into the vault when he went to get something he was working on. He would open up the dark velvet jewelry cases with their shiny rings and necklaces and pretty pieces of jewelry. It was delightfully mysterious to us.

It was not unusual when grandfather was changing his windows for passersby to look up and find Blanchie Mae and me putting on a show in the window. And we would sing, which made poppa happy. I sometimes called Grandfather Clooney "poppa."

When my first movie, *The Stars Are Singing*, was premiered in Maysville, Blanchie Mae rode in the open convertible with me in a parade down Market Street. We both had a lot of memories to share that day. We'd come a long, long way from those early times in poppa's window.

Maysville had three movies and one Catholic church, and I spent about equal time in each as I grew up through elementary school. Saturday afternoon was always kids' time. For a dime we saw gangster and western pictures. Edward G. Robinson, James Cagney and Buck Jones were more familiar to me than the great singing stars of the time. And of course, things like *The Clutching Hand* and all of the *Buck Rogers* outerspace serials.

The great treat was—whenever mother and daddy were together and things were good with them—going to the Russell Theater on Sunday night where they had the musical movies. I remember daddy always bought Beechnut gum for me to chew in the theater.

My Grandfather Clooney, I'm sure, had a tremendous effect on my early life. He represented stability to me long before I knew what the word meant. He was a very outgoing man; a very strong, idealistic man who accomplished a great deal. My brother Nicky reminds me of him more and more as time goes on. He did a lot of things really well. Jeweler and politician, as I've said, and he even had a free newspaper. His views, I believe, were really quite socialistic. As a matter of fact I recall a conversation I had about that with Justice Stanley Weed, who was a close friend of my grandfather's and also came from Maysville. I had a chance to talk to him once when I was in Washington singing at a Democratic fund raiser when John Kennedy was president.

After I arrived at the Mayflower Hotel I called the justice. He was having a party and invited me up to his suite. I couldn't because I had a commitment someplace else, so he said, "Let me come downstairs and talk to you."

We met in the lobby of the Mayflower and found a quiet corner and talked. I asked him, "Tell me what my grandfather's politics really were. What did he believe in?"

"Well," he said, grinning benevolently, "I would say that your grandfather was a socialist—or he was well on his way to that. He believed that all the energy things—the electric and gas companies, the oil industry, things under the ground—should be provided, along with water, without charge to the people of the country. He believed those things belonged to everybody, not just a few corporations."

"Well, what do you think he would be today?"

"If he continued the way he was," he said, in all good humor, "I would say that you, your sister and your brother would be living in Soviet Russia probably."

Perhaps Grandfather Clooney's philosophy would have changed had he lived longer. I don't know. But I do know he was a warm and compassionate man to us children. He used to tell Betty and me stories after we went to bed at night. In the darkness I guess he could drop all the pretenses of running a city and righting the wrongs that people did to each other and upholding his ideals. He would tell us stories about doodle bugs. Actually it was one continuous story with a different chapter every night. He would tell us about the cobbler in Doodle Bug Town and what he had to do. The doodle bugs, he explained, lived under the ground somewhere, but they had this magnificent society that was blooming. So we heard about the doodle bugs every night while we lived with Poppa Clooney. All about their marvelous system of living.

I loved that man very much because he showed us that he loved us very much. His love had no strings attached. He expected things of us, but his expectations did not take the form of demands. They were brought home to us, instead, by the fact that he was not surprised when we accomplished something. He would show great pleasure in our accomplishments, and even our simplest progressions were looked on with interest by him, but he was never surprised.

Grandmother Clooney, on the other hand, adored me on the surface but I don't think, as I've said earlier, that her love was entirely healthy. Not only did she lavish too many material things on me, but even at that young age I knew it was wrong when she had things to say about my mother which would make me unhappy and put me in the position of choosing. Children don't want to hear unpleasant things about their parents. I sometimes think my mother and my father's mother had some things in common in that respect.

I remember one time when mother was giving me a bath. It was during one of those intervals when I was living at my Grandmother Guilfoyle's, so it must have been one of those periods when she had broken up with daddy and gone home to live with my grandmother. As she bathed me, I said to her, "Mother, there's a boy by the name of Andy Clooney who works at the ten-cent store on Second Street."

"Yes."

"Well, it's kind of funny, because he has blond hair and he looks like me."

My mother, without any preparation at all, perhaps through an immediate anger at my father, blurted out, "That's because he's your brother. He's your father's son. Not mine. Your father's son."

I'd known Andy all my life and nobody had told me he was my brother. I had to find out when my mother, in a moment of pique, just let me have it cold without any prep- aration. I was only about four or five and not old enough to assimilate anything that traumatic. He was my father's son by an earlier marriage, obviously something my mother was unable to forgive for reasons I never knew. My Grand- mother Clooney had never approved of daddy's first mar- riage, so as far as she was concerned neither the marriage nor the child really existed even though he bore the same name as her husband and her son.

It created a great deal of confusion for me. Why would I have a brother and not know about it? It had to be some- thing my father had done wrong, because the way my mother put it to me, it sounded wrong. So it must be wrong.

After that I sort of stayed away from my brother Andy be- cause I wasn't sure I was supposed to know that we were re- lated, but he always was very nice to me. Even after I was older I was not allowed to see him a great deal, but we had very warm feelings for one another.

Andy later went into the army and when I lived with my father in Cincinnati as a teen-ager he came to visit us before he went overseas. He was then stationed in New Jersey and had a friend who knew Frank Sinatra. I was crazy about Frank, and through his friend he got me an autographed picture of him and sent it to me.

Andy's life was not meant to be a long one. When he came

home after the war he married a girl who had gone to school with my Aunt Chris. Her name was Nancy, and they had a son. Andy was so happy about having a son. But early one summer while swimming in the Ohio River he drowned. It seemed like I'd just discovered him and I didn't have any chance at all to really know him before he was taken away.

When I was in fourth grade and ten years old a lot of things happened to me that live in my memory. For one thing, I had my debut as an actress. I played the wicked witch in *Snow White and the Seven Dwarfs*. I enjoyed that. I felt like the wicked queen and the transition to the witch was an easy thing to do. I really loved it. Although I was disappointed at not being Snow White, I really wasn't the Snow White type. My disappointment was mainly because my third cousin, Joe Breslin, whom I had a terrible crush on all the way through grade school, was playing Prince Charming and I couldn't be his Snow White. I don't think I much cared for the darling little brunette girl who got that part, but being in the same rehearsal with Joe was better than nothing. The *Maysville Ledger* duly reviewed our fourth-grade effort, and that review has been duly lost somewhere along with time. But I was a big hit.

It was during this time that radio became a real attraction to me. We didn't have a station in Maysville, but Cincinnati had a 500,000-watt clear channel station, which is and was a fantastically strong station. Both of my grandparents' homes had big console radios in their living rooms—Grandmother Guilfoyle for the soap operas she lived by and Poppa Clooney for just about everything. I used to hear "Amos 'n' Andy," "Jack Armstrong," and I would hear Bing Crosby on his radio show. He was my father's favorite singer; my father used to listen to him religiously. That was my first introduction to Bing—through his songs on WLW out of Cincinnati.

The dime store sold songsheets, the kind with only the lyrics to all the popular songs of the day, which were printed on green paper and came out every week. I bought them regularly and learned the lyrics to all the songs I heard on the radio. I couldn't read music, but had an uncanny way of learning the songs very quickly.

The year I was in the fourth grade was also the year my Grandmother Clooney died—and I couldn't cry. I have a memory of the funeral. It was the first funeral I'd ever been to. I don't know why, but I didn't feel very much. Maybe I wasn't allowing myself to feel much. Maybe I really felt so much that I didn't think I could handle it, so I backed off from it. I don't know, but my attitude outwardly was surprising to other family members.

After Grandmother Clooney died, poppa didn't do too well, physically or otherwise. I think her death left him with a broken spirit and he never really recovered from it.

So I went back again to live with Grandmother Guilfoyle. I finished elementary school at Saint Patrick's Grade School in Maysville, and the summer after I graduated from sixth grade we all moved to Ironton, Ohio, because my Uncle George and Uncle Chick were going to open up a service station there and life would be better for all of us.

Living with Grandmother Guilfoyle, as I explained earlier, was the antithesis of living with the Clooneys. She was a marvelous cook and kind of fat. Very earthy. She came from a farm before she married my grandfather and had taught in a one-room schoolhouse—eight grades in one room—before her marriage. She had nine children—actually twelve, counting Betty, Nicky and me—to raise, but she took good care of us and she loved Nicky desperately. I have no complaints about those times I lived with her. They weren't always the easiest for her, and therefore for us, because my mother was always away in a different city, working, and all the uncles and aunts contributed as much as they could to keep my grandmother's house going.

While we lived in Ironton tragedy struck me personally. My Aunt Ann, who was such a good singer and always encouraged my singing, died at the very tender age of twenty-five. She sang in a sultry, dramatic voice that must have been a sensation to hear in a nightclub. I had been impressed with the lovely evening gowns and beautiful luggage she owned, but I guessed she didn't get along too well with her boy friends, because from time to time she would have a big fight with her current flame and come home to her mother until her hurt feelings healed.

I loved those visits. She added excitement to my life. She was superdramatic, terribly emotional, and while as a kid I didn't really understand the depth or the importance of her feelings, I delighted in her. She'd have screaming temper tantrums with my grandmother and there were some fiery verbal exchanges. It was very exciting to Betty and me, but it must have really worn both of them down.

One time she came for a whole week and I remember we were all out of shoes—all of us kids needed shoes. Full of life and vibrancy she said, "Come on. Come with me. We're going downtown and put some shoes on your feet!" She was a very generous lady, always doing things for us, and she always encouraged Betty and me with our singing. Most people just liked to listen to us. Aunt Ann thought we had something and should nurture it.

Getting something new, though, was always a big thrill to me. In those days my main interest in clothes was getting something that fit. I had to have clothes that fit so I could go to school. I had hand-me-downs from cousins, but I was getting to be as tall as they were, so clothes that didn't fit them didn't fit me either.

Aunt Ann's death was very sudden, and shrouded in mystery. The cause was never discussed around me, but I suspect that in a moment of depression and heartbreak over just one too many a romance that went wrong, she may have accidentally overdosed. Somebody said she had a fight with her boy friend and was "punishing him," which made no sense to me at all.

She died on a Saturday night. My Uncle George was a young man then, just graduated from high school, and I remember him getting on the phone and calling his brothers and sisters and saying: "Hello, Ann's dead!" That shocked me—I thought there must be a more subtle way to break that kind of news. Each time, after George's opener, there would be a long pause on our end of the line and I knew somebody on the other end must be having trouble believing what he'd said to them.

It was also the first time I had ever seen a corpse in the house. I had been to the funeral home when Grandmother Clooney died, but on Grandmother Guilfoyle's side of the family they still held to the tradition that country folks have of bringing the body home for viewing by family and neighbors because of long distances into town.

Aunt Ann's death had a tremendous impact on me. The dynamo of the whole family was gone. The spark had gone out—and only twenty-five years old.

Ironton itself was a big change for me. A change of schools —now I was in junior high school—a bigger city, and away from the place I'd been born and brought up in, the only place I'd ever known. That meant making new friends, always difficult for young people who are shifted from one city to another. But I never really had that many close friends in Maysville. It was probably harder on Betty and Nicky in that respect.

When I was about ready for high school some strange things began happening in Ironton. We were renting a house that seemed jinxed. Four weekends in a row we had bad things happen. One weekend my mother got sick, another weekend my Uncle Chick had an automobile accident, and of course it was on a weekend during that time that Aunt Ann died. There was some other misfortune, but I can't remember what it was. It just seemed that we were not destined to live there.

I'd like to talk a little about my Grandmother Guilfoyle's children—my aunts and uncles—because after we left Ironton the family began to scatter and they were all terribly important to me at the time.

My Uncle Neal was the eldest. He was in insurance and also owned racehorses in Lexington later on. Aunt Rose is my cousin Phyllis's mother, married to Uncle Isadore—both of whom I love very much. They now live in Dayton, Ohio. Uncle William was a career army man and after he retired he went to work for the city of Jacksonville, Florida, doing computer work, and is very well placed. There was Uncle William and then Aunt Jean who lives in San Bernardino with Uncle Roy and has five grown children of her own. Aunt Chris lives in Washington, D.C. Uncle Chick, who was between Aunt Rose and Uncle William, had a glass eye and had lost a finger. We thought he was marvelous because he used to take his eye out for all the kids in the neighborhood. We all loved that.

Of course there was Aunt Ann who died, and then the youngest boy, my Uncle George, who would play a very important part in my life and Betty's in years to come.

I remember when we first moved to Ironton with Grandmother Guilfoyle there was some strain between my Aunt Chris and us three kids who moved in with them. Aunt Chris was only three years older than I, and the baby of the family. We were close in age and close in growing up, too. Closer, once we were away from all that. There was sibling rivalry there, and she had a right to resent us. We were intruders moving in on her territory, and worst of all she was no longer the baby—Nicky was. It must have been a trying time for her, but all turned out well because she married a trombone player, my Uncle Dave, who played with Tony Pastor's band when Betty and I were singing with him and who also really resented our being with the band, as you'll find out later on.

The Guilfoyles all seemed to follow the lead of my grandmother in those days, and so when Uncle George and Uncle Chick went out of business in Ironton and she decided that Cincinnati was a greener pasture, the clan moved en masse on down the river to the Queen City. I was in the last semester of eighth grade at the time.

I liked Cincinnati. We lived in a neighborhood where the

houses were lined up like those in a Monopoly game, but there were back alleys where we kids could play tag and hide-and-seek. I recall a very warm summer's night when we were playing hide-and-seek and in the dark I ran into a guy wire running down from a power pole. It whacked me right across the face and left a nifty cut all across my face.

My father was off somewhere. I didn't see much of him during that time because he and mother were not together. I was now becoming more interested in music, however, and never missed the "Hit Parade" Saturday nights on the radio. I knew all the top tunes, but I wasn't really doing any singing. Betty and I just sort of kept abreast of what was popular.

My cousin Phyllis and I started as freshmen together at Withrow High School. Phyllis, always a beautiful girl, was the best-dressed girl in the school and also an excellent student. While she had all of those things going for her as a freshman and I had none of those things, I was never jealous of her. Had it been someone else, I probably would have hated her. But I always loved Phyllis, and the feeling has always been mutual. She was wonderful to me when I moved to Cincinnati. Warm and giving.

Once again I didn't have too many friends, but I was very close to Phyllis and Betty, who was still in junior high school. Even though we moved from place to place under difficult circumstances, we were always together growing up in Cincinnati during our teen years.

Betty immediately adopted the Cincinnati Reds and was one of their most dedicated fans. I became a fan when I developed a terrific crush on Grady Hatton, their hot third baseman. He was quite young and a fantastic ballplayer—also a college man on a baseball team, which was rather uncommon in the Forties.

No sooner had I finished my freshman year at Withrow than we moved again. That summer, following my freshman year, a lot of things happened. My mother got a divorce from my father in Maysville, which was a terribly important event to me at the time. I didn't really understand at first why she wanted a divorce. After all, they had a marriage like a merry-go-round. They got on when they wanted to and got off when they were tired of each other. Why get a divorce when they might go back together at any time?

Daddy was working in a defense plant in Cincinnati by this time and making good money. Usually when daddy was working and "behaving himself" he and mother would go back together, but not this time.

It wasn't long before I discovered the truth behind the divorce. Mother had met a sailor who was now stationed in California and she wanted to marry him. It was a marriage I would not approve of. I didn't know the man, but I didn't like him. Maybe I was jealous. Maybe my Catholic upbringing had something to do with it. Or maybe, and probably more truthfully, my anger and hate was for my mother. But I couldn't vent it on her. She was my mother, and I'd been brought up that mother was mother and that was that. Very frustrating.

Mother was now working in Cincinnati, and we were living with her again. I had an instinct for knowing that something was going on behind my back, but I couldn't quite put my finger on it because mother was being her manipulative best, very secretive and deceptive about her plans.

Grandmother Guilfoyle had also moved again, to a kind of country place at Indian Hill outside Cincinnati. I remember there was a big meeting at my grandmother's house—a lot of my aunts and uncles were there along with my mother, and of course we kids. I overheard one of my aunts saying to my mother: "You've got to take care of these children. They're your responsibility, not mother's. You can't expect mother at this time in her life to do these things for you."

Somehow my mother's response is blocked out in my memory. Maybe it was something unpleasant and I don't want to remember it. Maybe not. In any event it seemed she just wanted to leave Betty and me with my grandmother, but it was more than grandmother could handle and my aunts wouldn't allow it, which was rightly so.

My mother's mind was made up, and when she made her mind up to something, somehow or other she got her way. I don't know how she finagled my father into doing it, but somehow she persuaded him to move into her house to take care of Betty and me, while she would take Nicky to California with her. I shall never forget the day the taxi pulled up in front of our house, and mother, bags packed, with Nicky by the hand, told us goodbye.

"Your father will be coming to live with you, so there won't be anything for you to worry about," she said, almost as if her departure with our beloved Nicky were nothing more than passing the time of day.

They got into the taxi and drove off. Just like that. My mother never turned back—looked straight ahead as the taxi drove away. But Nicky, God bless him, turned and in his youthful, innocent manner, was waving goodbye to us all the way down the street until the cab was out of sight. My heart splintered into a million pieces that day. Oh, how I loved my brother—and how I hated my mother's soon-to-be new husband for taking him away from us—and for taking our mother.

Betty and I stood there, both of us angry and hurt. We both knew that mother was just doing the convenient thing for her. We didn't matter. It was what she wanted to do that counted.

I didn't see my mother or Nicky again for four years.

CHAPTER VI

"The Clooney Sisters"—Big Band Singers

While Betty and I had always been close, mother's departure brought us even closer. We decided to close ranks and face the world together. Whatever we had to do to survive, we would do just that. That adhesive bond we formed in front of our house that day grew ever stronger and lasted until she died in August 1976 from a very unexpected aneurysm. I don't know many sisters who have had the closeness we had.

Betty could forgive me anything. There wasn't anything I could do that would be bad enough for her to say, "That's really a terrible thing." Never. She would find a way out for me—a verbal way out. Truly a remarkable human being, and she proved that in the time that was immediately ahead of us.

My father came to live with us. We did not go to be with him; we were solid and felt completely competent and able to take care of ourselves. Still my father was trying, and I don't think he was doing too badly. It was wartime and the economy was booming. Daddy was on the wagon and working in a defense plant. But there was another adjustment Betty and I had to make. All our lives mother had told us what a rogue daddy was, how impossible he was to live with; that he was irresponsible. Now we were suddenly told that good old daddy was the salt of the earth, the Rock of Gibraltar and maybe even Old Glory poured into one supermold. I never understood why mother changed her mind about him. Maybe she didn't. Maybe it was just the easy way out for her.

But we would make the best of it. Daddy was sober, and as I've said, sober he was the greatest. One of the first things that changed was our residence, which was getting to be routine with us anyway. Daddy thought the place was too expensive, so we moved to a less expensive apartment in a kind of run-down neighborhood. The people around us were nice, though, and we had a pretty good view since our new place was on top of a hill and the streetcar line went right in front of our apartment house. That's where we lived when we started back to school that fall.

Daddy made us the best home he could and he was enormously funny at times. I can honestly say we had some really good times there. Big bands came to Cincinnati and played the Albee Theater. We always went on Saturdays to see them, which was a real treat for both of us because we were so crazy about band music.

With every plus there has to be a minus, and we had our share of both. Sometimes I think the minuses won out, but we managed. I was in high school and Betty in junior high. We'd get dressed in the morning and leave the house together. Betty's school was a few blocks beyond the high school, so I got off the streetcar first and she continued on. It was a routine.

One day a man came to my Latin class and beckoned me out of the room. Right away I knew something was up when he asked, "Where's your sister Betty?"

Having already acquired some street sense, my immediate

reaction was to protect Betty. "Betty isn't feeling well," I replied.

He nodded. "I see. Well, I think we ought to have a talk with her doctor and your father because three months is a long time to be out of school sick."

My bewilderment must have been plastered all over my face. The person who was closer to me than anyone else in the world skipping school for three months without my knowing about it? I couldn't believe it. We had shared everything together. Yet she had played hooky for three months and I had to hear it from the truant officer.

When it all came out, finally, she told me what she had been doing with her time. She had been going to the Keith Albee Theater every day to see the big bands, using her lunch money for streetcar fares both ways and the price of admission. On her school pass she could ride the streetcar for a nickel provided she caught the returning car home before five o'clock. After that time her school transportation pass was invalid for the day and the fare went up.

She'd gotten away with it for an amazingly long time, but now the jig was up. Different arrangements were made to be sure that Betty skipped the Keith Albee instead of school during the week.

The war was in high gear now and defense plants were going twenty-four hours a day. Daddy was making more money and we moved again—this time to a better neighborhood and a better apartment. It also meant a change in schools. Our new neighborhood was called Price Hill and we went to Western Hills High School which, to me, was an improvement over my last school.

On Sundays Betty, daddy and I would go down to the big chain drugstore on Fountain Square where they had those little individual jukeboxes at the counters and in each booth.

You could put a nickel in and listen to records that were popular. I think there was a selection of ten or twelve to choose from. We'd sit there and play Harry James records—"Velvet Moon," "It Seems to Me I've Heard That Song Before" and "I Had the Craziest Dream." Daddy loved the music.

Daddy, too, was musically inclined. He played ukulele, and played it well, and sang in tune. Mother, on the other hand, really always wanted to be a singer and performer more than anything, but she had no sense of timing when she sang. If you don't have that, you can't learn it. I remember when I was just three or four years old and would sing, mother always got upset with my pauses. They were natural to me, but not to her. She would say, "Don't wait all that time at a pause." I didn't know how to argue with her about it. I only knew I had to wait and in my mind beat out the end of one phrase until it was over before I started the next one. Mother thought the pauses were nothing but "dead air." One time daddy said to her, "You're telling her the wrong way to do it. Leave her alone. Let her sing the way she feels it."

Thursday, April 12, 1945. How well I remember that day. President Roosevelt was dead. I was on my way home from school when I heard the newspaperman on the corner selling extras all about the president dying in Warm Springs, Georgia. I was shocked and hurt. It was like losing somebody right out of your own family. He had been president as far as I could remember. I had been too young to remember anything about Mr. Hoover. I felt very sad that day, and everybody else seemed to share my sadness.

VJ Day came. The war was finally over. Betty and I were going to high school and daddy went out with some of his friends from the defense plant. They started to tease him. Someone said, "Aw, come on, Andy. You haven't had a drink the whole war. You mean to say you're going to let it go by without one beer?" One beer to daddy meant getting off the wagon.

One beer—and all the progress of three years went down the drain.

When daddy got home he was drunker than drunk—he was a different man. Betty and I were really sick at heart about it. We saw all our good times ending, because when daddy drank he didn't stay around. Anyway, he came home and gathered up all the defense bonds we'd saved throughout the war. After cashing them all in he had several thousand dollars. He took a cab and kept it for something like ten days.

Betty and I were left alone with no money and no explanations. Daddy just couldn't help himself when he drank. He never meant to hurt us or deprive us, but his mind worked differently under the influence. After a week or so, we collected all the pop bottles around the apartment, and there were quite a few, fortunately. We were great junk-food addicts like all teen-agers, and Coke was high on the list.

We could have called any number of our relatives in Cincinnati because practically the whole Guilfoyle clan lived in the area, but we were firmly against involving the rest of the family. We had grown up a little bit during those three years of daddy's sobriety and were even surer now that we could take care of ourselves. We were blessed with one great thing— we'd had three years under a roof with at least one of our parents and certainly the best years available from daddy. It had been wonderful, and if it was ending we were the stronger because of it.

So Betty and I would do whatever we had to do together. I was strong, but Betty had more moxie. She'd get out, for instance, and audition for things that I wouldn't have the nerve to. She was three years younger, but had so much more nerve. I guess it was confidence in herself.

We kept on going to school, and the money from the Coke bottles was spent on food at school. You could get a sandwich and a glass of milk for fifteen cents. That went a long way. I have to laugh when I think how I watch my diet now in order to keep the weight down. Neither of us had that problem then.

Speaking of Betty's nerve brings to mind something that happened just before all of these things came to a head, because it was a forerunner of things to come. Betty had heard they were auditioning talent for a show at the high school and she tried out. I didn't have the nerve to try out, but she did and she got a part singing. I put all my efforts behind her. We borrowed an evening dress from Phyllis, and on the night of the show I'll never forget the pride I felt when she walked out on the stage. Betty had dark hair and always looked older than she was. She wasn't quite fourteen but looked twenty up there on the stage singing "Temptation." She sang like a grown-up woman and it was hard to believe that was my "little sister" up there. But she did it and she was good. The audience gave her a big round of applause.

As I pointed out, Betty had a nose for auditions. We were running out of money because we were out of pop bottles. The telephone had been turned off and we expected the utilities to go any day because they hadn't been paid. Our rent had only a week or so to go until it would be due again, and we had no promise of any financial assistance in our immediate future.

When things really looked their bleakest, Betty came through, as usual. She'd heard that they held open auditions at WLW radio station every Thursday. The two of us had the sum total of about three songs that we sang well together. Betty had a very good natural ear for harmony and she had a lower voice than I did, so she sang the second part in our duets. I had a higher range, so I sang lead.

We figured it out together: If we ate no lunch, after school we could go down to WLW on the streetcar for a nickel, using our school pass. But we'd have to be on the car home before five o'clock or walk, and it was a long walk to Price Hill from downtown Cincinnati.

Nothing deterred us. After school we caught the streetcar, went down to the station and walked into the studio where the auditions were held. When our turn came, the piano player asked us, "Where's your music?"

We didn't have any music.

"What song are you going to sing?"

Betty said, "Hawaiian War Chant."

We didn't even know the real words, but we thought we could mimic them from having heard them, and I remember the wrong words even today. After that first song they asked for another, and we sang one of Ella Mae Morse's big hits, "Patty Cake Man." One called for two, and two called for three. They wanted just one more song. We picked a Johnny Mercer tune made famous by Tommy Dorsey and the Pied Pipers—the song was "Dream."

In fact, one time not long after Betty died I was in a car going from Manhattan to Brooklyn where I was doing a concert and they had an FM station on and two of those three songs came up back to back on the radio. I said to myself, "Old Betts must be letting me know there's something she wants from me right now so I should keep my ears and eyes open."

At any rate, on that day we auditioned, the talent coordinator —and I'm sure they didn't call him that in 1945—was up in the booth with the engineer. His name was Mort Weiner. He called in the program director and we did the same three songs again for him. Then somebody higher up was called in, and once again we did our trio of tunes.

While these great brains at WLW were deciding our immediate future, I was worrying about something far more practical and far more immediate—the clock on the wall was getting closer and closer to five o'clock and I felt like Cinderella just before midnight. I whispered to Betty, "This is all great, but how do we get home?"

We had our secret, and our secret was we had exactly ten minutes and ten cents to get home in and on.

I said, "What are we going to do, Betty?"

Betty, with all her great moxie, said, "If we get the job, I'll get an advance. If we don't get it, then we'll walk home. That's all there is to that."

I don't think we had to wait very long for a decision, but it seemed like a long time to me. Finally Mr. Weiner came over to us smiling and said, "We like you. How about twenty dollars a week—apiece?"

How about it? That was a lot of money to us at that time. Now we would be able to call up a relative and say, "We can pay our own way."

Almost in unison, before he had a chance to change his mind, we said, "Yes!"

Mr. Weiner said, "Well, you'll need your parents to sign for you because you're too young to sign for yourself."

For a change I had moxie. I said, "Our mother and father are in California and we live with our aunt."

"That's all right," he said. "You get your aunt to sign the papers and you can go to work."

That, we assured him, would be no problem. Now Betty made her big play and said, "Mr. Weiner, since we've got the job, I wonder if I could have a dollar advance on my salary." That took some nerve. I would never have done it. I would have cut my tongue out first. But she did what she knew she had to do.

"Why don't I just make a personal loan to you, and you can pay me out of your first paycheck? How would that be?" he asked.

That would be just fine. Mr. Weiner smiled. He understood.

We didn't go to school the next day. Too excited. But that evening we went to the corner and called Aunt Jean and explained that we had a job at WLW and between us we would be making $40 a week.

"Aunt Jean, do you think we could come and stay with you?" We explained the whole thing about daddy, and she wondered why we hadn't called sooner. We told her how we felt about supporting ourselves.

Aunt Jean was very excited about our job, but more excited and pleased that we were taking care of ourselves. She'd always worried about us. Even though Uncle Roy was still in Germany in the service and Aunt Jean had two little children of her own to take care of, she would have taken us in without a job. But we couldn't impose on her that way. We wouldn't.

Aunt Jean said it was all right for us to come and live with her, and so we *were* solving our own problems.

The day following our conversation with Aunt Jean we packed up what we could. We had a few clothes. Daddy had been wonderful about clothes. He knew we loved cashmere sweaters and we usually couldn't afford them, so for Christmas he had gotten us each one. For our birthdays he got us cashmere sweaters, too. We'd get different colors so we could switch off. Cashmere sweaters were very popular in the mid-Forties. What I wanted more than anything else was one of those Junior League strands of pearls. We wore bobby socks and penny loafers and were right in style with the current teen fashions.

Our apartment was on the third floor so we had to walk three flights, dragging our belongings behind us. There was a taxi coming to get us because we couldn't take all that stuff on a streetcar. Aunt Jean lived in Green Hills and paid the taxi driver when we got there. We would reimburse her out of our first paychecks.

A major crisis developed as we waited in front of our building for the taxi to arrive. We were making trips back and forth carrying our bags down this long walk to the curb when the streetcar stopped at the corner—and who should get off but my father! He looked sober, but we couldn't be sure, so we hid around the side of the house until he started up to the apartment. Daddy, when he was sober, would always whistle the first few bars of "Kentucky Babe" when he came home. Now he hit the porch and opened the door and as he went inside he started to whistle "Kentucky Babe."

Betty and I looked at each other. The cab turned the corner and was coming down the block. We had to make an instant decision. Betty said, "We're not sure if he'll stay sober."

I said, "That's right."

The cab was there, and as he was going up the stairs we raced down the walk, got into the cab and went to Aunt Jean's.

The die was cast. That part of our life was behind us. It was a long time before we saw daddy again, but Aunt Jean insisted we call him the following day at work to let him know our decision. I think he was hurt. He told us he didn't have to drink; he could stop if he wanted to stop. But that was something we had heard for a long, long time early on.

"Why don't you come back and let's try it again?" he said.

"No, daddy. We can't do it." I didn't allow myself any open display but I was crying my heart out inside. My mother was gone. My brother. And now my father. I'm sure Betty felt the same emptiness. Aunt Jean, who basically liked my father, left the decision to us. She was very wise because she believed daddy was a good person who had a weakness.

We had a whole new life now—living with Aunt Jean and working for WLW as singers. What more could anybody want? At the time WLW was newly owned by a company that manufactured airplane parts for Curtiss-Wright during the war. The Crossley Corporation had sold the station. What this meant to us was that we had to take a physical and carry identification badges like they did in defense plants for security. Betty had never had a blood test and she was scared to death of needles.

"I can't do it," she told me.

"Sure you can. I'm scared too, but I'll do it first."

I let them take my blood and said to Betty, "See? It's all right." They took some blood out of her arm and she said, "I'm going to faint."

The doctor said, "Put your head between your knees." She did and rolled right off the chair, just did a somersault—out like a light.

When we started singing at WLW we didn't know any songs, so they got us a coach. We were sent to a lady named Grace Raines, whom Doris Day talks about all through her book. She was a vocal coach rather than any specific kind of teacher, a marvelous lady who was very helpful to us, though we didn't stay with her very long. We learned about six songs at first so that we could do the "Moon River" show. It came on very late at night, but it was summer vacation now, so we were able to do it.

It was the perfect sort of show for very slow, romantic ballads and things that would lend themselves to thirds for the two voices. We did songs like "How Deep Is the Ocean?", "Talk of the Town" and "My Silent Love." That was our contribution to the first show we appeared on.

We started living what seemed to us a marvelous life. Aunt Jean didn't have an extra room so we both slept on the couch—a three-piece sectional. We were now enrolled in Our Lady of Mercy Academy which was right downtown and close to WLW. Neither of us was a great student, but we got by. The important thing to us was that we were being productive. From school we'd go directly to the station and work, and then come home on the bus to Jean's. After dinner we had the whole evening to do whatever teen-agers did, and for the first time really had some kind of a normal life.

Aunt Jean, who has always been a whiz with money, said, "Now, you've got to budget yourselves so that you can buy some clothes and put some money away every week."

We did it on $20 a week. I suppose I saved more money then than I did when I was making $20,000 a week. In your early days, when you start making money for the first time, you have a tremendous respect for it. That was an astronomical amount of money for us. You lose respect for money, though, as it comes in in greater amounts. Familiarity does breed contempt in money matters.

We bought summer dresses and saddle oxfords and that sort of thing, and it wasn't too long until we were doing outside jobs. We started working with a local band which was fronted by a trumpet player named Billy Petering, who was also my first boy friend. I was really crazy about him. It was schoolgirl love with the leader of the band, and there is absolutely nothing to compare to that. We basically played high-school dances, but it was wonderful for Betty and me. We were band singers.

We were out front doing it. To sing with a band was the big thing, no matter how small the places you played. I was a band singer, and it carried a lot of prestige.

We stayed with WLW about two years and a few months, making a good name for ourselves in the greater Cincinnati listening area, and we were making extra money with the extra jobs. Billed as "The Clooney Sisters" we would sometimes get checks from WLW for as much as $130 each in a week's time after everything was taken out. Some big-band singers were lucky to be making $125 a week, so we fared quite well as local celebrities.

Barney Rapp had a big band around Cincinnati. Doris Day had started with him. Barney heard us and liked us. He hired us for his band and sort of acted as an agent for us as well. We didn't do very many outside jobs, just worked with the band, so I don't know that he ever got much in commissions.

With Barney we played our first big club dates. One was the Beverly Hills Supper Club—which recently burned, killing almost 200 people. I had pangs of close association to that fire, not only because I played there many times but because my brother Nicky, who is now the anchorman for ABC television news in Cincinnati, went over to Kentucky and spent the night covering that tragic fire. You touch base with the past in strange ways.

We played Castle Farms for a week, which was a big club job, and also the big downtown Cincinnati hotels like the Netherlands Plaza which always had remote network broadcasts when the big bands were in town. On a local level we were highly successful.

The big problem with us was that both physically, financially and as personalities, we were growing. We needed someone to take care of our affairs for us—an adult. But Aunt Jean had a husband coming home from the war and her own children growing and needing her full attention.

Things have a way of taking care of themselves. My Uncle George had been a bomber pilot in Europe and was also freshly back from the war. Betty and I loved George very much. He was young and enthusiastic and we felt he could relate to us, probably better than anybody else because of the closeness in ages. Aunt Jean thought so too, and Uncle George became our guardian. Somebody had to be able to go down to the station with us, be with us when we played clubs and make sure our contracts were correct and proper. Aunt Jean, in addition to her home duties, just wasn't up to handling all of that because her mind wasn't oriented in that direction.

Uncle George's was. He also didn't have a job yet, just getting out of service. He would get our salaries and generally take care of our career. We were happy to do that because we now had a manager, more or less, and we had faith in him because we loved him. He was always right on top of everything; indeed he took his job so seriously that he became the biggest tyrant in the world as far as our behavior was concerned. He wasn't going to have either of our young reputations spoiled. Any boy who looked at us was suspected of bad intentions.

This was especially true after we went on the road. Even at that young age we were permitted to smoke at Aunt Jean's, but when we went out of town Uncle George did not permit smoking because he thought that would give us a bad image. No nun in a Catholic convent took better care of her girls than Uncle George did of us—often to our total frustration.

All of this began to happen at one time. We were singing with Barney Rapp, and that's how we became big-band singers with Tony Pastor. Charlie Trotta was Tony's road manager and a close personal friend of Barney's. Tony's home manager in New York was a man by the name of Joe Shribman who came from the famous Shribman family of big-band fame. Si Shribman had started Glenn Miller. George Tobias played him in the movie, *The Glenn Miller Story*.

Tony was looking for a girl singer for his band and was coming into Cincinnati to play a date. Trotta came as advance man for Tony, and since Cincinnati was a breeding ground for new singers, it was logical that he look there.

Barney told him, "I've got two little girls singing with me and they are really great little singers. Would you be interested in hearing them?" I'm very grateful to Barney because he could just as well have been selfish and let it pass and we might not have had that big break—certainly not at that time. But he was not that kind of man.

We were at WLW singing and Barney called us and said, "Come on and sing for this gentleman." He didn't tell us anything about who it was, just told us to come and sing.

The first thing we did was call Uncle George and ask him if it was all right. He said, "By all means." So we went down to Barney's office and, without any accompaniment, we sang. Evidently Charlie was just knocked out. The next move, then, was to have him talk to George and make the necessary financial arrangements and work out our contract. I think our first salary with Tony Pastor was $250 a week each. Out of that we had to pay our room and board—for us and for Uncle George. Nobody had told us it was Tony Pastor, but we knew it had to be because we know that Charlie was Tony's road manager.

I can tell you we were soaring. Buttreflies fluttered in our stomachs. The big band. This was it! We were in the major leagues now. Tony was in town to play a one-nighter at a big ballroom in Cincinnati and we met him, and everybody was happy about the arrangement.

It was all set that we would join the band in two weeks at Atlantic City, New Jersey. Our first engagement with the band would be at the famous Steel Pier. Betty and I had never been out of the tri-state area—Ohio, Kentucky and Indiana. We'd never seen an ocean.

Then there was the question of clothes—what we would wear while singing with the band on the road. My dear, sweet Grandmother Guilfoyle came through like a trouper as she always did. She was absolutely without peer as a seamstress. She said, "Well, girls, pick out the clothes you want to have made. Show me the styles and I'll do it."

My grandmother, having so many daughters, really knew

how to whip up a quick creation. They would bring her some material and a pattern in the morning and say, "I need it for a dance tonight," and she'd have it ready, most of it finished by hand with the tiniest stitches you've ever seen in your life.

She was now going to make everything in doubles for Betty and me. Uncle George came up with a hell of an idea, and it was really the added touch we needed. Uncle Roy had a brother, Frank, who was a medical student—and is now, incidentally, a very successful pediatrician in La Canada, California. Frank was a wonderful painter, very artistic. Uncle George went out and bought some white material which was almost like denim—cotton, with a lot of body. Frank painted flowers all down one side of the material, and my grandmother made blouses and skirts out of it. She found sequins of the same color and sewed them around the flowers. Perfectly gorgeous outfits that would be gorgeous today.

Then there was a plaid taffeta that was very young and chic, an off-the-shoulder outfit. And we each had a long black skirt with about three blouses. We didn't have anything like a strapless bra, so we were continually taking our bra straps down and pinning them on the inside of the off-the-shoulder dresses. We were very big with safety pins on the road.

Betty was so funny, because she was built much smaller than me. I was very thin but I must have been a 36-C by the time I was eighteen. Betty was always smaller-busted, shorter and smaller-boned. She decided that she didn't have enough up front where it counted, so she went out and bought falsies to wear on the road. There was nothing stingy about Betty and she didn't stint on the falsies either. Where most girls would gradually increase the size of their busts, Betty went from absolutely nothing to a 38-C. Invariably on the road guys would be standing down below us in front of the bandstand with their eyes and tongues popping out, saying: "Look—the blond is obviously wearing falsies because she is so skinny, but that brunette—wow! Is she built!"

That used to drive me absolutely crazy. She damned near

killed herself, though. She wouldn't just slip the falsies inside of the bra like everybody else did; she had to tape them right onto her body and I had to listen to her moaning and groaning when she'd take that adhesive tape off every night before she went to bed. You can't imagine the grunts and groans that came out of her throat. But she would do it—for vanity.

Anyway, we had our dresses and we were ready to board the train for Atlantic City. Planes were too expensive. Today it is the other way around. We were fascinated by the train ride, but most of it was after dark. The only other time we'd been on a train was from Cincinnati to Maysville and back. There was one crack train that went through Maysville, the Chesapeake and Ohio's "George Washington." That depot in Maysville today is on Rosemary Clooney Street. Every tourist who comes through on a train sees that sign.

We were so excited we never slept. Just studied our lead sheets that Tony's manager had left for us to learn. Songs the band was already playing. One solo, which Betty would have been the logical one to sing, went to me because it fit my register better. It was too high for Betty. It was a song made famous by Pearl Bailey called "That's Good Enough for Me."

Our grandmother had prepared box suppers for us—fried chicken and other goodies. It was like having a picnic at seventy miles an hour. We were on our way with all the good wishes of Aunt Jean, Grandmother Guilfoyle and all our professional friends like WLW and Barney Rapp.

It was make-it-or-break-it time.

CHAPTER VII

On the Road

There are two kinds of big-band leaders—the administrator and the musician. Tony Pastor was the latter, having served a long appenticeship under the baton of Artie Shaw before going out on his own. His band was sort of unique because it was very good musically and yet had the reputation and flavor of a performing band. It was the kind of orchestra that could play an evening for a party or prom and the following day be able to put together an hour show right out of the orchestra. Betty and I would learn a lot about performing, as well as music, during the Pastor years.

It was also my first real introduction into the world of jazz because Tony was very jazz-oriented. Some of his singing recordings are jazz collectors' items because of that marvelous kind of light jazzy way he delivered a lyric.

When I joined the band in 1947 his arranger was Ralph Flannagan, who later went on to make quite a name for himself with his own band, which most people considered to be in "the Miller style." Truthfully it was the "Flannagan style." Under Ralph's tutelage Betty and I learned the Tony Pastor arrangements quite rapidly for our opening in Atlantic City.

We looked like anything but big-band singers when we stepped off the train at the end of the trip. There we were, two sisters from Kentucky and their managing uncle. Cardboard suitcases filled with street clothes, band clothes and framed photographs of all our relatives. There was no big publicity buildup, no press to meet us, and it was just as well. The Atlantic City papers did have a small caption in the Steel Pier ad which read simply, "featuring The Clooney Sisters."

Some feature. We were housed in a very small hotel, the Albemarle, about a block away from the beach in Atlantic City. The entire band stayed there. I'll never forget the place— which was typical of a lot of hotels that big bands were quartered in during their reign as the top attraction in contemporary music. The walls were tissue-paper-thin, the floors were slanted, and there were no bathrooms in the rooms.

Betty and I were climbing the walls because Uncle George had made it plain he intended to enforce his ban on smoking with no exceptions. Dying for a cigarette, like all teen-agers with something taboo, we began scheming to circumvent his rule. There was a young boy singer with the band, about sixteen, who seemed to show an immediate interest in Betty. His name was Tommy Leonetti. I picked up on his attentions toward Betty and got an idea.

I said to Betty, "Listen, I think that boy likes you."

"You think so?"

"I really do."

Betty kept her eyes open, and my brain was in first gear. He did indeed like Betty. He liked her a lot. It was understandable. She always felt so easy with people and was so pretty. If you can say a kid of fifteen is sensuous, she looked sensuous.

After a couple of days in Atlantic City without a cigarette Betty and I were in the ladies' john, down the hall from our room, discussing our intolerable situation. As I explained, the walls were like tissue, and next to the ladies' room was the men's. Betty and I were in two separate booths and talking underneath to each other, never realizing that Uncle George was on the other side in the men's section and could hear every word we said.

Betty said, "You know something?"

"What?"

"I'll bet Tommy would buy me a package of cigarettes—if I asked him."

"My thoughts exactly. So go for it."

Unaware that a third party was on to our scheme, Betty made her pitch to Tommy, and the cigarettes were forthcoming. Uncle George never said a word to us about it. He let us hang ourselves. When Tommy handed over the pack of butts to Betts and she started to put them in her purse, Uncle George stepped out of nowhere and very calmly stuck out his hand and said, "I'll take those." He caught us every time. We felt as though he had ESP. Both of us were humiliated at being caught —and especially in front of Tommy.

When we joined Tony it was our first experience with our own dressing room. Betty and I were as one, so it was really like having a dressing room alone—something I've had hundreds of times since. Neither of us were rowdy in our dressing room. We were so used to living together under all sorts of circumstances that we had developed an instinctive respect for one another, so our dressing room was always quiet.

At the Steel Pier, however, you could hear everything that was said in every other dressing room, just as you could hear through the walls of our hotel. Betty and I were putting on our makeup when we overheard one of the men in the band mouthing off about us. It was Dave Maser (who later married Aunt Chris and became our Uncle Dave) and he was really heated up. He hadn't struck me that way before; he'd seemed like a nice guy. But there were no niceties in the way he was talking to the other guys that night.

"This is a fine thing," he said. "We end up baby-sitting two little kids on the road, for God's sake. This is supposed to be a professional organization. What the hell is this with a fifteen-year-old kid on the road? I think it's the most outrageous thing I've ever heard of in the band business."

He was really upset, and we were both deeply hurt. We didn't want to be with the band if nobody wanted us. So we went directly to Uncle George, and Uncle George went to Dave and told him we'd heard his comments and how we felt about it.

"But do you know what can happen to a kid like that, on the road with a bunch of musicians?" he asked Uncle George.

"I'm going to assume that the musicians in this band are gentlemen. My nieces are ladies and I'm here to see that they remain so. You'll just have to have a little understanding."

"It's quite an adjustment, but I'll try. You'll also have to consider the boys' feelings."

He didn't make any effort to apologize to us, but he got to know us pretty well and found we were just as Uncle George described us. Actually, Dave was thinking of us as well as the band. Life on the bus can and does get pretty boisterous, and the boys were wondering how they were going to relax on the band bus with two little girls and their overly protective uncle.

Dave Maser and Aunt Chris have been married thirty years now and we've laughed about that incident at family reunions over the years.

Opening night for the Clooney Sisters in Atlantic City. A big-name band and a crowded ballroom at the end of the pier. Whatever you get on first nights, I had. Backstage is a blur to me. The first thing I can remember about that night was Tony making the announcement, "And now—the Clooney Sisters." I went out first, Betty came out from the other side of the stage, and we sang our first duet together with the Tony Pastor Band. It was appropriate that we did it together, and the song also fit the occasion—"It's a Good Day"—because it was a very good day for us. The place was jam-packed and the people applauded a lot. It was good, and there was so much excitement attached to it that it gave us a kind of extra push.

I followed that with my solo, "That's Good Enough for Me."

Tony put on quite a show. In addition to himself and the Clooney Sisters he had his brother, Stubby Pastor, playing trumpet and singing, and the famous drummer, "Paradiddle Joe." The band played for three hours with appropriate intermissions. Tony's band was like our outfits that Grandmother Guilfoyle made for us—there were a lot of combinations: singing with Tony, dueting together, singing separately and singing with Tommy Leonetti. Most of Tony's arrangements were originals, which made it all the more interesting for us and for the people who came to dance or just to watch and listen.

We had a string of one-nighters following our two-week stint at the Steel Pier, and the first one-night stand was in Harrisburg, Pennsylvania. When we got there Betty and I unpacked everything in our suitcases. We put all the family photographs out, and barely had them set up when it was time to go to work. When we got back to the hotel it was after midnight and we just fell into bed, dead tired. We arose about six, bleary-eyed, stuffed everything back in the suitcases and were back on the road again at seven. We learned not to unpack until we got at least a week's engagement.

I remember one particular string of one-nighters that went on for ten weeks. It was difficult when I was a teenager. I think it would be impossible now.

We got in on the tail end of the big-band era. Many of the big bands had already started to break up, so the future was predictable. Singers had already started out on their own in many instances, and it became obvious that a band singer's career had to go in that direction, or go nowhere at all. That meant if I was to have a future as a singer, I had to make the best of my time with Tony Pastor—which ended up being about three years.

I remember the first recording session with Tony. It was with a record company called Cosmo, but I don't think the album was ever released. It was an album of songs from the big hit Disney picture *Song of the South*. Betty and I sang "Zippety Do Dah" with Tony and Tommy, and I sang "Sooner or Later" by myself. Although the album was forgotten, the review given me by *Downbeat* magazine lives on as a bright milestone in my career.

They said: "Rosemary Clooney has an extraordinarily good voice, perhaps the nearest thing to Ella Fitzgerald we've ever heard."

Not only did I flip out, but every guy in the band took a second look at my ability. Suddenly I was getting an awful lot of respect that I hadn't gotten before. That was the time I thought to myself, "Maybe I'll just be a jazz singer." It was an amazing and rewarding feeling to be accepted by these musicians. Up to that time I felt they had only been tolerating me. After that review everything changed.

A lot of things happen to you when you're on the road. Crowds are totally unpredictable. We traveled a lot and appeared before thousands of people, but one event stands out in my mind about those one-nighetrs. In the spring of 1949 we did an outdoor concert at VMI and one of the boys got very cute. He was standing in the crowd that had gathered around down in front of the bandstand, and as we were singing he tried to grab Betty's ankle. We were wearing spike-heeled patent leather pumps, and without missing a note or a word of the song, Betty raised her heel and put that spike right through the back of the boy's hand. Just came down on it as hard as she could, smiling all the while. The boy took off holding his hand, yelping like an old hound dog chasing a rabbit in the backwoods of Kentucky. You just didn't mess around with Betty.

Betty and I always dressed alike, but in fact we should never have worn the same clothes because our personalities were totally different, as was our coloring. Uncle George, however, thought it a nifty idea that we not only dress alike on stage, but offstage as well. So we were stuck with the same clothes—and both of us hated it.

I should mention here that while we were on the road, my mother had returned to Cincinnati. She knew we were singing with Tony, but we had no direct contact with her. We did talk to our grandmother on the phone often and she would tell everybody what we were doing and tell us all the latest family gossip.

In 1949 we also took our first plane trip, as did some of the guys in the band. We were going to Hollywood to play the Palladium. The plane we flew to the Coast on was probably a DC-3, but it looked like a giant to me. We made four stops en route, and I thought it took forever—I was deathly afraid. But when we got to California, after going through the three-hour time change from the East Coast, and I got off the plane, I fell in love. I've never felt anything so soft in my life as the air out here. I loved it then and I still do.

Along the way I had also fallen in love with one of Tony's musicians, a guitarist. It was my first mature love affair. We weren't really dating, because Uncle George was still riding herd on the romance department, but we saw each other behind George's back. The only person who knew about us was my sister Betty. I knew that Dave (I'll call him) planned to leave the band in California, and he wanted me to marry him. I said yes because I really did love him. He was a tender man. I don't think there could have been a better introduction to any kind of lovemaking than through him. He was extraordinarily kind and gentle with me, all the good things you read and hear about a first lovemaking experience. All the things that don't usually happen.

Dave was also extremely bright and a very good musician. All in all, everything I liked in a man. So it was easy for me to say yes to him. Betty always covered for me when I saw him. When Uncle George checked us at bedtime Betty would say,

"Rosemary's asleep," or "Rosemary's in the shower." Whatever was necessary, she did it. No questions asked.

In Hollywood we stayed at a place which still exists on Vine Street. Less than a year before Betty died we went to the Villa Capri for dinner one night—just the two of us. Afterward we decided to get into my Corvette and drive over to the Vine Lodge just for kicks, to see what it was like now and share a few memories. It was pouring when we got there, and the young man who was the night clerk must have thought we'd lost our way. He recognized me and said, "Hello, Miss Clooney, are you sure you're in the right place?" It was not the same Vine Lodge it had been in 1949.

I said, "My sister and I lived here a long, long time ago. Could we look at the courtyard?"

We stood in the courtyard, in the rain, and remembered how we used to wait for June Christy to come home with her husband from her gig with Stan Kenton while we were playing the Palladium. She would come in wearing a suede trench coat and we thought she was just about the most stylish thing we'd ever seen and loved the way she sang. We were big fans, and she was always very nice to us.

We worked the Palladium every night, and Ava Gardner used to come by and listen to the music. I remember how beautiful she was. Just exquisite. That was another thing we learned about Hollywood on that trip: Having been brought up in the Midwest and South, we discovered that California was the land of beautiful people. There were an awful lot of beautiful boys and girls out here—and logically so, since they all came from somewhere else looking for a big break in the movies. The beauties all came out here to get "discovered," and they still do, with the result that there are some absolutely gorgeous people here.

We were established band singers now, and our first recording date with Columbia Records came up during that stay. I had a solo to do with Tony and the band, and Dave played the introduction and guitar interlude on the session, so it was very special to me. The song was called "I'm Sorry I Didn't Say I'm Sorry When I Made You Cry Last Night."

As I made the record—all during the time I was singing at the session—I had in the back of my mind that I wasn't really going to leave the band; that I was going to leave Dave in California. I hadn't told him, but I knew by then that I was going somewhere and a husband would only impede my progress. I was doing more and more solos with the band and less and less singing with Betty. Betty was very proud of me. I'm sure it was about this time, although she never really expressed the sentiment, that she began to become less interested in the band and more interested in a private life. She had a lot more drive and ambition than I did, and career was important to her, but it would not take precedence over her whole life.

I had the tenacity to hang in and probably more talent—I sang better than Betty—but I could not do what Betty could do with an audience. She had charisma and such immediate rapport with an audience that she could wrap them up when she first walked out on the stage. And she cared about people, too, in a way that I didn't. I was a little more aloof. Ambitious and aloof—always just a little bit apart from the audience, holding myself in reserve. They had to come to me a long way before I gave back of myself.

When I did that recording session I was not able to sing above a whisper. Fear. Fear and this thing I was feeling inside about Dave. But the music critics misinterpreted it: The consensus was that I had a new, revolutionary style. The people at Columbia Records agreed and began an intensive promotion with the disk jockeys, starting with Martin Block, who also thought I was a great new singer with a brand-new style.

Martin was very important because he had "Make-Believe Ballroom" which was one of the top record radio shows in the country. He was one of those people who could make or break a record overnight. There were a few around who could do that, and the record companies would fall over themselves trying to please them because they knew if these guys played something it would sell enough records to recoup company costs right away—whether the record became a hit or not.

We had about six dates on the West Coast after the Palladium, then would fly on to Texas to do one-nighters through Texas on a bus.

The time came to tell Dave I was going on with the band. I kept telling him right up until the day before I left that I was going to run away and we'd get married. But we were leaving the next day and I had to tell him I couldn't stay. My main excuse was that I couldn't leave my sister. Excuse number two was that because of my family I couldn't afford to leave the band just yet. A third, rather lame excuse was that I hadn't given the band the required two weeks' notice. I was full of excuses. I wanted to draw it out because I didn't want to lose him, but I didn't want to stay either. I wanted to have my cake and eat it, too.

Whether he ever understood, I don't know, but he was gracious and let me go to Texas with the band. We made a pact that he would write me care of General Delivery in all the towns that I would be in so that I could take casual walks to the Post Office and get his letters without Uncle George finding out. As you know, however, Uncle George was quite an investigator, and it wasn't long before he knew about the whole thing.

We got to Virginia Beach—and it was summertime. The band was booked into the beautiful Cavalier Hotel. I was back there about a week after Betty died. They no longer had the big bands coming in, but I went to that deserted ballroom and remembered the big crowds, Betty and me singing and the applause. I sat down on the edge of the bandstand and cried, remembering that we faced the ocean the night we were there. Memories are around every corner and in every niche in this business.

While we were playing the Cavalier that night I met an incredibly handsome young man. He was named something-

something the Third and I remember him as being very rich and just the prototype of the handsome boy that I never had a date with in high school. Blond, blue-eyed, tanned and from the right family. He had a gorgeous car, too. Our love affair, torrid as I thought it was, lasted one night.

Still, I hadn't thought I could be with anybody but Dave, and that night awakened me to the facts of life. One of those facts was that Dave was just a passing part of my life. I was obviously becoming more sophisticated. Dave and I would never be, and I knew it. The age of innocence was leaving. Naïveté was going—that time when you're sure it is forever was over. The handsome stranger was not really an important thing in my life except he showed me where my future was, and it was not with Dave in California. If he could so easily distract me from Dave, then something or somebody else could and probably would.

My career was suddenly taking on enormous proportions. The record we made in California was now released, and the reaction, critically, was tremendous. It was a Tony Pastor record so I never knew the commercial profits it made, but it was certainly played as much or more for the time than anything I've ever had. That's when the whole thing came out about my "brilliant style." They expected me to continue singing that way, but I couldn't—the fear was gone. I busted out of the style a little at a time and soon got to singing the way I do now—the Rosemary Clooney way.

Betty decided to leave the band, and that put me in an even more prominent position. She wanted to go back to Cincinnati. She was eighteen years old and had never been to a dance except on the other side of the bandstand. She had met a football player named Bob Bueresch, so she went back home and did all those things that she had planned to do and missed. But she found she missed singing, too, and pretty soon had her own show on WLW, the station where we got our start. That led to other things and New York again for her . . . but that's getting ahead of ourselves. Betty made up her mind to leave the band one day and she was gone the next morning. Uncle George also went home.

It was time for me to make a move, too, and I knew it. I stayed on with Tony to honor the two-week notice required in the contract we had with him. Before I left Tony, however, Columbia set up a recording session for me. The record was under my name with Tony Pastor's band—my first single as a singer on my own. It was a number called "Bargain Day," written by a younger man, Billy Roy. A fantastic song, but very sad. Kind of a Billie Holiday-type song.

Singers were already coming in very hot, and Frank Sinatra, of course, was the hottest. For a long time Bing Crosby had been about the only big singer recording solo. Before long the field would be crowded.

I finished out my two weeks' notice with Tony at the Deshler Hotel in Columbus, Ohio—not far from where I had started it all in Cincinnati. I went home to Cincinnati to just sort out my priorities and regroup before launching myself as a single entity in New York. I was twenty-one. I was a woman now, not a child. I still had some rough spots ahead, but I didn't know that—not yet.

CHAPTER VIII

Success

I left the band and the one-nighters for New York and frugal living. I had little money and few prospects. Now that probably sounds ridiculous considering all the plaudits for my singing that I've described. The truth is, it cost a lot of money to maintain myself on the road with the band. Clothes, food and hotels were the big drain on my salary. As long as I was drawing a paycheck from Tony I had security. When that stopped, so did my security.

Tony's manager, Joe Shribman, became my manager. Joe and his roommate, Joe Galkin, had a one-bedroom apartment on West 57th Street, but they had a living-room couch, and that's where I bunked. I lived out of my suitcases, and whatever money I made, which was very little for quite a while, was spent on hunting the wholesale houses on Seventh Avenue trying to get clothes cheap.

A lot of people were helpful. I did a lot of shows with

Vaughan Monroe who had the "Camel Caravan" radio show which was a weekly. His producer was a lady named Louise and she was enormously considerate and helpful. I would go wherever the band was on a weekend to do the radio show and then fly back to New York to do other things during the week. A lot of little things began to happen for me.

In 1950 television started coming in a great big way, and a couple of good things happened to me all at once. For one thing I had a regional hit in Philadelphia. I had recorded a song called "The Kid's a Dreamer" that was written by Doug Arthur, a disk jockey. As a result of that song becoming number one in Philly, I could play the number-one clubs in the Philadelphia area and get more money than I could anywhere else. Manie Sacks was heading up A&R at Columbia when I signed with them to do records and he was guiding my recording career. However, that was right at the end of his tenure there. Shortly thereafter he left Columbia and became president of RCA.

Manie did a lot for me, though, and deserves a lot of credit for my getting off the ground. He was trying to find a hit for me. While Manie was still at Columbia, Frank Sinatra was looking for a girl singer to do a recording date with him. Manie suggested me, and Frank said okay.

We did two sides on that first date together, but later on we did some other things. That first session with Sinatra was the thrill of my life because I had always been such a big Sinatra fan. I remember once, in high school, I had somehow or other gotten the telephone number of Frank's manager and I called up, hoping to hear Frank's voice on the other end of the line. My mother later found the call on the bill and raised no little hell with me about it, but what did I know? I thought I could call this number where his manager was and Frank would be in the office. I had no idea about things like that. Some nice lady answered the phone and was immensely amused by my call. I suppose she hadn't even met him herself.

Enter Mitch Miller, who probably had more to do with establishing me as a permanent part of the singing scene than any other person. My initial contract at Columbia was nothing terrific. I don't remember all the details, but it was renegotiated when Mitch Miller came in. I think my new contract was for five years with options. I knew so little about business—Uncle George had handled everything on the road. I do know my new contract was a long-term one and that they were now putting an enormous effort together to find material that would break me out in the open in a big way.

A lot of us started together. Tony Bennett and Guy Mitchell at Columbia. Patti Page at Mercury. Doris Day and Dinah Shore had both been in the Columbia stable before me. Dinah and I are the greatest friends and I am often a guest on her television show. During those early days I met her once, and I've never discussed that meeting or my feelings about it with her. Manie took me to the Waldorf to see her. I was a little jealous of the fact that he was so obviously crazy about her. Dinah was a big star. I was just the new kid on the block.

Mitch Miller, however, swept into Columbia like a strong spring breeze. It was during the summer of 1950, and he would make a fantastic difference on the Columbia label. Goddard Lieberson was the president of Columbia and an enormously charming man. Married to the very beautiful film star Vera Zorina, he was a most urbane gentleman.

Lieberson had replaced Ted Wallerstein who really had made me feel like a welcome member of the Columbia (and his) family. He and his wife had a summer house in Westport, Connecticut, and they had a forty-foot ketch. I crewed on that ketch the whole summer. I'd go up for the weekend and he'd treat me like one of his kids. He took me to my first opera and my first ballet. All of this helped to make my beginnings in New York much more warm and comfortable. Ted Wallerstein—a terribly nice man.

Where Manie was kind of a quiet man, and soft-spoken, Mitch Miller was anything but. Here came this bearded musician who was a total extrovert. He had positive opinions about everything. In a recording studio he would take the arrangement and turn it around and change something and do some little thing to it if he didn't like the sound. He put his mark on the product at once. He knew exactly what he wanted and had exactly the right way of doing it.

My first hit at Columbia was "Beautiful Brown Eyes." It was an old standard in the country field, but I had given it a plaintive, folk song interpretation which appealed to the popular chart people. It eventually sold in excess of half a million copies. Mitch felt I had better things to come and he wanted to find them for me. The record that really made me, though, was almost not made by me.

I listened to a demonstration record of "Come On-a My House" by Kay Armen. It had been written by William Saroyan and Ross Bagdasarian who later became David Seville of "Chipmunk" fame. Saroyan had written a collection of essays and published them under the title of *Dear Baby*. This particular essay was called "Highway U.S.A." and was inspired by a cross-country trip that Saroyan and Seville had made by automobile. Traveling across America they saw all the riches of this country. That's why they said, "Come on-a my house, I'm gonna give you a peach and a plum and an apricot, too." They saw all the things that could grow here that did not grow in Armenia where their parents were born. So that's what it was really written to convey.

I think it was a musically snobbish time of my life. I really hated the song. I hated the whole idea, and my first impression was, what a cheap way to get people's attention. When Mitch caught up with me to set the record date, I told him I didn't want to do it.

Mitch, who was usually very kind and sensitive, said, "Well, let me put it this way. I will *fire* you unless you show up tomorrow."

Needless to say I was at Liederkranz Hall the next day ready to record. Columbia used Liederkranz for much of its recording because of the fantastic natural acoustics.

The song was not exactly a hymn to America. The lyrics

were supposed to be sung as though I were singing to one man only, my husband.

We had quite a few takes before Mitch was satisfied with the recording. This was before any kind of electric piano and he wanted a harpsichord sound. We had to rent the harpsichord from a place that didn't have too many in stock and we waited one whole session. I remember Stan Freeman and all the other musicians waited with me for one full three-hour session and the harpsichord never showed up so we couldn't make the record. Then, once we had it, to get the sound of the harpsichord amplified to the point where Mitch was satisfied, we moved microphones and harpsichord all over the studio. The mixes also had to be adjusted.

He finally got the sound he wanted by trial and error. Joe Jones was the drummer, and Mitch didn't like the sound of the drums. After some finagling he finally said, "Get rid of the drums. Just use the case."

And that's the way it was done. He wanted Joe to use the brushes but to use them like sticks in order to get the slap sound he wanted. Mitch never had any compunctions about doing what was necessary to get the desired results.

It didn't take me long to do my part because by that time I knew the song really well—after two sessions. My goodness, I never took that long for anything. Most of the time I couldn't afford to take two sessions because of too many other comitments. I wouldn't dream of going in for one record session, which was three hours, get the musicians and just work on one song.

I had Mitch's instructions in mind when we recorded, and ended up with an Italian accent for an Armenian song because it was the only kind of accent I knew. Thanks to all the guys in Tony's band who had always taken me to meet their families on the road, I was very up on Italian accents.

With "Come On-a My House" recorded I went on to other things with hardly a thought that anything good would come of that session. Too many things had gone wrong, plus which I still didn't like the song. Which says a lot about my ability to select a hit.

In addition to recording in the pop department of Columbia, I was also doing a lot of things in the children's department. I had been doing that before any of my hits came along. I have always enjoyed doing children's records because you have to be totally honest. There are no tricks and no cutesy-pie things like the way you can get by for adults with things like "Come On-a My House." The double entendres—you just don't do that with kids. Just sing it straight and in tune to get the story across. Those records continue to sell and I continue to receive royalties from them. Instead of making new records for the kids, the old records find new audiences. Every week Captain Kangaroo plays one or two of my children's records.

I followed "Come On-a My House" a couple of months later with "Tenderly." Mitch asked me what I would person-ally like to record and I said, "I'd like to do 'Tenderly.'"

"All right, let's do it."

I remember going into the recording studio and singing it correctly. It was a hard song to sing because it had a very wide range, but I thought I had sung it quite well. It was a beautiful arrangement by Percy Faith and had a million strings and all that. But Mitch flipped the talk-back and said, "I'll be out to talk to you." That's something else I appreciated about him. He would never embarrass you or put in in any kind of un-comfortable position the way a lot of A&R men would do. He would come out of the booth and talk to you privately. He was a marvelous recording psychologist.

"Now,"he said, "You really are being intimidated by this song."

"I'm very fond of the song."

"That's because it's been recorded by so many other people."

He was right. Mine was the twenty-second recording of "Tenderly." Randy Brooks, a trumpet player married to band-leader Ina Rae Hutton, was the first to make a record of it, with a beautiful trumpet solo. Many others had followed, in-cluding Sarah Vaughan and Nat King Cole.

"I just want to sing it right," I insisted.

"What you're doing is letting the song sing you. You've got to fake. You've got to approach this as if it were the first time a recording was ever made of 'Tenderly.' I want *your* interpretation of it."

That's what I needed. He had a way of explaining so that I understood exactly what I had to do. We did it in about five takes. They didn't piece songs together then, like they do now.

"Tenderly" was not an immediate hit. That one was for the long haul and it has served me well both in prestige and financially. It still sells.

Right after I recorded "Come On-a My House" I went to Florida. Buddy Rich, who had been a drummer in the Tommy Dorsey orchestra, was a good buddy of mine and still is. Buddy said to me, "I'll go to Florida with you." You have to understand—Buddy wasn't a lover. Not even a one-night affair. He was my friend—that's all. So we used to hang out together sometimes.

He said, "Now if I can get a job down there, I'm not going to play drums, I'll just dance and sing." Which goes to show that no matter what you do well, there is always something else you'd like to do. Buddy is one of the most naturally funny guys in the world. He has a reputation of being brash, but if you understand his sense of humor you know that isn't true. It's just his style.

So Buddy and I split for Florida and played an engagement at the Olympic Theater in Miami. We were doing something like four shows a day, but it was an easy job and the weather was nice.

Now Miami is a little remote as far as instantaneous reaction to hits and things like that. You don't get the pulse of what's going on in the rest of the country. It sort of trickles down.

My manager called me about midway through the engagement and said there had been some fantastic reaction to the record. Mitch had shipped 300,000 records on consignment, which means if they don't sell the dealers can return them. Mitch Miller had the kind of power to more or less do a little dictating to distributors. He had a charisma that brought everybody together and he was a hit-maker, so people listened to him. That's really what makes a good producer of records—getting everybody to cooperate.

I couldn't get very enthused about the news because it sure wasn't getting any play in Miami. Jackie Sherman, my roommate in New York, was down there with me and at her suggestion when I finished my engagement we flew to Cuba for a couple of days. We checked into Havana's Hotel Nacional and I enjoyed going to all those marvelous nightclubs that abounded before Castro became premier. It was the first time I'd ever been to that kind of resort, so it was a very relaxing experience for me.

Returning we had to change planes in Miami because there was no direct service from Havana to New York. But we finally arrived at La Guardia and went by cab to Manhattan. I had an overwhelming surprise in store for me. As we drove up Broadway every single record store (and there must be dozens) was blaring out over the loudspeakers, "Come-On-a My House." I couldn't believe it. But there it was.

It is amazing what a hit will do for a singer. Let me illustrate. All the time I was recording in New York and working on television and radio—whatever I could get a job at—I was introduced, always, by the local emcee wherever I was working with a lot of qualifying statements. He would go through all my credits to sort of lock me into the people's minds. Just to let them know it was not an amateur hour and that I held some promise of ability to entertain them for the next twenty minutes or whatever.

The first big job I had after "Come On-a My House" hit the charts was a date at the Chicago Theater in Chicago with Frankie Laine. Frankie had left Mercury and was now also recording for Columbia, and we did seven shows a day because Frankie was very, very hot. The shows were short, but you still had to be in the theater all day from nine o'clock on. At the same time, you just couldn't escape hearing "Come On-a My House" because it was everywhere—wherever there was a radio or record store. A lot of my friends were sick of hearing the song before it ever reached its peak. It was amazing to me.

I knew I was somebody the first day. There was another act on, then I came on and was followed by still someone else before Frankie. The emcee said, "I'd like you to meet Rosemary Clooney"—no qualifying of any kind—and the audience went crazy. They knew who I was. I was halfway home when I stepped out on stage. I felt wonderfully warm. It was the first time I'd been introduced that way.

I must tell you I did not feel like a star. Mostly I felt confused. It is very difficult to see yourself in the star position for the first time. After years of being a fan, the transition is awesome. The only thing I can think of that is comparable is going from Miss to Mrs. *That* takes some getting used to also.

I have to tell you a little something about my living accommodations because up to this time I was not exactly rolling in money. We were living at Hampshire House because Jackie came from a very wealthy family and her mother owned an apartment there. So we had a very nifty address, but often didn't have any money to buy food.

From the moment we arrived back at Hampshire House I felt as though I were on a merry-go-round. There was just a constant stream of things to do. For the next eighteen months I had more jobs than I could fill, the cover of *Time* magazine, a big story in *Life*, and every newspaper had feature stories on my success. The publicity thing was just enormous. It was all of this attention that brought me finally to the realization that I was a star. That, and the fantastic money. Fantastic when I had only been making something like $150 a week doing all sorts of odd engagements. Later it would skyrocket.

I was recording all the time because they now wanted product. You had to follow up a hit with some albums and things like that. Put the hit with an album and milk it for all the traffic allows. Just one thing after another. I didn't seem to have much time for anything. Not until I went to California.

By this time I had met Jose Ferrer—Joe. I was dating some, but mostly I was developing an interest in Joe.

I had met Joe at a television show that Robert Q. Lewis had. At the time I was doing all those television and radio shows during the summertime, before my hit with "Come On-a My House," and getting the equivalent of peanuts for each show, more or less. Robert Q. had a daily television show and I was on it as a singer. Joe was there publicizing his film, *Cyrano*, and a play he had just opened in on Broadway with Gloria Swanson called *20th Century*.

I was immediately impressed with him. He was charming and terribly talented. I had been going out with Robert Q. occasionally and so one night we went to see *20th Century* together. Bob seemed to know that there was some attraction between Joe and me. I don't know how he knew it on Joe's part, but he knew it as far as I was concerned. Because of that, I think he deliberately left me in Gloria Swanson's dressing room while he went over to see Joe and congratulate him on his performance. Miss Swanson was quite charming and nice to me, but I felt very left out and mildly uncomfortable.

But it was inevitable. Joe and I kept running into each other at parties, and every time we were at some function we exchanged small conversation. One time he asked me out for lunch.

Robert Q., in addition to the daily show, had a Sunday-night show on television, which was local in New York. It was sort of a celebrity thing where he wandered about this big room talking to well-known personalities in the audience. This was around Christmas of 1950, I know, because I had a red dress on that I wore to a Christmas party. Joe was also on Robert's show that night. I remember I had my little sister, Gail, with me and she was about four years old. She was visiting me at Hampshire House and I took her to the show with me. Joe

Shribman was with us, too. After the show we were waiting in the hall outside and Joe came up and said, "Who is this?" I introduced him to Gail. Later on he told me he had been enormously relieved because he thought she was my child and that I was married.

The following week we had lunch together and discussed an idea he had for a show about George M. Cohan. He was interested in me playing Mary. We lunched at a steakhouse on 56th Street called Al & Dick's, and Joe did something that astounded me. He'd polished off a shrimp cocktail, a steak and a side order of sliced tomatoes, and when the waiter asked if he'd like some dessert, Joe said, "No. I'd like to have the whole thing all over again." And he had another shrimp cocktail, another steak and another order of sliced tomatoes. It was the first and only time I ever saw him do that.

We saw each other occasionally after that. Many of our meetings were not planned. New York is a surprisingly small town when you get to know people. Somebody would have a cocktail party and both of us would be there. Jackie and I had one giant cocktail party, more or less to celebrate the success of "Come On-a My House." We decided to invite all three famous horn-rimmed-glasses people to the party without telling any of them that the other two would be there—Dave Garroway, whom I had also been dating for a long time, Steve Allen and Robert Q. Lewis. The idea just knocked Joe out. He thought it was hysterical.

Let me explain about Dave Garroway. I'd met him in Chicago maybe two years earlier, before I was there with Frankie Laine. Dave had a TV show in Chicago called "Garroway at Large," an innovative type of show that came out on NBC. He also had a late-night radio show that was strictly jazz, and Dave had me on the show. Buddy Greco did an arrangement of "My Funny Valentine" for me and there was a great orchestra with a couple of guys from the Tony Pastor Band which played it brilliantly. I sang the song, and after the show Dave invited me out and we started seeing each other. Often when

I finished a job anywhere near Chicago I would stop off and see Dave the way some people go home between engagements. We never got tremendously serious. I don't think either of us ever thought of anything like marriage.

I was still seeing Dave, who was now in New York doing "The Today Show," in which he started, and I was seeing other people, too, but I found myself getting more and more attached to Joe as time went on. I wasn't terribly thrilled about the fact that Joe was married and obviously working at it, but I wasn't all that impressed either. It was his second wife and they had no children. He had earlier been married to actress Uta Hagen and they had a daughter. There was never any confrontation between us about his marriage, but it was always there, and we both knew it. We had discussed it, about how painful it was for everybody. I never asked if he was in love with his wife.

It was after I moved to California that Joe finally separated from his wife.

While I was working in New York—even before I met Joe —I made a friend who has always been there when I needed her and has given me more good advice and counsel than any other woman I've ever known. That friend is Marlene Dietrich. When Manie Sachs went from Columbia to become president of RCA, RCA was making one last-ditch attempt to survive television and to pull everything out with a radio show called "The Big Show" with Tallulah Bankhead. It was on an hour every Sunday night and had a huge orchestra conducted by Meredith Willson. This was before I had any big hits or any reason to be on the show at all, but Manie liked me and decided to do me a favor. I was doing a song called "Taking A Chance On Love."

I hadn't done many network shows, and the night before dress rehearsal I was really frightened. So I went to a jazz place where a good friend, Art Tatum, was playing piano, and I sought some counsel for my jitters.

"You'll be fine," Art assured me. "Don't worry."

I said, "I don't feel as if I have any right to be on the show, because these people who are on it are big stars and I haven't done anything. I don't even know whether I'll be wearing the right clothes." I just kept going on with all those negative thoughts, and Art kept assuring me that my fears were foolish ones and I'd be great.

The next night when I got to rehearsal there was a big bouquet of roses from Art Tatum. Musicians are the greatest people in the world. I have great respect for them, and I think it's mutual. I understand them. I understand their sense of humor because I have very much the same sense of humor. It's just something that I grew up with and it's like second nature to me. I'm more comfortable around musicians. I hate to generalize, but I think musicians are the only men I've come across who can have a totally friendly relationship with a woman without bringing sex into it. Of course, they're always open for that, but if you're not, that's fine. They don't push it. They can really be your buddies and have been so with me for years.

Anyway, at the dress rehearsal I had seen Marlene Dietrich on stage with Tallaluh, but I hadn't spoken to her. There was no reason to. I had barely spoken to Tallulah, who was not overly taken with me—not terribly friendly, but professionally nice. She was busy with a lot of her close friends, and Dietrich was one of those.

The show was done before a live audience, and on the night of the show, after dress rehearsal, this woman came in the back door of the theater. I didn't know who she was. It was pouring outside and she was wearing this big scarf, galoshes and a long, funny raincoat. Out of this strange cocoon came a beige chiffon dress. Out of the galoshes came gold strappy sandals and the most beautiful legs you'll ever see. The scarf came off and here was this beige-blond hair—and there was Dietrich all pulled together. Simply a vision. She didn't care how she looked in the rain, but she was going to cover up the stuff that she had to take care of. She is an enormously practical woman.

I once said to her, "Everybody talks about that time when you were a presenter on the Academy Awards and stole the whole show because everybody was froufrou from here to China and suddenly you came out on the stage in a black, long-sleeved, high-necked wool dress that was down to the floor, but slit up to the hip, mostly on the downstage side where everybody could get a really good look at the legs. No jewelry, nothing. You knew that everybody else would be silver-and-gold-laméed to the teeth, and you came out in a black wool dress."

She said, "Well, my darling, it was very practical because I had a terrible cold."

That's what I mean when I say Dietrich is practical. Moreover, she is immaculately clean and neat, even when she's doing housework—and you've never seen an apartment cleaned until you've seen Dietrich clean.

On the night of the show, as she was unraveling herself from all these outer garments, she said to me, "You sing very well." She had heard me at rehearsal.

I said, "Thank you."

She asked, "What have you done?"

I told her I was recording for Columbia but hadn't had a big hit.

"You will. You will." And as she turned to go to her dressing room she added, "Now we really should keep in touch, because I think you have a great future."

That started our ongoing relationship which is still very much alive. I saw her again after I had the hit record, and Mitch Miller decided that Marlene and I should record together. He knew her and was recording her, and he knew we knew each other. Mitch thought the chemistry was right, so he got us into a studio and we did four sides. Among them were "Too Old to Cut the Mustard" and "That's a Nice, Don't Fight." It was great fun because she's so professional. The records, I might add, sold quite well.

Meanwhile Marlene and I saw a lot of each other and became enormously good friends. Marlene is the kind of woman who, if she is your friend, will walk the plank for you. Friends are very important to her. When I came to California to make films, of all places for me to end up was Paramount Pictures. Marlene helped build that studio and was one of their biggest stars—ever. She sat down and wrote personal handwritten notes to the heads of every department at Paramount as a way of introducing me—makeup, hair, props, wardrobe—including Edith Head. What an entry into the world of motion pictures.

After "Come On-a My House" it was inevitable that Hollywood would take notice of me—and Las Vegas. I played my first date in Las Vegas at the Thunderbird Hotel. There were not that many hotels there at the time and they gave me my first offer. It was not an enormous amount of money, considering the money I would make later on—only $5000 a week—but for me at that time it was a bonanza.

I tested at Paramount and was given one of the leads in *The Stars Are Singing*, which is not the most memorable film ever produced in Hollywood.

While all of these things were happening I was still recording, my records getting more and more air play and my singing career becoming one of the hottest in the country. Joe was doing a play, *The Shrike*, in New York, and we talked a lot on the telephone.

Mitch Miller was continually looking for new things for me to do on records and, like Bing Crosby, he often left little mistakes in a recording session that added originality to the number. I remember when I did "Botcha Me" Stan Freeman was playing harpsichord and Percy Faith walked in during the recording and was teasing Stan. Right in the middle of a take, the music fell down on Stan's hands. You can hear the fumbling at the harpsichord on the record. Yes, it's there. Mitch left it in for effect.

The Stars Are Singing was completed in 1952 and released in March 1953. What a year that was! It was destined to be one of the most active and important years of my life—in every department. The little girl from Maysville was a star.

CHAPTER IX

Mrs. Jose Ferrer

I'd finished my first picture at Paramount and was being highly touted as the "next Betty Hutton," which in truth wasn't me at all. Pitted against Anna Maria Alberghetti and Lauritz Melchior you can see where "Come On-a My House" would fit in, but Paramount, like Columbia, was getting a lot of mileage out of the big hit.

Publicity on the picture took me back to New York before starting my next film, *Here Come the Girls*, with Bob Hope. Joe had departed for Europe to make *Moulin Rouge* and New York seemed empty without him.

I didn't have time to think too much about Joe, though, because I was immediately sent on an extensive promotional tour after my first picture was premiered with plenty of fanfare in my hometown, Maysville, Kentucky. Paramount was giving me the star buildup, which entailed lots of travel, interviews and photo sessions, plus which I was spending an awful lot of time in the recording studios. There was no letup in my schedule.

Before we started shooting *Here Come the Girls* we had three or four weeks of rehearsal, and it was while I was making this picture that I decided to make California my home. I couldn't find a house right away so I was renting an apartment that belonged to producer Bill Dozier on Wilshire Boulevard.

About the time I finished the picture, Joe returned from Europe and we met in California. There was one big difference now—Joe was separated from his wife; they had parted just before he left to do *Moulin Rouge*. We had been in constant touch by telephone and letter all the time he was there, but we were by no means totally locked together as great lovers. He had been seeing a lot of ladies on the Continent, and I was dating in Hollywood.

It was during that separation from Joe that I met a marvelous man, Dante Di Paolo. Dante was a dancer I worked with in *Here Come the Girls*. We didn't have a chance to go out much alone, but we were together a lot in a group from the film. By the time I was making my third picture at Paramount, *Red Garters*, we were seeing an awful lot of each other. We were rehearsing dance numbers together every day and we had to work closely because it was an enormously stylish picture and the musical numbers were intricately interwoven, like a fabric, as part of the story.

I found Dante a sensational guy to be around and he was practically my own age, whereas Joe was sixteen years older. Because of our age difference—and also because of his work, which I thought was terrifically important—I always felt I had to be a lot more dignified when I was around Joe. I assumed it was expected of me. Joe has always been very serious about his work, but the way I should act around Joe was all my idea, not his.

Anyway, I was having fun with Dante while doing *Red Garters*. He was a fantastic man with a great sense of humor and he had a marvelous family—Italian—which really took me back to my days of working with the Tony Pastor band. It was a very easy relationship and there were no demands made on me, ever, by Dante. We made no big plans about each other. I felt sad because I knew nothing could come of us; by that time I was very wrapped up in getting married to Joe. Although Joe and I had never actually sat down and discussed marriage—he never formally said, "Rosemary, will you marry me?"—it was an understood thing between us.

It was easy for my relationship with Dante to take on a surface significance, however, because, although Joe and I began living together upon his return from Europe, he left almost immediately for Hawaii to film *Sadie Thompson* with Rita Hayworth. Happily, he went directly from that to *The Caine Mutiny* at Columbia. That meant he would be in town part of the time he was shooting, and I spent that time with him.

Even though Joe and I were living together, I continued to see Dante while Joe was on location. It's true Joe was working out of town so much that he spent precious few nights in my bed, but there has to be some other basis for this kind of behavior on my part, and I'm convinced it goes back to my childhood. I was shifted around so much as a kid, never having any genuine roots, that as an adult I was hanging on for dear life to everything that had any meaning to me. The end result had to be some sort of disaster at worst and confusion at best. I sincerely believe that it was during this period of my life that certain seeds which had been planted early on were beginning to take root, like weeds in a lovely garden. Unfortunately there was no human horticulturist nipping them in the bud.

I had a big house at 709 North Bedford Drive in Beverly Hills. I like big houses. By the time I finished *Red Garters* I had once again moved. That was an interesting set of circumstances because I didn't move into the house I wanted directly. There was a detour first.

I had looked at a house on Maple Drive and fallen in love with it. Came the week I was supposed to move in, I was told by my manager that Judy Garland and her family were still living there and really couldn't get out right then. I think it was one of the times when Judy was not feeling too well. It was okay with me. No rush. I was finally told I could move in, that everything was set, and I showed up at the front door. Judy was still there, and I remember the real-estate man with me was irate. "This is outrageous," he said. "This can't be done."

I had a vision of Judy Garland, whom I admired tremendously, sort of being hustled around, and it offended me so deeply I backed away. "I'll live anywhere," I told him, "except I don't want to disturb or bother her or have her discommoded in any way." So he found me a tiny little house on Doheny Drive in the interim, and when Judy was finally out, I moved in.

My brother Nicky was visiting me then, and Dante and my brother became very good friends. It got to the point where Dante was always around the house, and that didn't make it very easy for me. I rationalized that he was Nicky's friend, so what could I say? He was a truly good friend and I really loved him, but my plans to marry Joe were set. Joe, of course, had no idea about Dante and me.

Very few people knew that Joe and I were planning to marry. The press had reported us seeing each other, but in the Fifties it wasn't exactly kosher to say two people were living together unless you were doing a hatchet job on them—and there was no reason for anybody to do that to either of us. We were both Catholic, and Louella Parsons, a devout Catholic, had always been friendly to me and kind. With all her power, and with all her disdain for any kind of immorality, Louella would never put a Catholic in a bad light. It just wasn't her style.

Edith Head knew, of course, because she was working on a wedding outfit for me. But Edith is one person you could tell you murdered your mother and if you said, "Edith, don't breathe a word," Edith might live in agony about it, but she'd keep the vow once she made it. She never once mentioned to anyone that Joe and I planned to get married.

Edith designed and made me a beautiful suit from some lovely light-gray wool tweed Joe had brought back from England for my wedding outfit. I'd like to let Edith know here just how much I appreciated both her silence about our plans and the pains she took to see that I was exquisitely dressed for the occasion.

It was the summer of 1953 and Joe was going to do *Kiss Me Kate* at the Texas State Fair in Dallas. It gave him the opportunity to do something he'd always wanted to do—sing. I would join him there and we would get married.

I remember packing for the trip. Dante and Nicky were lounging at the pool. When they came into the house I still didn't say a word about my upcoming nuptials. I told myself that marriage was a happy occasion; why make it a sad beginning by just bluntly telling Dante my plans? That, I theorized, could wait until later. Once again I was shutting away decisions that would someday come back at me full force, like opening a closet bursting at the seams and having everything fall out on your head.

I left without telling either of them my intentions. Meanwhile, the newspaper people were on the alert to the fact that we might get married because Joe's wife had just been to Juarez to pick up her divorce papers. Speculation among members of the press was not if, but when, would we do it.

In Dallas Joe and I mapped our strategy. We got up early one morning and drove to the closest town in Oklahoma, Durant, where we could get married quickly and be back in Dallas in time for Joe to take care of things he had to do in connection with his show that night. It was about ninety miles each way. We had the blood tests and went to the courthouse where a justice of the peace awaited us. He was a very old man, about eighty-five I should think, and his eyesight was not the best. We stood before him along with Joe's agent, Kurt Frings, and his wife Ketti, who went with us, and the ceremony started.

The one thing that stands out prominently in my mind about that day was when I heard the justice say, "Rose Mary," which reminds me of the way they say it in Kentucky, "do you take Vincent Turner to be your lawfully wedded husband?"

He'd read Jose Vicente Ferrer, put an "n" in there and somehow turned it into Vincent Turner.

I said, "No, sir. I take Jose Ferrer, but not Vincent Turner." He looked closer at the paper in front of him and replied, "Oh, is that it?" Then he started all over again and Rosemary Clooney and Jose Vicente Ferrer were joined properly in the eyes of God and the law in holy matrimony.

I remember feeling very much in a daze. Joe had been married twice before; I don't know how he felt. But it was my first and only time. Everybody, I think, feels somewhat ambivalent on their wedding day. They want to and they don't want to when it gets right down to the wire. There's a lot of commitment there, and I felt it. It's like when your baby is born and you see it for the first time. There's an awesome responsibility involved.

We were married and had managed to give the press the slip. But by the time we got back to Dallas the whole world seemed to know about it. At our hotel it was impossible. The lobby was filled with press and people waiting for our return. Just bedlam. And it carried over to the theater that night. Joe was playing the director in the show and made his entrance from the audience. Well, there he came down the aisle toward the stage, and instead of striking up the proper music the band began to play "Here Comes the Bride." The whole audience fell down in hysterics. Joe, always the professional, marched up onto the stage, out through the wings and back around the building where he made a second entrance from the audience, this time to the proper music. He may have been a bridegroom in the A.M., but he was an actor in the P.M.

After the show that night we celebrated at Mario's, an Italian restaurant owned by Brenda Vaccaro's mother and father—a really supergreat Italian restaurant. A big party had been planned for us there and it went on into the wee hours of the morning.

We had only been married a few days when I had to go to New York to be a guest on Ed Sullivan's show. Joe went in the opposite direction, to La Jolla, California, to begin rehearsals on a play he was doing with Olivia de Havilland called *The Dazzling Hour*. Once again our careers took us on separate paths. But not for long, because I finished up the Sullivan stint and joined Joe in La Jolla. I fell in love with the place and have been ever since.

It was only a matter of weeks until Joe and I moved into the house I've lived in now for twenty-three years in Beverly Hills. As soon as Joe finished *The Dazzling Hour* we went house hunting, and both of us knew immediately this was our home. We moved right in.

The house has a musical history. Russ Colombo, who was the big crooner of his time (Crosby was just coming into his own), accidentally shot and killed himself in the den of this house in 1934. George Gershwin lived here and wrote "A Foggy Day in London Town" in what is now my living room, as well as his last composition, "Our Love Is Here to Stay." Ira Gershwin is our next-door neighbor, and Joe and I purchased the house from Ginny Simms (another singer) and her husband, a very wealthy man by the name of Calhoun who had actually gutted the house and redecorated it attractively.

The only thing the house needed was our own personal touch. There were some reproductions on the walls, but no paintings until we started putting them up. We did our own redecorating gradually. There was no dressing table upstairs and Joe had one made for me at Universal Studios—gigantic, and done with antique mirror. Touches like that took a little time, but it was fun planning all those personal things.

Who our friends were depended on whom Joe was working with. If he was making, say, *The Caine Mutiny* then we were seeing a lot of Fred MacMurray and June Haver, Van Johnson, and Bogart and Betty Bacall. Bogey was tremen-

Rosemary at approximately age four in a first photo taken on an excursion to the local dime store.

At sixteen Rosemary sat for her first gallery shot in Shillito's Department Store in Cincinnati.

Rosemary with her father, Andrew Clooney, Jr., and best childhood chum, Blanchie Mae Chambers, at the mayor's home in Maysville.

Rosemary on stage with a young Charlton Heston.

Rosemary and Mitch Miller before their relations became strained.

Rosemary Clooney and Jose Ferrer leave the courthouse in Durant, Oklahoma, following their marriage on July 13, 1953.

Rosemary and Jose record "Man and Woman."

Rosemary and Joe with their first-born, Miguel, at Harefield, Sussex, England, in 1955.

Frank Sinatra and Rosemary were the guests on Bing Crosby's first television special, "The Edsel Show."

Bing Crosby and Rosemary rehearsin for "The Edsel Show."

Bob Hope and Rosemary rehearse for th movie *Here Come the Girls.*

Rosemary and her sister Betty in the Ferrers' New York apartment. *(Photo by Lew Merrim, courtesy of author's collection.)*

Rosemary puts finishing touches to Tennessee Ernie Ford's makeup just before facing the cameras for her television variety series. *(NBC photo by Herb Ball.)*

The late William Bendix and Rosemary doing a song-and-dance turn for "The Rosemary Clooney Show." *(NBC photo by Gerald Smith.)*

The late Charles Laughton and Rosemary discussing his guest appearance on "The Rosemary Clooney Show." Laughton was responsible for the title of Rosemary's autobiography. (*NBC photo by Elmer Holloway.*)

Rosemary and Perry Como bantered at the piano.

Rosemary with her father, Andrew Clooney, Jr., and her mother, Frances, on a visit to their home.

Rosemary putting a song across at Harrah's Club in Lake Tahoe, Nevada.

Rosemary on a fishing expedition in Vancouver, British Columbia, just prior to her breakdown.

Miguel, Maria, Dante, Rosemary, Rafael, and Monsita arriving in London for Rosemary's return engagement with Bing Crosby at the Palladium. *(Photo courtesy of author's collection.)*

dously kind to me always. I first met him when Joe was doing *The Caine Mutiny*. I'd been on the set with Joe and met him only briefly. But the Bogarts had great Christmas Eve parties, and I think it was our second Christmas together that we went to the first one.

I recall many things about Bogey, but one incident stands out quite vividly. We were at a party given next door by Ira Gershwin. Bogart could be very mischievous and sometimes he would use word games and word trips on people. At this particular party Sid Luft was there with Judy ·Garland, and Bogey happened to be passing by when Sid said, "Culturally speaking . . ."

Bogart stopped and said, "How can you say 'culturally speaking'? Your background doesn't merit that kind of an expression. Now if I said that, there would be some credence to it because I had a very, very good education. I was brought up on Park Avenue. My background gives me the right to say that, but yours certainly doesn't."

Sid's face was reddening more and more as Bogey went on, until he was absolutely furious. It was obvious he was about to slug Bogey, who quickly put on his glasses and said to the irate Luft, "Are you going to hit me? An old man? How can you possibly take a poke at a man who wears glasses?"

Realizing by now that Bogey was doing one of his numbers on him, Sid said, "I'm sorry. I lost my temper and I'm sorry it happened."

Bogey, delighted with himself, turned to Luft in parting and said, "But seriously, how can you say 'culturally'?"

Outrageous but wonderful. That was Bogey. And Betty Bacall? I love her. She's one of the most straight-ahead ladies I've ever known in my whole life. A very honest woman. I've found—and once again I find myself generalizing, which is not my habit but in this case does seemed to hold true—that really beautiful women don't have many hang-ups about being perfectly straightforward. The deviousness seems to come when a woman doesn't really feel all that beautiful, when she's really done it on her own. Somebody who has been really fat and lost a lot of weight looks in the mirror and still sees the fat girl. Lacking confidence, she still needs a lot of external ego-massage. A terrifically beautiful woman doesn't need that, and her confidence frees her to be perfectly honest and have better relationships with other women. Not many women, however, have really beautiful women as best friends. Not many, and they should, because they are more trustworthy than other women. There are no games going on with these women. They don't have to prove anything to somebody else's husband or boy friend, nor to themselves. They know who they are and where they are coming from.

We had parties at our house, too. Things like sit-down dinners for eight or ten people. Nat and Maria Cole were very close friends and came to dinner often. Nat was a tremendously genial man. He would get up from the dining-room table, which is across the foyer from the drawing room, and during coffee, while people were quietly chatting, he would seat himself at the piano in a corner of the drawing room where Gershwin had composed and start to play. I thought to myself during one dinner party, Just imagine, Nat Cole playing after-dinner music where Gershwin once sat. Nat was one helluva good friend.

Joe was working very hard during the fall and early winter months of the year we got married. He was trying to raise money for the City Center in New York and did four shows, back to back, rehearsing one while he was performing in another. I had completed *White Christmas* with Bing Crosby and was in New York with Joe. He did *Cyrano*, *Richard III*, *The Shrike* and *Charley's Aunt* in succession, which was really a backbreaking schedule. So we had Christmas in New York. Joe gave me a diamond-and-sapphire bracelet for Christmas. It was just gorgeous. But it was the first time I'd ever spent Christmas away from my family. Usually at Christmastime I was around some member of my family, even if Betty and I had to spend it alone together. Christmas didn't seem to mean too much to Joe then, and all the things I was used to doing we just didn't do. We spent Christmas in the New York apartment that Joe had before we were married, and it was a very sad Christmas Eve for me. I had done all the shopping and sent all the presents to my family and talked to them all on the phone, but it wasn't the same. I missed being there with them.

Joe, not very sentimental about Christmas and unaware of my feelings, had some friends in, people he liked very much but I didn't know very well. I don't think he really noticed, and maybe I didn't show it to him either, because I was very adept at hiding my personal feelings.

However, the sadness of Christmas was quickly replaced with the New Year and my first trip abroad. Joe had planned it as the honeymoon we'd been too busy to take and he scheduled everything to make me happy—the best hotels and the most beautiful circumstances. It was a lovely, lovely time. Not museums and that sort of thing, but visiting old friends, fabulous houses and people in the various countries. We were initially going to spend two weeks in London and ended up spending seven weeks. It was my introduction to Claridge's, the hotel that others try to compete with.

I remember we went over on BOAC, so it was all very British from the time we set foot on the plane. Joe immediately had a bit of a British accent. He's such a linguist (speaks seven languages fluently) that he can hear almost anything spoken and immediately switch into that language, even picking up on regional accents. It's second nature to him. His French accent changed, for instance, when we moved from Paris to the south of France. It was a perceptible change, even to me, because Parisians speak very differently from those in the southern part of the country.

Anyway, we were on board the airplane for London and they were serving caviar and seven kinds of wine. In those days planes had berths, and we had berths on opposite sides of the aisle from one another. The steward was near us and he leaned over and said, "Madam, your berth is on the left."

Joe looked up and said, "Don't be surprised if you find us both together in one berth or the other." Then he added, "Which side is the sunny side?" Meaning, of course, on which side will the sun come up? He wanted to be awakened by the sun coming in the window of the berth.

The steward, very straight-faced, replied, "Whichever side you prefer, sir!" Which was hysterically funny to both of us. It was that kind of trip.

When we arrived in London we were met by Kevin O'Donovan McClory, an old friend of Joe's who is now a producer. He had been a boom operator on *Moulin Rouge* and in honor of our arrival he'd rounded up about twenty Irishmen at Paddy Kennedy's pub. When we entered they were all kneeling in their shoes with Toulouse Lautrec beards and bowlers on, lined up like a royal reception committee. I couldn't believe it. Even Paddy's German shepherd sported a Toulouse Lautrec beard and a bowler. Joe had a wonderful sense of humor, in his own style, and it was certainly reflected in the humor of his friends. I loved every minute of it.

There was a tremendous amount of press coverage of our visit. I had been a big, big seller of records in England—at one time even more so there than in the United States, with five songs in the first ten more than once. So every little nuance was recorded by the press and at times completely misinterpreted, as the media are wont to do on both sides of the Atlantic. One front page read: "ROSEMARY CLOONEY ARRIVES WITH THE INEVITABLE MINK COAT."

Another one, the same day, said: "WHAT IS MISS CLOONEY TRYING TO DO, PULL A GARBO? She had on a gray flannel skirt and a gray cable knit sweater which seemed a little quiet for the kind of glamour we're used to."

First off I get it for the mink coat, which was also gray, and then the sweater and skirt. It was very hard for me to deal with. And they didn't miss out on Joe, either. Particularly difficult for him to swallow was something that was totally twisted out of context. Joe was being very nice to me. And as a generous notion on his part he leaned over my shoulder as I talked to a newspaperman and asked, "Can I draw you a bath?"

I said, "I'd love it, Joe. Just what I need."

That came out in the newspaper as: "He fetches and he draws baths," intimating that Joe was little more than my lackey. The implication was not nice, but it was our honeymoon so we soon forgot about it.

I enjoyed meeting some of Joe's friends for the first time. Emlyn Williams and his wife Molly. I was familiar with his writing—*The Corn Is Green*, and *How Green Was My Valley* as well as other important works about the Welsh people. He was also a brilliant actor. I remembered especially *Night Must Fall*, which he wrote. Robert Montgomery starred in the film. It was the one where he carried the head around in a hatbox. Kept me on the edge of my seat. Socially, Williams was one of the wittiest men I've ever known in my life.

Ruth Gordon and Garson Kanin were a couple I got to know well on that trip. When I was in New York not so long ago with Bing Crosby at the Uris Theatre I ran into Jones Harris, Ruth's son by Broadway producer Jed Harris, and he reminded me of something. "You know," he said, "one of the funniest things you ever did that nobody ever heard of except my mother and me happened when you were in England on your honeymoon. Do you remember?"

Of course I remembered. We were standing out in front of the Kanins' house after dinner and Ruth was saying goodnight to everybody. It was wintertime and we were walking out into the cold and I was walking backward saying my goodnights. Ruth said, "Goodnight, Rosemary."

I, a little happy with wine, I suppose, said, "Goodnight Ruthmary!" which struck Ruth and Jones as terribly funny.

Ruth is a very bright woman and a tremendous wit as well as great actress. Garson is also a great raconteur, so wonderful stories were told that night.

John Gielgud was also at the dinner party. He was very quiet, but when he spoke it was in that marvelous voice. There is a kind of emotional quaver in it and it is devastating to hear on-stage. You can imagine how riveting it is when you're his dinner partner.

Joe's friends welcomed me warmly into their homes and their hearts. Mary Lee and Doug Fairbanks were exceptionally nice to me, and you haven't seen anything like Joe and Sir Laurence Olivier trying to thaw out a frozen toilet bowl.

I enjoyed all of these people because they were people I had always had great admiration for, most of them, and especially because they were friends of Joe's. But I was never awed by meeting them. What did impress me was the marvelous way I was received and their interest in me. It's true, I was one of the most popular singers in the world at that time, so I had some sense of my own professional worth, just as they did. I knew what I had accomplished. Professionally I was always secure. That was my big problem: I didn't feel secure away from that. But I'd found out by being friends with Bing Crosby that being in awe was the surest way to put off somebody you wanted to be friends with; you had to relax around people before you could get close to them and enjoy what they had to say. Besides, if you start out with friends like Crosby and Dietrich, where are you going to go from there and be awed?

So I relaxed and met a lot of really nice people, like Peter Ustinov and Carol Reed, the great English director—and thoroughly enjoyed the fantastic restaurants. I do love good restaurants because I like good food. And I like food served well. Served beautifully. I love good china and lovely linen, all the accoutrements that go with good food. That comes from my Grandfather Clooney because he had lovely Limoges and Devonshire and Wedgwood china both in the jewelry store and on the table for special occasions, so I was always around things like that growing up.

England having been a tremendous success, we moved across the Channel to Paris. There was a big party for us there and loads of press. It was really quite funny because there was a man at the party who was the head of the European division of Columbia Records and who had been an ex-boy friend. It was like walking a tightrope—I liked him and wanted to be friendly with him, but I also didn't want Joe to know anything about my past. So I was nice—but cool. He got the idea.

It was the same basic thing I'd always been programmed to do as a child. Couch everything in the right terms and don't say the wrong thing. My first instincts were to ask myself, What is the coin of the realm? What will be the means of exchange? What is the currency in this country—with this person? Then I would work from that. It had nothing to do with my feelings, it was just instinct. It didn't even go through my brain. I never went around and spoke my mind like I do now. I wouldn't think of offending anyone by being truthful.

We were staying at the Plaza Athenée in Paris and the very first night we went out we were robbed. We went to the opera and I was quite foolish. At Claridge's in London I would take off my jewelry and leave it on the dressing table and the maid would put it in the jewelry case for me. But it didn't happen that way in Paris.

Of course we called the French police the next day when we discovered the robbery. We were very high up—the eleventh floor—so it was not exactly a ground-floor job. Whoever it was had walked past and must have had to slip out with only those things they could carry in their pockets because there were thousands of dollars' worth of camera equipment and mink coats that they skipped. Just took my jewelry—everything, including my Christmas gift from Joe. There was a canary diamond ring, a brown-and-white diamond—all sort of things. I've always been very fatalistic about things like that: If it's lost, it's lost; no use worrying about *things*. I love pretty things and I love to have them, but I will not worry about them. I only care that much for people.

Well, the police—it was like a French farce. They came in and looked out the window as though a human fly might have walked up eleven floors on the outside of the building. It was absolutely ludicrous the way they handled the investigation. I expected Inspector Clouzot to come in any moment followed by his prefect. Unbelievably badly handled.

But they wrote up their reports and that was the last we heard about it or the jewelry. But then, some of the most classic crooks were Parisians, so what can I say at this point?

We rented a car in Paris and started driving toward the south of France. It was a gourmet experience. Joe knew all the out-of-the-way places, all the little exciting detours and, of course, all the best chefs. Away from the pressures of work, we took our time and enjoyed ourselves.

When we got to the south of France we stayed with a friend of Joe's who owns La Reserve in Beaulieu, which is one of the best hotels in all of Europe. We took the owner's cottage, which was kind of old-fashioned. There was a sitting room on the first floor and bedroom on the upper floor—no doors; the rooms opened up to a kind of swirling staircase so that the hallway was like one giant room from bottom to top with a staircase curving up. A very enchanting arrangement. The walls, I remember, were stone or some other sort of masonry.

With our bedroom just above the sitting room, one night I received my first hint of what would perhaps become a way of life later on. Joe met an old friend while we were there. They were terribly good friends. Most of the time they spoke to each other in English, but they would lapse, from time to time, into French for long spells. It was generally boring to me since I did not speak nor understand French. On this particular evening I got the feeling of being left out and finally said, "If you'll excuse me, I'll go up to bed."

In bed I started to read, but that staircase became a sound chamber and I could still hear every word they said. During the conversation they lapsed back into English. I've often thought how unfortunate that it happened to be right at that time, on our honeymoon, but I heard them start to laugh and then I heard Joe start to describe very graphically a sexual encounter he'd had with a woman who came backstage to see him while he was in New York preparing for our trip. He went into great detail about her physical attributes, and both men seemed to think that was worth another jolly good laugh.

I was crushed. Just crushed. I was on my honeymoon. All of that had happened while I was rushing to finish *White Christmas* in California so I could be with my husband in New York. I started to cry and was still crying when he came up to bed. He knew that I had overheard their conversation, but he asked me, "What's the matter?"

I said, "I heard your conversation, Joe. *All* of it."

I'll never forget the look of dismissal in his expression when he said to me, "Maybe we should call it off right now."

It wasn't ever going to be that easy. I wouldn't allow it and I found myself saying, "No. No. Let's try." I couldn't bear to fail that soon. I couldn't bear to say, because of one instance, that it was all over. I couldn't quit on my honeymoon. "Infidelity" is not exactly an alien word where I come from, but it seemed awfully early in our marriage for it to be happening to us. It was the way I learned about it that really took its toll on me. Two men together describing it in a very crude, brutal way. I've heard men say that sort of thing has nothing to do with their marriages, that it's just something in passing. I don't believe that. I believe there is an underlying, significant reason for it to happen. I truly do.

Also, I had sudden visions of the kind of marriages my mother had. Even though there were only two, there were other men. I couldn't see myself doing that for the rest of my life.

But the book of revelations had been opened to me. That would be the pattern in our marriage, really, although I didn't know it then. My instincts, being a young bride, were to wonder what was wrong with me. Why did he need somebody else? I was young and healthy and eager. But I would find out later on about some dalliance and Joe would always say he was sorry and that it would never happen again. Being sorry can be a momentary thing to extricate yourself from an embarrassing situation.

Joe never said he was sorry that night. I wanted him to. Of course I did. But I didn't make a big scene.

It's funny how, in my lifetime, I've always picked up unimportant things attached to important events. The next day I went out on the beach—and at Beaulieu there is no beach per se; there are just small rocks leading down to the water. I was walking alone down by the water. The Mediterranean looked so beautiful and I felt very hopeless that morning. I picked up a piece of rock that was almost crystal but had been worn so that it was opaque on the outside because of the water, and I said, "This will remind me of this day. I won't always feel this way, but this will remind me of the day I did feel this way." In a sense it was a rather poetic way of marking a demoralizing milestone in our marriage.

But there were other things to do. That was yesterday and now it was a new day. We went to see Marcel Pagnol—at his house for lunch I believe, where we met his wife and children. A great writer who had written a trilogy from which came *Fanny*. A great novelist. We returned later after one of our little side trips and stopped to see him again and his child was in the hospital. The hospital was situated high up on a mountainside overlooking the sea. We found Pagnol sitting inside an archway and he wouldn't leave his post. Just sat in silent vigil. Joe said he looked like all the characters that he wrote about, and later on, having read a lot more of his works, I realized how true that was. The men from the south of France always have cigarettes in the sides of their mouths like Jean Gabin. He had a beard and a kind of cap on, just sitting there.

"You will excuse me," he said. "I cannot leave. It is my daughter. Subconsciously she knows when I am not here even if she cannot see me when I am. When I go away even for a moment her temperature rises. I cannot leave."

I applauded the devotion. It so affected Joe that he obtained some canvases and some paint and painted a picture of the man sitting on a bench outside the hospital room, just waiting. It's called *L'Attente* and hangs in my drawing room in a prominent position today. He's a wonderful painter and can paint quickly and easily. I envy that. My children also do it.

That kind of attention to a child, and Joe's being touched by it, seemed to heal the wound of a few days before; somehow it didn't seem as important as the fact that he was moved by that man's emotion—and indeed, later on, Joe had that same compassion for his own children. It was a moment of truth, that painting, because Joe is and has always been an excellent father. A very caring father. So my judgment about that was right.

So the honeymoon was over and we'd saved our marriage from an early dissolution. We went back home to face other challenges—work, and the beginning of a family. Things far more important to both of us than some indiscretion resulting from a moment's temptation.

CHAPTER X

Family

After returning from Europe, Joe and Stanley Donen were immediately busy working on a new picture—something they were writing together. Stanley and Marion Donen (she later was married to Bob Wagner) were always very close friends of ours, and their babies were close to our children's ages. Their son Peter is just a little older. That summer we spent a lot of time together. We went to Las Vegas and to La Jolla, traveling about southern California quite a bit. I had let up on my work schedule. It wasn't as hectic as it had been before my marriage. I just wouldn't allow it. I was doing a few personal appearances and continuing to record regularly at Columbia. It was a very relaxing time for me, being a wife more than an entertainer.

Not all my friends and business associates approved of my marriage to Joe, which is kind of funny because when it ended they all stood around and shook their heads as if to say, "How could such a perfect marriage go sour?" But it was my marriage, not theirs, and I wasted no time letting everybody know that being Joe's wife came first. Everything else would have to be worked around that or forgotten.

Being a wife didn't entail very many duties at that point. I didn't have the responsibilities that would come later. We had a cook, a butler, an upstairs maid, laundress, gardener and secretary. It was a big house. It was like living in a very grand hotel, and I'd lived in hotels for a long time. But it was the way Joe liked things and it gave me more time to be with him.

Joe and I went up to Lake Tahoe to see Nat Cole who was working at the Cal-Neva Lodge. We'd been fishing out on the lake, just having a great time, when I noticed I wasn't feeling too well. It was nothing major, but when I got back to Beverly Hills I called my doctor for an appointment. When I saw him and explained how I felt, he sent me to Dr. Leon Shulman—a wonderful man who delivered all five of my children. He lives in La Jolla and has an office in Santa Monica next to Saint John's Hospital.

So I found I was pregnant, but the way I found out was amusing. Louella Parsons had a direct line to every laboratory in the area and often had people's expectancies in the paper before the doctor, woman or her husband had the results back from the lab. That woman had more connections than a switchboard operator at Ma Bell's.

Now that kind of item in a gossip column could be disastrous for someone who was either in the middle of a film or getting ready to start one, so my doctor aware of all this, did a fabulous thing: He sent out the specimen to be tested on the frog in the name of Louella Parsons. Louella thus had a positive test for pregnancy. I thought it was a great joke on Louella.

When I got the positive report I didn't pussyfoot around like they do on the television commercials. I just told Joe, without any embellishments: "Joe, I'm pregnant."

I got many reactions. From Joe there was absolute joy. From my business associates a long moment's silence. It would mean curtailing my activities even more than I already had. Of course every one of them went through the motions of being happy for us. They really had little option. My pregnancy was a fact of life—literally.

I didn't gain much weight with my first pregnancy, but found I was easily winded quite early on. I remember Joe and I went to San Francisco because Mary Martin had asked him to come and see her in *Peter Pan*. Adolph Green and Betty Comden, also friends of ours, had written some new songs for the production. I used to love to walk in San Francisco, but I couldn't walk up the hills. Joe, trying to be helpful, put his hand in the small of my back and said, "This will make it easier." I didn't want to disappoint him by telling him it wasn't helping a damned bit, so I said, "Oh, that's tremendous. Let's walk up another one!" Talk about being programmed to please at all times!

There were, however, a few very select people along the line that I was totally honest with, and Dante was one of those. He always knew exactly how I felt. In fact, he almost didn't need to be told—he was so sensitive to my feelings.

My pregnancy went along just fine until about the third month, when I started having symptoms of possibly miscarrying. I was terrified and the doctor put me on a regimen of shots to prevent that from happening. I had to have one injection a day for all those months until the baby was born.

In the meantime I stayed around Hollywood and started working with Bob Hope on radio and television. I was also working a lot with Bing Crosby.

As the months wore on I was getting very edgy, as every woman does in pregnancy, and especially with her first child. Not knowing exactly what to expect, it is that fear of the unexpected and the discomfort of those last couple of months that create more anxiety. I had been working, and the baby was due in late January or early February. At the end of January the baby had not come yet and I received a hurry-up call from Mitch Miller at Columbia. He said, "Columbia has bought the rights to all the recordings and the cast album for *Pajama Game* and they want some hit records from it. So far we haven't had one. I think you can change that."

I knew Johnny Ray had recorded "Hey There!" but evidently the treatment wasn't right or something wasn't appealing about the record. It wasn't selling, so Mitch wanted me to come in and cut a side.

"Mitch," I said, "I'm waiting for this baby to be born momentarily."

In his usual fantastic, outrageous way he said, "I'll send an ambulance for you and you can record in a wheelchair, but I've got to get your voice on 'Hey There!' "

So I went down to Columbia Studios in Hollywood and we recorded "Hey There!" On the flip side I did "This Ole House," just to fill in a side. I seriously doubted either song was going anywhere. If Johnny Ray couldn't pull "Hey There!" out, I didn't see how I could. "This Ole House" was just tossed in. The record made, I went back to the business of having my baby, and just a week later I started labor. The record wasn't released until almost a month after Miguel was born.

February 6, 1955, was a Sunday, and there was an awful lot of tennis being played at our house every Sunday. Joe was playing tennis. Several people were at the house that day, among them a very dear friend who recently died, cartoonist George Baker who drew "Sad Sack," the cartoon that bolstered our troops in Europe throughout and after World War II. I have a fantastic drawing he did of me in his GI style. Henry Nemo, the songwriter who wrote "Don't Take Your Love from Me," was there. Nemo, as we called him, started a lot of the popular dialog of the Fifties and was just the hippest-talking guy that ever lived. A marvelously funny and sensitive man.

I remember I was supposed to stay away from salt and I loved tomato soup but couldn't have it because of the salt. Nemo, always ready to help, said, "Don't worry, you shall have your tomato soup. I have a recipe, salt-free—just delicious." Nemo went to work in my kitchen putting fresh tomatoes in the blender with milk and some other things and made me some tomato soup—sans salt. It tasted pretty good, but more importantly I just liked him so much for trying to satisfy my hunger for it.

The tennis went on all day. I remember my grandmother, or maybe it was Aunt Jean, saying, "Just before you start to have the baby, before you go into labor, you get this tremendous burst of energy." I hadn't evidenced a lot of energy. My mother was living with us now, but I never thought of asking her anything about having my baby. I would have talked to Aunt Jean about it, but there was always that something with my mother that prevented me from having that kind of mother-daughter relationship with her. I guess it was too late at that point to try to have something I hadn't had as a girl growing up.

Anyway, that day I suddenly got this urge to clean out the bureau drawers. The floor of my room was a holy mess with all the litter. I went through a lot of things that day. I alternated between that and being downstairs with Joe and our guests. Someone was playing chess, and Nemo was still there in the evening. I'd been in the kitchen doing something and decided I'd sneak up to my bed and lie down for a while because I was getting kind of a backache. It didn't occur to me that all of this could be early signs of labor. You know, you read all the things and you know all the things, but you don't really put it together the first time until it starts to happen.

I think Stanley Donen and Joe were playing chess—there was always a chess game going and Stanley was one of the most constant players. Stanley and Joe always played chess on Saturday nights and Marion used to say, "Well, here we are. Another big Saturday night and we've watched Charlie Chan again while these two are playing chess." It wasn't the most exciting way in the world to spend a Saturday night, but Marion and I did a lot of laughing about it.

After I went upstairs, Joe decided to move the chess game

upstairs, so that meant everybody in the house came up, too. Joe never liked to be far away from me, and that has carried over to the children; it seems to me that whatever room I'm in is the center of the household.

I really didn't feel like having much company, but there we all were. I was uncomfortable and trying to watch the "Ed Sullivan Show." I had been quietly timing some pains from the beginning of the show and now knew something was happening because they had become quite regular. About nine o'clock I said to Joe, "Let's call the doctor and see if I shouldn't go to the hospital because I've been having pains now for the last hour and fifteen minutes."

I caught Joe by such surprise that all he could say was a rather overmodulated "Right!" But he went immediately into action. He'd already made two trial drives to the hospital to see how fast he could get there. Joe is a very good New York driver. He could get there very fast—so fast that I could have a heart attack, maybe even have the baby from sheer fright en route. I couldn't see myself having a baby in a Jaguar, however. He had the sports model with two seats and it wasn't made with birthing babies in mind.

My bag was packed and I was ready to go, but Joe must have thought he was going to be there for six months because he took four books, a chessboard and the chessmen—plus his friends, who followed us in separate cars. I remember asking Joe, "Do we have to have all these people?" He seemed to think we did.

As we were leaving, Nemo was coming out of the house, and Nemo is a little bit rotund and thought he was making too much noise on the driveway with his feet. I remember looking around and seeing him tiptoe on the grass down to his car. He was so funny it took my mind off my own immediate problem for a moment. He was trying not to disturb the baby.

We arrived at the hospital about 9:15 in the evening and I went into the prelabor room. Joe was allowed to stay with me until I started needing medication, which must have been about an hour later. Miguel was born at 1:33 A.M. on February 7th. A new day of the week and a new baby.

I remember the doctor saying, "Mrs. Ferrer, here's your son," and he was upside down. I turned my head to look at his face. I'd wanted a boy and I'd wanted him to look like Joe. If I ever doubted the existence of God and having prayers answered, I had no reason to doubt any further because Miguel looked like Joe at birth and has looked more like him every year.

Humphrey Bogart and I had a $50 bet. He said to me while I was carrying the baby, "What kind of a child do you want?"

I said, "I'd love to have a boy."

He grinned and replied, "Well, I'll bet that it's going to be a girl because I've never won a bet with a pregnant woman in my life."

The morning after Miguel was born, very early, the first flowers that arrived were about three dozen coral roses with a note which read: "Okay. You win. Bogey." I got cards and flowers from about half of Hollywood. I remember one agent's card said, "He's got an open contract when he reaches the age of consent."

People have a misconceived idea that women want boys first in order to please their husbands. I don't think that holds true at all. I think it is more old-fashioned than that—at least it was in the part of the country I came from. A boy that's older, if anything happens to his father, could be responsible for the family, could take over as head of the household. I intended to have a big family and so it was right and proper for me to have a boy first. I also predicted I would have five children. That, too, came to pass.

After five or six days I was home. I had to do a "Person to Person" with Edward R. Murrow at the end of March so I had to lose weight and get myself back in shape. I nursed Miguel as long as I could—about two months—and went to New York to do the Murrow show. On the show I was presented with a platinum record. "Hey There!" and "This Ole House," back to back, had sold two million platters and gone platinum. The platinum record was presented to me with the following inscription: "To Miguel Jose Ferrer on the occasion of his mother's 2,000,000 sale." Columbia would later split the records and issue them separately so they could get the full run of it.

When I recorded "This Ole House," Mitch hadn't wanted it to come through as it eventually did, otherwise I would not have done it quite as raucously. But who argues with hits? Stuart Hamblen wrote it, and after Miguel was born and the record had been an immediate success, Stuart was out in California and running around everywhere with my manager. He came over to the house one day and wanted to see my nursery. Then he went out and returned with a bassinet that had about 125 yards of pink tulle—and a pink satin house embroidered on it. It was the most beautiful thing you've ever seen and became the bassinet for all my babies. Generous thoughts like that have become a storehouse of pleasant memories for me.

Returning from New York, the next thing I had to do professionally was to sing at the Academy Awards. It was interesting because there were a lot of people involved that year whom I knew well. It was the year Grace Kelly won for *The Country Girl*. Judy Garland was up and I was going to sing "The Man that Got Away" from *A Star Is Born*, which was a nominated song.

Judy's son, Joey, was born on the day of a rehearsal for the show, and forgetting that she had once been married to David Rose, who was conducting the orchestra that year for the awards, I popped over to him and said, "Gee, did you hear that Judy had a baby boy?"

I got a very flat, "That's nice." Then I remembered.

Marlon Brando was up for *On the Waterfront*, and his biggest competition was Bing Crosby for *The Country Girl*. Brando won. I was sitting in the audience early in the evening because my song was late in the program, and I saw Bing come into the theater with a very pretty brunette girl—Kathryn

Grant, who was a member of the Golden Circle at Paramount. I thought she was very pretty and terribly nice, but I didn't know whether they would be together very long. It never crossed my mind that they might be serious. I had never met Dixie, Bing's first wife. I think she was already quite ill when I started singing with Bing.

Another incident that comes to mind about the day of the awards involved Grace Kelly. Grace and I had the same hairdresser at Paramount, Lenore Weaver, who was one of the best. She was working on a film, but we were told by the head of the department that she could be sprung to do our hair. We'd have to come into the studio to do it, though. We went to the studio, but something went awry—Weaver could not be pulled off the picture.

Grace and I were left to the helpful, but not as talented, ministrations of the lady who was head of the department. She was a good administrator but not as good in the hair department. With my hair there is not much you can do to hurt it—it just falls into place naturally. Grace, on the other hand, had a very special dress and she wanted her hair done a very special way. She actually wept as we walked out together.

"Rosemary, what am I going to do?" she asked.

"You've got time," I said, "to stop somewhere and get it done."

"You really think so?"

"Yes, if you do it now."

"Maybe Saks. I'll stop by Saks and maybe they can throw it up so that I'll just wear it up. It'll look all right if it's done up and simple."

And that's the way she wore it when she got the award that night. They had done her hair at Paramount in what only can be described as "early mess." Saks did a nice salvage of a bad situation.

I was backstage when the award for Best Actor came up, and when I realized that Brando had won instead of Bing I was disappointed. I'm sure it was a hard choice but Bing had been fantastically good in *The Country Girl*. He'd done a lot of singing pictures, but nothing comparable to this great dramatic performance.

Joe was in Portugal doing a picture called *The Cockleshell Hero*, and after the Academy Awards I flew there to be with him for about a week—I had Las Vegas coming up shortly. My manager was with me and we were going to stop in England to do some promotional work for my upcoming engagement at the London Palladium. All in all, 1955 was a very busy year for me.

For once in my life I didn't overpack, just took a few things. As a result of that I only had one pair of black shoes—and crossing a cobblestone street in Lisbon one day I broke the heel on one of them. Joe let me borrow his car and driver the next morning to go into the city for a new pair, but someone neglected to tell me that women aren't on the streets of Lisbon in the daytime—at least there weren't any in the summer of 1955. Here I am with my summer clothes designed by Jax and the car and driver. Because of the narrow streets the driver had to drive around the block while I went into the shoe store. By the time the car got back I had collected, I suppose, forty men in a circle, all talking in Portuguese and pointing and patting while I tried to kind of look above it and think pleasant thoughts.

I returned to America via London and went to Las Vegas for my opening at The Sands Hotel. It was my first big Vegas thing. Frank Sinatra had started playing The Sands and had asked me to play there, too. I, of course, said yes. Frank, at that time, was building the group of people who would work The Sands.

The show went very well and I was well received. I used one song of Cole Porter's, a most charming man with whom I had recently had dinner in Lisbon. The tune was "It's Delovely," from *Red, Hot and Blue*, which had starred Bob Hope and Ethel Merman. The first verse is about a courtship, the second about a marriage ceremony, and the third about the birth of a baby. It was perfect for me.

My reviews were excellent and the audiences were fantastic. Edith Head had done my clothes—which is another story. We almost didn't get the clothes because Dietrich decided she was going to go to the fittings with me and she is so very particular and so very knowledgeable. When Dietrich fits clothes she walks, sits and bends in them to see the way they move. She'll say, for instance, "Move one bead over a quarter of an inch."

My clothes were beautiful, but they were simpler than Marlene's things and yet had to enhance anything I had to offer in the show. I'm primarily a singer, though, so I didn't have quite the same approach to clothes that Marlene did. The poor fitters would just stand there when Dietrich would say, "This doesn't stand out. This moves very strangely." They'd be backed up then for four more weeks working on changes that Dietrich came up with, and meanwhile I was going crazy along with them.

So anytime Marlene and I got together I tried to arrange it so that I wasn't fitting clothes that day. It became a game. I finally did get my wardrobe, with certain positive suggestions from Dietrich, and of course Edith Head does a superior job without any assistance.

After a fantastic stay at The Sands, I got everything together to take to England for my engagement at the Palladium. I had a baby nurse, Harriet, whom I liked a lot because she was so marvelous with the baby. But she didn't like to fly, so I said, "What a good thought. We won't fly. We'll sail." I had some business to take care of in New York so I flew on ahead. The baby, Harriet and my mother came east on the train and we all met in New York. Shribman was to accompany us, and we all sailed on the *Queen Elizabeth*. I must say, I favored Cunard Lines. They have wonderful ships.

Joe, already in England, met us at Portsmouth sporting a bowler, a wonderful English suit and an umbrella. Under his arm he carried a copy of the *London Times*. I thought he looked extraordinarily British. He had found a great country house and we spent the summer there. While Joe cut and edited his film, I was getting ready to open at the Palladium. I was going to break my show in at The Empire in Glasgow with Buddy Cole, my conductor, playing the piano.

Kevin O'Donovan McClory was once again in evidence, and when Joe had to fly back to New York to do some publicity, Kevin asked me if I'd like to go out. He had planned a special evening for me.

I accepted and he picked me up early in the evening. To my surprise he took me to a small theater in an area of London that I'd never seen before—and here we were, dressed in dinner clothes. Kevin must have arranged it with the manager of the theater ahead of time because I was presented with a large bouquet of flowers. We were sitting in the last row of the theater, my lap full of flowers, when on the screen flashed: "*The Blue Angel*—starring Marlene Dietrich." One of Dietrich's greatest films and I'd never seen it before. What a treat for me!

From there we went to the Café de Paris where Dietrich was appearing in person. I'd known she was there, but hadn't seen her and had no idea that I was going to. Kevin had given me an extraordinarily pleasant surprise and a divine evening.

We had an Italian couple cooking for us that summer and gave some big dinners. I remember Dietrich came out to see us at the house on one of those occasions. The place was called Black Jack's Mill and had indeed been an old mill before it was converted into a house. It had five bathrooms, which was and is unusual for an English country house. There was also a mill run underneath the house and there were canals. The whole inside of England is lined with these canals—most of the shipping is handled that way—and the people who live on the canal boats are a breed apart. If you live on the canal and somebody on one those brilliantly painted boats gets sick, you are bound to take care of him until he is picked up on a return trip.

Anyway, we had lots of places to fish including the Cone River and half a lake on the property, so this particular time Dietrich, who loves to fish, came out to go fishing. Now Dietrich approaches fishing in the same practical manner she does everything else. First, Dietrich is always dressed correctly for the occasion. And second, dressed in pants and a shirt, she did something I couldn't do—she baited her own hooks with worms. Worse yet, as they wiggled she would talk to them. I can still see her impaling a worm on a hook and saying, "Now this isn't going to hurt. Just think how nice it's going to be when a big fish sees you and ends up on the table. Won't that be marvelous?"

She never ceases to amaze me.

I should mention that the night I went to see her at the Café de Paris, Burt Bacharach was her conductor. He was with her for years. I remember one time when they were in my living room and she said to me, "You've got to hear some of Burt's songs." As usual my judgment in songs was bad. I said, "Very nice," when he played, but wasn't too impressed. I can't even remember what he played.

Another time Joe called me from Paris and said, "You know, George Auric has done this fantastic score for *Moulin Rouge* and there's one song that Zsa Zsa sings—with another lyric it would be fantastically good for you to sing."

I remember thinking to myself, Now you're a wonderful actor, but stay out of my department. I know music.

But I said to Joe, "Oh, that really sounds interesting." And I promptly forgot it.

Percy Faith sold something like two million records of "The Theme from Moulin Rouge."

The Empire in Glasgow is a sketch in itself. There is a saying, "If you're a hit in Glasgow, you can be a hit anyplace in the world," because they are notoriously discerning. Anything that is phony will get a thumbs-down response from them. They also talk back to you from the audience. Like the Palladium, they had the two-a-day vaudeville policy—one show at 6 and one at 8:30. During the first show the house was composed mostly of working people from the mines, sitting up high with their lunchboxes tucked under their arms.

Opening night, when the curtains opened for the second half the orchestra was playing "Tenderly" and I remember *feeling* the roar of the crowd. My manager was standing in the wings and later told me I gave him a scare. He saw me flinch, but didn't know why until the sound reached him— a split second after it reached me. It was simply a wall of sound. I've never encountered that particular sensation anyplace else.

About a week into the run, at the early show, I was singing a ballad and way up in the top I heard a voice, loud and clear in a thick Scottish burr: "Rossseee . . . marrrie!" I tried to ignore it and it happened again. That voice would cut through anything—my singing—the music. Finally I stopped singing and said, "What is it?"

His reply was loud and clear: "Come On-a My House!"

He didn't care what I was singing. That's what he wanted to hear, and it brought the house down. I turned around to Buddy Cole, looking for support—my one ally on stage—and he was leaning over the piano absolutely convulsed.

So I sang "Come On-a My House" which was usually my finale.

I also found out in Glasgow that I wasn't the best-known Clooney in the area. During that time the BBC was only allowed to play individual records a number of times a day, and so even a hit record you didn't hear that often. My brother Nicky, on the other hand, was in the army, stationed in Frankfurt, Germany, and had a disk-jockey show on Armed Forces Network which was beamed across the Channel. It was a very popular show, and since most people couldn't afford to buy Gramophones and records, his three- or four-hour show was the hottest thing in Scotland. I was one of the biggest singers to come out of the United States, with all the attendant acclaim and hoopla, but in Scotland I was Nick Clooney's big sister. I thought my little brother was very sneakily taking over the record world. But I was damned proud of him.

I opened the Palladium—and at the six o'clock show, sitting in the third row, were Noel Coward and Marlene. I'd known Dietrich was coming, but I hadn't known she was bringing Noel. They liked the show, but of course had some suggestions—all good. At the end of the show the ushers bring up flowers that are sent to you; you don't get them in the dressing room as you do in the States. So these young ushers were piling the flowers all around me, and one handed me one small nosegay and as I was taking a bow I could see the card. It said: "Have a great success. Larry and Vivien." Laurence Olivier and Vivien Leigh. I said to myself, Lady, you've come a long way from Maysville, Kentucky.

It was a wholly successful engagement. One night Bea Lillie came in with Joe. He was going to a show, ran into Lady Peel and brought her back to the dressing room. She was a charming woman. We sat around laughing and talking and she did an imitation of Marlene that was hysterically funny. Probably one of the funniest women I have ever known.

I must relate an incident of an earlier trip that took us to Ireland to visit John Huston, after Joe had finished *Moulin Rouge*. We froze the whole weekend, with nothing but peat fires in this great manor house that John had outside of Dublin. Huston is a big man, both in size and in thought, and also in the accumulation of important people. He would hold court in front of the massive fireplace, and as a result of this, being such a tall man, he got most of the heat on his backside while the rest of us huddled around freezing to death. I loved every moment of it—especially in hindsight.

The trip to London for the Palladium show was a lovely time for me because of the friends we made—and those I had made before with Joe. We also acquired an addition to our entourage on this trip—a basset hound named George. We all got on the plane home together, since Harriet had decided she'd try winging it this time and the airline allowed George to be in the cabin with us. I made a deal with Joe, "I'll take care of Miguel if you'll take care of George." (I always took care of my children when I had time away from work.) George was impossible. Miguel behaved beautifully. George kept everybody up, and Joe was steaming because the deal we'd made ended up with him having all the headaches.

Back home in Beverly Hills George continued to behave so badly that we couldn't even keep him in the backyard. With those great big feet and giant floppy ears he was adorable and funny, but he finally got to be too much and one day Joe said, "Why don't we retire George to the East? We'll put him in the country house in Ossining." I agreed it was a good idea because George was just making a mess of everything. I think George must have liked Ossining. Located in New York's Westchester County, it was and is a beautiful place. I never spent the night there because it was a house that Joe had had for a long time, so there were a lot of memories attached to it that had nothing to do with me. I didn't want to invade those memories, nor be reminded of them. I couldn't handle that.

During the fall of 1955, after our return from England, my agents, MCA, wanted me to go into television. I didn't want to do a live show, but I agreed to do it if it was on film. The Maysville Corporation (after my hometown) was set up and we filmed thirty-nine half-hour television shows with a pre-recording technique that was just as good as records. It was an amazingly good series.

I got pregnant with Maria in December after our return from England. We spent Christmas at home, and Joe's daughter, Lettie, from his earlier marriage spent Christmas with us. We also had my mother and my sister Gail with us.

Mother and Gail had come to live with us before Miguel was born. While Joe and I were on our honeymoon I got a call from mother, who was by then divorced from Gail's father and living with Betty in New York. Betty was marrying a Latin bandleader, Pupi Campo, and was breaking up housekeeping in New York. Mother didn't know where they were going, but wherever it was they were going to be traveling a lot and she wanted my advice about where to put Gail in school. She called Claridge's and they finally tracked me down at a little pub we'd gone to in the country near Pinewood Studios.

I said, "Okay, mother. Let me talk this over with Joe and call you back."

I went back to the luncheon table and told Joe that mother needed our advice about boarding schools for Gail. Without hesitation he said, "Why not have her come and live with us in California?"

I thought that was very generous of him. I felt great that he had such compassion for my sister, but I am no longer surprised by such things in Joe. Children have always held a warm spot in his heart. Joe has a great feeling for people. The fact that it was his suggestion, of course, settled it to the delight of everyone.

Betty did a television series in Detroit not long after that, so mother ended up living with us soon after Gail arrived. Mother had no place to go and I don't think she got along well with Betty's husband. Actually I got mother an apartment not far from us, but she spent more time in our house than she did in her own. It's ironic—my mother lived with me longer as a grandmother than I ever did with her as a child!

As for Joe and me—at this point there was peace between us. Our work started taking us to different places and I found it easier to hide behind ignorance of any suspicions. If there was anything to be upset about, I refused to see it. If I didn't know, it couldn't make problems for me. Once again, of course, I was not dealing with things; I was shoving everything into that closet.

I worked all through my pregnancy with Maria. The television show was syndicated so it wasn't shot on a tight weekly schedule. It took us almost a year to do it, so I worked other engagements between episodes.

It was during this time span that I started taking my children on the road with me. It started with Miguel. I took him everywhere, and as we added to the family my entourage grew. Between my professional family and my private family, we were quite a sight to see when we unloaded ourselves at a hotel for one of my personal appearances. I was operating well within the image that the world had of me: first, as the sweet, unadulterated young singer from Kentucky; and now as the nice middle-America mother who also happened to be a singer who took good care of her family.

I have some very fond memories of being a family on the road. That was never a strain. It was always a joy.

CHAPTER XI

Duke, Billie and Judy

Nineteen fifty-six was the year I recorded "Blue Rose" with Duke Ellington—or without Duke Ellington, as I'll explain in a moment. People always ask singers which of their albums is their favorite, and they invariably name their most recent one. I am always high on the latest album I've recorded because it should reflect the progress I've made. "Blue Rose" stands out as a highlight in my recording career. I think that's because of the uniqueness of the album, the way it was recorded, because I was working with the fabulous Billy Strayhorn—"Sweet Pea," as all those who loved him called him.

The album date was set, but my doctor thought it would be better if I didn't travel back to New York to do the album with Duke. Duke, however, was scheduled to be in New York for the next few months and he couldn't come to the Coast with a full band. So Billy Strayhorn came to California and together we picked out the songs that I would sing on the

178

album. We used songs that Duke had recorded in the past and we worked out all the vocal arrangements—what we would do with the songs, how many we'd do, where I would sing in the arrangements and so on.

After working with me for two weeks, Billy went back to New York, sat down with Duke and wrote the instrumental "Blue Rose"—a tone portrait of Rosemary Clooney. The songs were all recorded instrumentally, and in three or four weeks Billy returned to California with the master. I worked with earphones—and with Billy—in a booth and did the album. Fascinating! It was the first time it had ever been done at Columbia, although now it is done quite often.

"Blue Rose" was a highly successful album artistically and also sold quite well. It was a well-integrated album, and people never got the idea that we had recorded it separately. Thanks to Billy Strayhorn, there was a perfect meshing of orchestra and voice.

There are many things that I remember about Billy Strayhorn. I remember him talking to me about "Blue Rose" and how he wanted me to sing it. He didn't want it to be a vocal per se. Instead, he said, "I want you to imagine that you're living in New York and you've got a really hot date and you're getting ready to go out and the radio is playing one of Duke's records. So what you're doing is just singing along with the orchestra. But I want you singing as though you're combing your hair."

And that's the interpretation he got.

Billy also became a close friend. I remember one of those days when I was feeling very pregnant and very much not wanting to work—not wanting to do anything—and Billy came over to my house with an apple pie which we both proceeded to eat upstairs on my big bed. There we were, the two of us sitting there with plates, knives and forks, and the pie in the middle, and laughing like kids playing hooky. He was one of the most generous, talented people I've ever known. He was also one of the greatest poets when you think of the lyrics he wrote—songs like "Lush Life." He was obviously a very complicated man. At times he could be very childlike in his ability to unravel himself in a very simple, beautiful poem which was only enhanced by being set to music. Indeed, it was entirely Billy Strayhorn's talent that made "Blue Rose" come off at all. Nobody else could have done it. However late, I think the world should know the tremendous efforts this dear man put into his work, from somebody who knows firsthand.

The title of the album was originally going to be "Inter-Continental." That's the title Duke had in mind, but Columbia didn't want to advertise the fact that we weren't together when it was recorded. So "Inter-Continental" became "Blue Rose."

An article appeared in the *Saturday Evening Post* about this time written by Pete Martin's wife, Virginia. It was a very straight-ahead piece and Mitch Miller was quoted as saying he didn't approve of my marriage. Joe was extremely upset about the article. I had my husband on the one hand and the producer of my records on the other, and they were not seeing eye to eye.

Mitch denied he ever said anything. I got him on the phone the minute I saw the article and I said, "Mitch, what the hell are you trying to do to me?"

"I've been misquoted, Rosemary."

I was a very hot property at Columbia, but I saw then that the handwriting was on the wall. Mitch and I could never have the kind of relationship we'd had in the past, because of Joe; he was just too upset by it. And if there had to be a choice, for me there would be no choice—I was Mrs. Jose Ferrer first.

From that day on, my relationship with Mitch started to disintegrate—evidenced by the fact that he could no longer call me at a moment's notice and have me in a recording studio twenty-four hours later. Before my marriage my work had always had top priority. Now I had a husband, I had a home, I had a child—and they came first, even if my career had to go by the boards. I had made the choice when I said, "I do," back in Durant, Oklahoma.

I've paid the price without regrets. I made a lot of records after that, but I never did have any more big hits. Nothing as mammoth as I'd had before. That didn't bother me then, nor has it ever. I never tried to paste the situation together again. Mitch was a very strong-headed man. So was Joe. My contract with Columbia and my relationship with Mitch would both have to die a natural death.

And that's the way it was. I did not renew my contract with Columbia. I received a very good offer from RCA which was the incentive I needed. I signed with RCA. I'd been with Columbia since the Tony Pastor days—almost ten years—but changes come, and that was that.

One afternoon Joe and I had been to the tennis matches at the Los Angeles Tennis Club. It was during the time when people like Pancho Gonzales, Pancho Segura, Ken Rosewall and Lew Hoad always played doubles so well, Pancho Gonzales looking more beautiful on the courts than any man had a right to look. Great-looking and a great player—and aware of both.

It was the day one of Pancho's serves would have decapitated me if he hadn't had the presence of mind to warn Joe of that possibility. When the Beverly Wilshire had a tennis court, sometimes you would sit right on the court, and that's where I was—sitting in back of the service line, very pregnant with Maria, in a chair next to Joe. Pancho was playing Don Budge in an exhibition match, and I was directly in line with his serve —which had been clocked at 150 mph. Fortunately, early in the match Pancho screamed out, "Joe, put a tennis racket in front of Rosie's face. If one of these balls hits her, it's going to be all over!"

Joe said, "Right!" And I'm glad his reflexes were good, because a couple of minutes later one of Pancho's serves came right at my face and Joe got the racket up in a split second. It would have smashed my face, broken my nose, my teeth—everything.

Outside of that incident it was a rather funny afternoon. Dinah Shore and her husband, George Montgomery, were sitting next to us, and then Doris Day—we occupied three boxes and there were two empty. Dinah quipped, "All we need is Patti Page and Jo Stafford and we'll have a chorus." It broke everybody up. Norma Shearer, as always, was there. I always admired her. She used to come wearing gorgeous silk turbans with parasols to match to keep her perfectly beautiful white skin white. So lovely.

Later that evening Dinah, George, Joe and I went to a little jazz club. We'd started out to get something to eat, but I don't think we ever did. We ended up in this little place just east of Vine Street on Hollywood Boulevard. Billie Holiday was playing there, so we decided to go in and see her. I'd met Billie Holiday in passing. One of those things of being in a jazz club and just saying hello. I'd never sat down to talk to her for very long. Of course I was a tremendous fan of hers. I always admired her work.

Billie was in very good voice that night. I'd heard her at times in the past when she wasn't. I suppose it had to do with her habit and her health, which couldn't have been great when she had abused herself—and been abused—as much as she had. She came over to the table and to my surprise she singled me out and said, "You're a good singer. I'd like to talk to you."

She didn't say much to any of the others and I felt a little uncomfortable and wanted to change the subject. Her biography had just been published, so I said, "I read your book and I thought it was wonderful."

She shook her head sadly. During the Fifties things were so pure, there was a lot one couldn't say in a book about one's life. She just stood there and shook her head. Finally she said, "That ain't half the story. Do you want to hear the *real* story?"

I said, "Sure."

"All right," she went on. "I'll come and see you tomorrow. Where do you live?"

As everybody else just sat ogle-eyed, I quickly scribbled my address and gave it to her.

She said, "I'll see you tomorrow. Don't forget."

"I won't," I assured her.

We left shortly after that. It seemed everything else would be anticlimactic. What could top what Billie had said?

She arrived at my house early the next afternoon and we went into the den. Our den opens onto the garden, but the windows were closed. I went behind the bar and asked, "Can I get you anything?"

She said, "I'd like a gin and orange juice."

I fixed the drink and figured she shouldn't have to drink alone, so I fixed one for myself. We sat down together and she started talking about her book, filling in what had really happened in her life.

She said, "You know, I got sick when I was down South once. Very sick." (She didn't say it, but I had a feeling it was a venereal disease from the way she discussed it.) "I couldn't find a doctor to treat me. I was singing with Artie Shaw's band. It was always a problem, you know, being black and singing with a white band in the deep South. We had lots of segregation. Tony Pastor—used to be your boss, didn't he?—Tony was playing saxophone and singing with the band. Tony, God bless him, found me a doctor so I could get some treatment.

"I was always a fan of Tony's," she went on, "and I used to listen to you when you were singing with him. I kind of got to feel comfortable with your voice, so I became a fan. I like the way you sing. You sing from the heart. I like that."

I've never been more honored.

Billie paced up and down all afternoon in my den. I was sitting in the chair and I remember looking out toward the garden late in the afternoon and being somewhat mesmerized by the haze from our smoking—just blue smoke hanging lazily there on the air like it does through the Blue Ridge and Great Smoky mountains. I somehow was struck by the incongruity of her conversation, the blue smoke, and the gin, which I wasn't able to handle too well anyway. It was really hard for me because every time I fixed Billie a drink I'd fix one for myself.

Billie was doing just fine. I was having problems, not being a gin drinker, but I was hanging in there because what the woman had to say was so fascinating to me. I can tell you, she was one hell of a lady, and from all she told me, I'd say she sure had a right to sing the blues.

We immediately had a kind of shorthand between us; she'd merely gesture and I knew exactly what she meant. I think I was surprised by the initial overture, but delighted because to know her, I thought, would be a tremendous plus in my life and I got to know her that afternoon in a way, I suppose, not many people ever did.

A man came to pick her up—I think it was her husband, but also her manager. He drove up in the driveway and we took our time walking out to the car together. She turned just before she got into the car and said, "That baby that you've got in your belly. What do you think it's going to be?"

I said, "I hope it's a girl because I have a little boy and I'd love to have a little girl."

She grinned and touched my shoulder. "Tell you what. I'll be the little girl's godmother."

I said, "I'd love that."

"Yes—I'd be a good godmother. It takes a *baaaaddd* woman to be a good godmother." She winked, squeezed my shoulder affectionately and got into the car and drove away.

It was the last time I ever saw Billie. I sent her a telegram when Maria was born. She was in New York, not working because she couldn't get a police cabaret card because of her narcotics record. It was a shame. The only place where she could make a good living and they wouldn't let her work. What a tragedy, not allowing someone, so victimized by a society she made so happy with her songs, to work. Such an injustice. It was not just Billie's financial loss, it was a cultural loss—to all of us.

A lot of things were coming down. Experiences that would always stay in my mind. Experiences that made me more a woman, more a person.

Maria's birth was not as complicated as Miguel's. For one thing, I didn't have that entourage at the hospital with me. For another, I went into labor in the middle of the night and was at the hospital at 7 A.M., before all the heavy traffic, so I was spared Joe's driving expertise. Also his chess-playing friends.

But he did repeat a strange thing he had done on the night Miguel was born. That night he'd had all his cronies there, and after Miguel was born they all went out and decided to lift an elbow to Joe's newborn son. By chance Joe ran into Georgie Auld, a tremendous saxophone player who did all the playing recently for Robert De Niro in *New York, New York*. Georgie was playing someplace around Santa Monica in the beach area where Joe went for a drink.

That had been a coincidence, but in August 1956 when Maria was born Joe again went out and had a couple of drinks, and then decided that after each one of his kids was born he'd have to find Georgie Auld to help him celebrate. It's so crazy, because he found him. Somewhere in the city of Los Angeles Georgie was playing that night and Joe found him. That went on for about three years—and three babies—but during the fourth year Joe couldn't find him and was terribly depressed about the whole thing.

I had to get back to work to finish the thirty-nine weeks of syndicated shows. That meant I had to get my body back in shape for my costumes to fit—and quickly.

When I was trying to do that after Miguel was born, Dietrich told me about a woman out in the San Fernando Valley by the name of Louise Long. Dietrich said, "I'm going to send over a lady who is going to get you back in shape from having your baby. She'll do it quickly." Louise was a legend in Hollywood for over thirty years. There was a kind of underground that knew about her and passed her name along. Everybody goes there—even now, although Louise is no longer alive.

That became my way of getting back into shape after my babies were born. Louise would come to me the first time, and then I would go to her salon. It was the hardest massage I ever had in my life. The first time when she came to my house I didn't have a massage table and she grabbed me as she sat on the foot of my bed. She grabbed me so hard I started rolling toward the headboard. Then she clasped my other side with her other hand and there was no moving after that. It was the hardest thing I'd ever experienced physically in my life. In combination with that "massage," Louise used a machine with an electrical impulse that put the muscles into contraction, a very strong passive exerciser. All of that treatment, plus diet, put me back into shape quite rapidly.

Louise's sister, Nanny is still alive and working wonders now with women who come to her out in the valley. I go there for my massages every day I'm in town. Louise's daughter-in-law, Winnie, works on me and I swear she's just as strong as Louise ever was—and about a third her size. That woman has hands of iron.

When I went back to work again I started my prerecording of the show—the songs—and Nelson Riddle was my conductor. It was my first meeting with Nelson, and for the television show he did one very outstanding arrangement for me of "Come Rain or Come Shine." He had a marvelous idea: He had me sing rather slowly but used a double-time, kind of bongo tempo in the background which kept it moving along in the most exciting way, creating a musical illusion.

Judy Garland later came out with an album, "Judy at Carnegie Hall." I heard it, and there was Judy singing an arrangement of "Come Rain or Come Shine" almost identical to mine. It was a Nelson Riddle arrangement. It didn't anger me at all.

Part of my problem was I couldn't show anger. It was the pattern and habit of so many years. That was the way I learned it.

Judy played the Palace that fall in New York and Joe and I were there, so we went to see her. After the show we went backstage. I was standing in the doorway of her dressing room. Judy was sitting in front of a mirror at her dressing table taking off makeup and she looked at me in the mirror and said, "Just what the hell do you think you and Mitch Miller are doing lifting my record?"

I had recorded "Come Rain or Come Shine" many months before, but it was not released until after Judy's record, so Judy thought I stole her arrangement.

I walked in and said, "Okay, Judy, let's get Nelson Riddle on the phone right now. Let's just get him on the phone and we'll settle it right now."

I caught her kind of flat-footed, but Judy could get out of anything. She was amazing that way. It was like she let her gears shift into neutral while she took a different tack and all of a sudden it was, "Darling, how are you?" Just like it never happened. But that was one time I did strike back because that was a terrible accusation she made in front of all those people. The room was filled with her admirers, all of them celebrities themselves and people I knew too.

Edie Wasserman (wife of Lew Wasserman who heads up Universal Pictures) was the first to know about the whole thing and went to Nelson Riddle and told him, "What a hell of a thing you started." Nelson may have started it, but it ended in Judy's dressing room that night.

In spite of what he had done about the song arrangement, I was beginning to find Nelson Riddle more interesting as we worked together. There was something about him that attracted me, but I knew that nothing would ever come of it. I would never pursue it, and besides, we were both married.

CHAPTER XII

And Then There Were Five

I spent most of that winter in England with Joe. We took Miguel with us but left Maria at home with my mother; she was still such a very small baby, not quite ready for world travel. We stayed at Claridge's again while Joe worked on one of his very best pictures, *J'Accuse*, which was the story of Dreyfus. Although Dreyfus was French, the French government would not let them shoot in Paris because they were still quite sensitive about the whole thing, so the interior shots were being done in London and the exteriors in Brussels. I was pregnant again, with Gabriel, and again threatening to lose the baby in the early months, but in England I was given the name of a doctor who put me on progesterone pills instead of shots. I was grateful for that.

It was a wonderful time because we spent weekends in the country visiting our friends, and when Joe finished the interior shots in London we went to Brussels together.

At the other side of customs in London Joe had to pick up some duty-free things he had purchased, and I was standing slightly away from him preoccupied with something else when I overheard one of the customs men saying, ". . . and this diamond pin, sir?"

I was amazed that he had a diamond pin, and instantly leaped to the conclusion that it must be for somebody else in his life—one of his "other" ladies. I was crushed, but said nothing.

In Brussels there was a tremendous dinner party and Joe gave me the most gorgeous diamond pin you have ever seen. It had a large diamond in the middle and other diamonds going out like a starburst. The mountings were invisible from the front, so that when you wore it against black velvet the diamonds looked as if they had been scattered in the air and just stayed there, suspended in space. I've never seen another like it.

In the midst of my pleasure, however, I suddenly had the greatest pangs of guilt you can imagine. I had to do some mental readjusting and I found myself wondering how many things I'd silently accused Joe of without questioning. Perhaps right then I should have said, "Look, Joe, you know what I really thought? I thought you bought this for somebody else." But I couldn't bring myself to be that honest. That was another time I could have done something to salvage myself, because at least it would have been a positive thing and maybe we could have laughed about it—together. But I didn't do it.

It was early summer when we started back home. We were returning by ship, and by this time Joe had replaced the diamond-and-sapphire bracelet that had been taken in the Paris robbery, so I was sort of loaded down in the diamond department. I remember the first night out, which is usually a very showy affair, I wore my diamonds—and lo and behold, another woman on the cruise turned up with the same bracelet, the only difference being that hers was set in rubies and diamonds instead of sapphires. There were only two of them made by Van Cleef, and of all things both of them wound up on the same trip aboard the *Mauritania* en route from England to America.

We both wore our jewels proudly. I, for one, was not about to put that gorgeous thing away, and apparently she felt the same way.

Miguel had a very unfortunate experience on that crossing which he vividly remembers today. There was a playroom on the ship that had a scooter on a track so the kids wouldn't fall off. It must have made him a little queasy, because when Joe took him to have tea with the captain and he had some vanilla ice cream, he promptly threw up all over the captain's cabin. Poor Miguel. I think to have such a vivid memory of an incident that occurred when he was only two and a half must be due to the fact that, though little more than a baby, he was horribly embarrassed.

I didn't feel up to snuff either on the voyage back. Joe tried to lift my spirits by doing a watercolor portrait of me in a pair of his pajamas. I always wore his pajamas when I was pregnant, and he thought it would be nice to capture me that way for posterity. It was a pleasant diversion.

Joe hadn't had to pay any tax on the diamond pin while leaving England, but he did have to pay the duty on it when we arrived in New York. His lawyer met us with his checkbook and was obviously not all that happy about it. He didn't like the fact that Joe was spending so much money.

We didn't stay in New York long because I was anxious to get home. I wanted to be close to my own doctor, who quickly assured me that everything was going along fine. I still didn't feel right, but if the doctor said I was all right, then I supposed I must be all right—especially where the baby was concerned.

A new television series was taking shape for me which would start late in the fall. It was going to be very close, in any event, because Gabriel was due in October. I would have perhaps two weeks after his birth to get myself ready to start rehearsals. But it was an NBC network effort slated for 10 P.M. and in color—one of the first shows in color—and was creating a lot of excitement. We already had a big sponsor, Lux Soap.

While all of these things were coming to a head, I was grow-

ing very concerned about the birth of my baby. It just seemed
to be calling the shots too close; everybody was assuming
everything would come off right on schedule. I just wanted to
have my baby in peace, but suddenly everybody wanted to
know when I was going to be ready to rehearse and when I
would be able to do this and when I would be able to do something else. How could I think about all that when I hadn't
even attended to all the things involving my forthcoming
lying-in. You really can't think along other lines when you're
working toward the last few months of your pregnancy. That's
really all a woman can truthfully concentrate on. Those final
months are demanding, and the concentration attached to it
was very important to me.

I don't know if all the traveling and the kind of stress I was
put under was responsible for it, but at the end of July I started
feeling very strong cramps in the middle of the night and they
weren't regular. Not regular, but quite pronounced, and it
frightened me. I woke Joe and called the doctor. He asked me
to come right to the hospital for an examination—he said he'd
meet us there—so we got into the car and drove to the hospital
where, after the examination, I was advised that I was already
in labor and the baby would be two months premature. Just
what I needed to hear.

I'd never had a great deal of anesthesia with my babies. This
time I wouldn't get any. That was all right because I was more
afraid that the baby would be too small to survive than I was
of pain—though I was damned scared of that, too. I remember
one labor pain that started and never ended. They put me on a
rolling stretcher and got me to the labor room just in time for
Gabriel to be born. He weighed four pounds.

Gabri was born at a time when hospitals were just starting
to use Isolettes. There had been a lot of problems with the old
incubators; some children had developed problems with their
sight because of them. The Isolette was far more efficient and
safe—but a very expensive piece of equipment. I think Saint
John's had three in service at that time, which wasn't many

considering the number of births at that hospital. Joe did a wonderful thing. He was so grateful to the Isolette for saving Gabri's life that he went out and bought one and donated it to Saint John's. I believe it is still being used.

Gabri was in the Isolette for about a month, and for the first time I was unable to take my baby home with me from the hospital. I had to go right to work and my baby wasn't even home. I was feeling very torn about the whole thing and would go to the hospital every single day to just stand in front of the glass and look at him in his little Isolette.

I remember once we were on our way to the beach to have dinner with Paul Newman and Joanne, and Gore Vidal, who was visiting them. We were bringing along Claire Bloom. Joe knew I had to see my baby every day and he was very good about it. Claire went to the hospital with us before we drove on to the beach, and I've never forgotten how nice she was about it. She didn't act for a moment as though it were an imposition. She went up with us and showed a great deal of interest in the baby. That gave me a good feeling about her.

Dr. Russell Mapes, the pediatrician who took care of all my children, was a kind of old-fashioned man, rather courtly, and I remember something he said about Gabri that proved prophetic. He said, "If a baby is premature, they fight very hard the first year of their life, but if they make it and they're healthy they never really stop achieving and they never stop fighting for what they want."

That is true of Gabri. He was four pounds at birth and the usual weight loss after birth brought him down to slightly over three pounds, but he fought to regain his birth weight and went on from there. He's tenacious in a quiet way even today—dedicated to his beliefs and ambitions, very purposeful, single-minded about things. When I see some of his tremendous accomplishments, like his ceramics work or his work with the church—anything to which I see his dedication applied—it reminds me of that statement by Dr. Mapes.

It was actually a matter of a month before I went into full

rehearsals for my television show for NBC. I didn't feel quite ready; I'd had three children in three years—actually the third had come less than a year after the second—and I was not coming back as easily physically. Thanks to Louise Long, I lost the weight I'd gained, but it was hard. Very, very hard. Each pregnancy was taking its toll, a little bit at a time, on my general health.

There was also that feeling of not being able to concentrate on my baby, being torn away before he came home. I was back to work by the time he was released from the hospital, so I wasn't able to give Gabriel the same postnatal attention I'd given my other children and I felt cheated. I felt the loss. That might have made me a little more nervous than usual, but I started the television show and was soon into the week-after-week grind.

Actually, I'd tried to avoid this television series because I didn't want to be held down to a specific time. The earlier series, which was filmed, was a lot of work but I could still take off in the middle of it if I wanted to and I could double up later. That allowed me to do some outside things and go on trips with Joe. MCA thought this new, live show was good for me professionally and they made some very strong points to convince me, so I said, "Okay, we'll do it." And we did.

I remember so vividly one of my early guests on the show, Wally Cox, who was a friend of long standing and a wonderful man. I came to a rehearsal one morning out at Burbank, and Wally came over to me and said, "You seem very nervous and overwrought."

"Well," I said with a sort of frustrated sigh, "I have so much to do at home and I drive the freeway to get here and right into work, then I drive the freeway to get home and it is right into home problems and responsibilities. It's very difficult, I can tell you."

"I know," he said, "but I have a good idea for you. I never drive freeways. I think when you leave the studio you should go over and get onto Mulholland Drive—that's the mountain road—and forget the freeways. It's a slow, leisurely drive and you don't have much traffic. The scenery is fantastic and by the time you get home you'll be so much more relaxed that home won't be all that much a challenge."

It was the best piece of advice I could have gotten. I started coming to work refreshed, and I would come home having left all the problems of work at work, because the break between work and home was pleasant and relaxing, rather than difficult and tiresome.

My show was going fine and I was just adjusting to not having had the time with Gabri that I would have liked, when about in the middle of taping the show, right after the first of the year, I got pregnant again. Once again the agents, managers and television people were fretting. I think outside of Lucille Ball who wrote her pregnancy right into her sitcom series, I was the first performer to ever work pregnant as much as I did —through two television series actually.

The designers found it a problem, but they met the challenge admirably, with the result that I had the most fantastic maternity wardrobe of any human being going. All those gorgeous evening dresses done by Worley and Edith Head. Also some things from Marusia. That part I loved.

After I finished the series something strange happened to me —I developed a fear of flying. I think it was all that traveling with my whole family—all the babies and everyone on one plane. Too much could happen. I was working all over and I just didn't want to fly.

As a result of that, on the final day of shooting of the television series Joe and I, two nurses and three babies went to San Francisco by train where we changed trains for Reno. In Reno we were picked up and driven to Tahoe where I had an engagement. After I finished there we rented a car and Joe drove us all down to Las Vegas where I was playing The Sands. He really was a hell of a good driver. We settled into Vegas like the Swiss Family Robinson. Ridiculous! But that's the way we spent the summer, my doing the nightclub circuit with all of us together. I made a tremendous amount of money on that trip. When you start talking Tahoe and Las Vegas you are getting into some very large dollar signs.

When I got back to Los Angeles I was tired, but not too tired to record, which I did. Joe was soon involved with a play, *Edwin Booth*, which was being tried out in La Jolla, so we all moved down there by the ocean for part of the summer. The play had an excellent cast: Joe, Lorne Greene, Marion Ross and a young actor by the name of Steve Franken who was tremendously talented and became very close to Miguel. My mother and Gail were with us, plus the two nurses to help with the children, so naturally we had to have two apartments. No one place would have held us all.

Marion Ross, who has been so successful along with my friend Henry Winkler in "Happy Days," became a good friend during that time. I saw her recently at the studio and she said something which must say a lot about today's fashions, since the kids really do mimic "Happy Days" which leads adults to do the same thing. "You see," she pointed out laughingly, "I'm still dressing the same way as I did when we were in La Jolla."

Not a lot changes, does it?

After we finished up in La Jolla we came home. It was shortly before Monsita was born, October 1958, and Betty was visiting me. In our backyard I had allowed the two older children to plant some radishes and other easy-to-raise vegetables so they could see how things grew, and on this particular day I was out back with the kids and they were showing me their garden. Betty was with us. It was about four o'clock in the afternoon, I think, when I turned to Betty and said, "I believe I'm in labor."

Joe was in the house because he wouldn't think of leaving when it got close to time for our babies to be born. He liked to be the one who drove me to the hospital. Betty all of a sudden got terribly nervous, and when Betty got nervous she tried all the more to take charge of things. She said, "Yes! Well, what will I do?" She was highly agitated and coming a little unglued. "I'll stay here with the children," she said, her voice getting just a little bit higher, "and you go tell Joe. Or do you want to stay here with the children and I'll go go tell Joe?" It was just hysterical watching her fall apart.

"I'll tell Joe," I said, and went into the house, leaving Betty pacing up and down the grass giving orders to the children.

It was at the height of traffic and to try to get down Wilshire to 22nd Street to the hospital seemed like an impossible task. Joe was dying from frustration. He tried running red lights, hoping a cop would pull him over and he'd be able to get a police escort. No such luck.

"Any other time in the world," he said impatiently, "let me make one mistake and red lights and sirens would be all over me. Today I can't buy one."

Labor with my fourth child progressed very quickly. That need not happen, but it did. We made it to the hospital—barely —and she was born within an hour. My beautiful little Monsita was perfect in every way, which was a great relief to me after all I'd gone through with Gabri.

But before it was over I had reason to worry again. The blood-platelet count was very low and my obstetrician called in Dr. Mapes right away. They might have to do a complete blood exchange on her. For twenty-four hours we awaited the decision whether to do the blood exchange or not. Finally the doctor came in to see me, smiling. The problem worked itself out as the count went up. Then I was able to sleep.

Once everything was all right with the baby and me, Joe went back to *Edwin Booth*. It was not a success in New York, however, and before long he was back in California doing something else.

Christmas was marred by the death of my Grandmother Guilfoyle. She had died at her home in Lexington, Kentucky, so the holiday season was not so merry. I was working and couldn't get back for the funeral, and that bothered me, but I thought a lot about my grandmother. I remembered going back to Kentucky when I was pregnant with Miguel and that she did something very typical of country people. When a pregnant woman was big and nearing the end of the pregnancy, she was never allowed, for instance, to bathe alone because it was feared she might slip and fall trying to get into the tub. Pregnant women are notoriously awkward anyway. So my grandmother insisted on helping me and she sat on the "convenience" and talked to me while I bathed.

She said, "You know, you better be sure to put a quarter on your belly button." I didn't know what she meant. I did know it was getting damned uncomfortable as my clothes rubbed against me and my swollen stomach. She explained, "If you tape a quarter over your belly button it will stop the irritation. Otherwise you'll rub yourself raw."

Those old people from the country had a lot of common-sense preventive medicine—in fact a lot of common sense, period. When Miguel was born she made little cotton flannel receiving coats for him just the way she'd made them for her own children. They were just wonderful because you just put them over a baby's diaper and shirt. They were made to fit a one-year-old, which meant the baby would practically be swimming in it, but you could turn back the cuffs when they were still small. I still have and treasure those little garments.

There's a mental block about my professional life during this period. Maybe I just don't want to remember and so I don't. I'm sure I was busy. I had a big family now, and that took a lot of my time—more and more with every new baby. My marriage, on the surface, was adequate. There were times when I suspected Joe was having little affairs, but they didn't seem to be too important to him and I had long since chosen to ignore them. He was being a little more discreet now. I think having a family made a difference. More responsibility. More caring.

More and more, though, Joe was becoming unhappy with California. He wasn't really appreciated by the movie industry in Hollywood and he knew it. Had he been born in England, that tremendous range that he has as an actor would have been far more appreciated than in America. We tend to hang on more to personalities that are usually pretty much the same in every picture. I don't think Laurence Olivier is appreciated by the people in middle America as the greatest living actor, which he is, the way he is appreciated in England. But then, we don't have that classical background, really, as a country for Shakespearean plays or anything in that vein. In England everybody goes to see Shakespeare, whereas it is quite limited here.

Joe always becomes the character he plays, which is the mark of a tremendously good actor. He has that unique ability to transform himself into that person. As a result of that, people can't pigeonhole him, and people like to do that. Even when someone does classify him, it is as a classical actor, despite the fact that he is a talented comedian, and had his beginnings in an out-and-out farce like *Charley's Aunt*. American audiences seem to prefer the stereotype, and unless you allow this to happen to you, people have a tendency to either dismiss you or have less interest in what you do on a running basis. Joe has suffered from that syndrome.

Disenchanted with California, Joe began to lean toward a move back to New York. That didn't make me very happy because I loved it in California and it was a great place to bring up my children. I never felt I had to be active in motion pictures to live in California. Joe did. I could take my work under my hat and go wherever I wanted to. There's a kind of security in that, which perhaps an actor doesn't have. Joe's work is a lot more complicated, so maybe that's the difference.

At any rate, my reluctance to leave California put a strain on a marriage that was already teetering in the wind.

By the fall of 1959 I was pregnant with our fifth child and feeling this strain more strongly than ever because Joe wanted to move back east with the children and told me so. The apartment we had in New York wouldn't begin to accommodate our family and entourage, so his lawyer, very anxious to make things right for me in New York, arranged to get an apartment for us in the Dakota. It's located at 72nd Street and Central Park West and they filmed *Rosemary's Baby* there. Those apartments were hard to come by, but because of Joe's stature in the theater they were happy to have us, so we got ten rooms with seventeen-foot ceilings, overlooking Central Park. Our neighbors were fantastic people, and it was perfectly beautiful so far as the view was concerned. But it wasn't California.

Joe Bushkin, a friend and someone I've worked a lot with over the years, moved into our house in California while we were gone. Mother, who'd never formally given up her own apartment, moved into it with Gail. Mother wasn't very happy about it because she didn't want to be away from the children—and in fact she became very important to her grandchildren; she loved my kids and they loved her dearly. I think she tried with her grandchildren to make up for all the things she didn't do with her own daughters.

Though I hadn't wanted to come to New York, once there I made the best of it—and there were some exciting moments. Joe was directing George C. Scott in *The Andersonville Trial* (so few people know he is such a talented director) and George used to come up to the apartment and they would work together in the den. Besides the children, I busied myself with television things in New York, but more than anything else I was becoming fascinated by the advent of the Kennedys on the political scene.

My interest had been growing since John Kennedy came in second best to Estes Kefauver for the vice-presidential nomination in 1956. My Grandfather Clooney had always been a staunch Democrat, so I knew about the Democratic party and knew what the Democratic presidents had done, and my own political feelings were in that direction. Through the Eisenhower years I was almost totally uninterested in government. I had been brought up more or less a Roosevelt-Truman Democrat and hadn't had a lot to get enthused about in the party until the Kennedys came along. I didn't know it then, but I would become very involved with the Kennedy bandwagon and in the not too distant future.

We spent that Christmas in New York at the Dakota. All the kids were there and we had a warm and wonderful white Christmas of our own. Still, I wanted to come back to California to have my baby. That was very important to me. I didn't want to go to another doctor. It's like a run of luck, and my luck, all things considered, had been pretty damned good up till now. I'd come through with four children at Saint John's with the same doctors and I felt comfortable with the same setting.

Joe was very understanding about it, so we all came back to California and moved back into our house. This, being the only real home I've ever known, has always been my anchor, my haven of rest and comfort—and my security. This house, where all of my children were brought up, is like family to all of us.

With Rafael I was feeling fine. I suppose we'd miscalculated the time of his birth because we were suddenly ten days late and Joe was hanging around the house, waiting for something to happen so he could take me to the hospital as always. Finally something came up that he could not avoid. He was taking a big French easel that he had promised to lend to somebody and he had it in the back of the station wagon on his way out the driveway when I returned from an errand. We stopped beside each other in the driveway and he said, "I'll only be gone for about an hour."

"No problem," I assured him.

Joe had been gone about fifteen minutes and I went into labor. I called the doctor and he said, "This is your fifth child. You better hurry along now, especially since our experience with Monsita."

The only person in the house who could drive me to the hospital was my mother. Now my mother had never driven a car until she came to live out in California with us. Her average driving speed was fifteen miles an hour. If she had to turn left at her destination she immediately got into the left-hand lane when she pulled out of the driveway, even if she was driving from Los Angeles to San Bernardino. Never went near a freeway. All in all she was one of the funniest drivers I've ever known, but when you're expecting your fifth child and labor is upon you, you're apt to miss the humor of it all—you are looking for safety and speed.

Nonetheless, I was stuck with mother. She slid behind the wheel and away we went. We got down to Wilshire Boulevard and at the corner of Wilshire and Linden, a good five miles from the hospital, she turns into the left-hand lane. (She knew she would have to make a left turn at 22nd Street in Santa Monica to get into the hospital.) There was a laundry truck in front of us and I said, "Mama, this laundry truck is going to wait to turn left, so why don't you get over into the right lane?"

She said, "Rosemary, please don't make me nervous."

I was thinking to myself, I'm in labor and we're parked in the middle of Wilshire Boulevard and she's telling *me* not to make *her* nervous.

When we finally got to the hospital, mother let out a tremendous sigh of relief—she was so grateful that we'd made it at all. She accompanied me to the prelabor room, and there my labor stopped. Nothing was happening. It was about eleven in the morning and Joe very shortly caught up with us. Here he came with his usual stack of books and concern.

Although the sharp pains had abated, there was still some discomfort. By seven that night I was worn to a frazzle, and still no baby. The doctor gave me a shot—perhaps oxytocin to step up the contractions, or perhaps calcium to give my muscles a little more strength—I don't remember exactly. But whatever it was, my fifth child was born at eight o'clock on the 23rd day of March 1960.

Rafael was small, maybe an ounce over five pounds, but he was a term baby so I didn't have to go through all that hassle with Isolettes that I'd had with Gabriel. Rafi was the smallest baby in the regular nursery, but he was healthy and I was happy.

I love my children tremendously. I think they've made my life important in a way that nothing else could. The sense of accomplishment, being around a child or young person when they turn to you for an opinion. To know and realize that you have the responsibility of perhaps being the one who gives them the first insight into something that will either stand them in good stead or cause them to look at things in a crooked way for the rest of their lives. That is an awesome responsibility, yet I get a great sense of satisfaction from that and from them.

They've been the most important events in my life, but believe me, it hasn't meant that I haven't done other things or that I haven't taken care of myself. I realize that is important, too. That's why, after Rafi was born, I started getting busy in the 1960 presidential campaign of John Kennedy. It was now time to do something for Rosemary that Rosemary had been unable to do before.

CHAPTER XIII

A Touch of Camelot

It was in the fall of 1960. The national conventions were over and John Kennedy had been nominated by the Democrats. Then came the famous Nixon/Kennedy debates on television. I had very strong feelings about John Kennedy as a candidate and I was drawn to his campaign. I opened the Waldorf Astoria that fall for a five-week run, which would keep me on the East Coast during the campaign. There were a lot of things I became involved in to help the Kennedy candidacy—just small appearances in different places where I would show up and say a few words, nothing really earth-rattling—all on the East Coast.

Toward the end of my engagement there was one big rally before the election in November. I was in New York and was invited to come to Madison Square Garden for the event, which the candidate would also be attending. I went and sang, and someone introduced me to Senator Kennedy, who was

very nice to me. Of course I was elated after his election. Like
so many others I felt a new hope for the country, and his being
Irish also warmed my heart.

Frank Sinatra hosted a tremendous inaugural gala in Washington the night before Kennedy was sworn in as president. A
year later, in January 1962, there was an anniversary party held
in Washington to celebrate the first year of the Kennedy administration. I was invited to sing. It was a gigantic party held
at the armory with thousands of people at tables. There was a
stage at one side of the room and on the other side a long, long
dais where the president, Mrs. Kennedy and other notables sat.
Everything was designed by Lee Remick's husband, Bill Col-
leran. Bill suggested I get up from one of the tables with a
microphone, start singing "Everything's Coming Up Roses"
from the center of the room and then make my way in one
mad dash to the bandstand.

I was wearing a black velvet Edith Head dress and did it
with great gusto. I remember hearing the president over the
public-address system cheering me on as if I were carrying a
football toward the goal line for the winning touchdown. He
broke me up so much and I was laughing so hard I could barely
continue with the song.

There was still another party afterward at the Jockey Club,
and a buffet. I sat down at a table and was joined by three people who later would have a great deal to say in the running of
the country: Vice President Lyndon Johnson and Lady Bird,
and Hubert Humphrey. My mind flashed back to that very
often after the assassination because it was like the second team.
Senator Humphrey was the majority whip.

The president phoned me at the buffet party and thanked me
for showing up at the celebration. He always took a very personal interest in thank-yous—never left it to subordinates if he
could do it himself.

Later, Attorney General Robert Kennedy and Ethel came
to see me at the Shoreham when I appeared there and I was
invited out to Hickory Hill for lunch. My first visit there left

me impressed with the homelike atmosphere of that lovely house with an awful lot of children all over the place and a great deal of very green lawn. I met and became friends with Undersecretary of the Navy Paul "Red" Fay and his wife Anita at Hickory Hill. Red, who was from San Francisco, would later write a very popular book about his service under Kennedy, *The Pleasure of His Company*. I liked them and their family very much.

Later on that summer I was going to Europe and I was asked to stop in Washington on the way, to sing at a fundraising affair at the Mayflower Hotel. Before the show, there was a cocktail party which was attended by former president Harry Truman. I have always loved and admired Mr. Truman, but there was something that day that sent chills down my spine. I just had great difficulty understanding some of the things he said. He would, at the drop of a hat, start talking about the decisions he had made and had to make during his time in the White House. We'd met before and it was always so surprising to me to hear him talk about momentous decisions in such a casual manner—especially anything so sensitive as his decision to drop the atom bomb, as he did that day.

With an audience Mr. Truman was quite a showman because he could segue from something that profound to something as amusing as the letter he wrote Washington music critic Paul Hume about his review of Margaret's singing abilities. He said, "I didn't send that as president of the United States, I sent that as a father. I even walked outside the gate and mailed it myself." He was a marvelously plain-spoken man.

Two presidents attended that cocktail party. And there was something else memorable about it. President Kennedy always walked very fast and it was hard for the Secret Service people to handle his security at times because he was usually right behind them. He would get out of the car and stride right to where he was supposed to be. He didn't saunter. He didn't hang back. He just moved straight ahead.

That was what he did at this particular party. This was a

small room and we were all there, talking quietly. When all of a sudden these men burst through the door. It was frightening because you didn't know whose side they were on; they were just as wild-eyed as any revolutionary about to wipe out all of the cabinet and the president along with everybody else.

The president followed them into the room and the mood changed immediately It was like a blast of heat followed by a pleasant spring breeze. Jean Smith, the president's sister, said very casually to me, "Rosie, do you know Jack?"

The understatement of the century. Did I know Jack!!

I did the show that night and afterward went up to my suite in the Mayflower and took off my evening dress. I was just sitting around talking with my Aunt Chris when there was a knock at the door. It was Steve Smith, Jean's husband, and he said, "The president would like to see you at the White House." I figured the only thing I could wear was the same gown I'd worked in that evening. I remember it had a long white silk coat.

It was very late, but I got into a convertible with Steve Smith and we drove into the White House grounds. It was very dark; there were no welcoming lights or anything like that. Steve drove up to an entrance and let me out of the car. "Wait here while I park," he said. I remember looking out in the distance and seeing the Reflecting Pool and the Washington Monument. Being all alone and that close to all that history —now *that* was an awesome feeling. I'm sure there were a lot of eyes around, but they didn't make themselves visible to me.

Steve returned and together we walked into the main floor. Only the small lights over the paintings lit the hallways. We went to an elevator and rode up to the living quarters of the first family.

After leaving the elevator, as we walked toward a sitting room, I caught sight of a rocking chair and from the back I could discern the president and his suspenders as they crisscrossed against the chair. In the room, besides the president, were Jean Smith and Peter Lawford. When I walked in, the president immediately got up and put on his coat.

I said, "Oh, please don't, Mr. President," but he did it anyway. As always, I was taken by the fact that he was so tall and so terribly handsome. He always wore a blue cornflower in his lapel instead of anything larger, and he was wearing it then. The blue of the cornflower was almost the color of his eyes. A very, very attractive man.

I sat on a small couch with the president, and Peter Lawford sat on the president's other side. We chatted about the Mayflower event and he thanked me for being there, and for coming to the White House. Suddenly he said, "Anyone for scrambled eggs?" He turned to me. "Would you like some?"

I said, "No, thanks," simply because I didn't know where to put the plate. If I put it on the small coffee table in front of me I knew I'd drop scrambled eggs all over the lovely floor, and to drop scrambled eggs on a nice Oriental carpet in the private quarters of the president of the United States just didn't seem right to me, so I passed.

He fixed eggs in a little kitchenette off the sitting room for everybody else, including himself. As he sat there and started to eat he dropped some egg on his shoe and I thought, Well, I guess if you're the president you don't have to worry about Oriental carpets in the president's living quarters.

Our conversation wasn't earth-shattering. He asked how the jacket to my dress stayed on because it was right on the edge of my shoulders. The dress was made of white lace, and I said, "Mr. President, there are snaps underneath the jacket which attach to the straps, so no problem." I'd heard that he was curious, but that was about the strangest thing for him to be curious about. A very inquisitive man about everything, I suppose.

Later on, after my visit to Hickory Hill to see Ethel and Bobby, I was working at the Shoreham and I talked to Ethel before my show on Friday night. She said, "I don't know whether Bobby's going to be free or not to come to see you tonight. I know he wanted to, but he's just been working so late recently and on top of that the president's coming back from a speaking tour because he's got a sore throat."

I would later know that all of this was a subterfuge so people wouldn't know what was really going on: the Cuban missile crisis.

However, at the very last moment that night the maitre d' at the club called me and said, "We have a packed house, but I've just received word that Attorney General and Mrs. Kennedy are coming to hear you. We'll put a table on the dance floor for them."

And that's what they did.

I saw Bobby just briefly after the show. Ethel laughed a little and said, "I don't think anything could have gotten him away from the Justice Department tonight except to hear you sing."

I really enjoyed knowing that Bobby was a big fan of mine, because I was certainly a fan of his. He was always extremely nice to me, partly, I think, because I am Irish.

The following night, Saturday, I'd been invited to a party hosted by Red Fay aboard the presidential yacht. He sent a car for me and they brought the yacht back to the dock to pick me up so I could spend my time there between shows.

The first thing I noticed on the yacht was that there were a lot of women without their husbands. I saw generals' wives without their generals, and admirals' wives without their admirals. It was almost like a hen party, with all the men apparently occupied at big meetings going on all over Washington. It was particularly noticeable because it was a Saturday night, when normally there were few business meetings and no reason not to go to a party. Washington is a big party town. Ethel was there—without Bobby. Red Fay was there, but he was the *under*secretary of the navy and it was his party. They may have told him to go ahead with the party as another diversion.

It was a very pleasant party nonetheless, and after I went back to do the second show Red surprised me by bringing the whole party to see my show. I remember Joan Fontaine and

Charles Addams were in the party. I'd met Addams once before in New York and was fascinated by the fact that he had decorated his home with a Santa Claus on a scaffold instead of a Christmas tree.

After the show, some of the people from the party came up to my suite to have a drink. I remember going into my bedroom to change clothes. Aunt Chris was helping me. The door was slightly ajar and two men were just outside the door with their drinks. As Chris was unzipping my dress I heard one man say to the other: "Here's to the invasion Cuba."

I looked at Chris and said, "What a ridiculous thing to say." But I soon dismissed it.

On Sunday Washington had a kind of nervousness about it. You could just feel it. There was a lot of tension and a lot of activity, all the signs of some kind of impending crisis. That day I traveled to Toronto where I had one show to do before going to London for a command performance. Somehow with all the packing and travel time that day I missed whatever news there was on the radio and television, but by Sunday night I knew what all the strange carryings-on in Washington had been about.

The president finally made his famous speech about the missiles, bringing America and Russia to "eyeball-to-eyeball" confrontation. I called Aunt Chris before I left Canada and told her there was a lot of tension in Canada. Washington, she said, was like a city running on raw nerve endings.

I didn't know what tension was until I got to London. On the way to Claridge's from the airport I had to pass by the American Embassy and there were groups of anti-American and anti-war groups—just a tremendous number of demonstrators—all angry and throwing rocks at the building. Having always felt so at home and in tune with anything English, I was shocked. I suddenly felt very much an alien. As an American, and as someone who strongly favored the Kennedy administration—in fact had helped in some small part to make it a reality—I think I felt personally involved.

The following night I had the command performance, and

I've never been more nervous before a show. I didn't know how most of England might feel about the president's position on Cuba—I'd only seen that group of demonstrators stoning the American Embassy. When you are working a club or doing a concert for money, that's one thing. When you do a command performance, that's something else again because you have a strong sense of representing your country. I wondered what kind of reaction I would receive from the audience.

To add to my jangled nerves—and probably because of that —I missed the first cue. I knew the arrangement, but I had to come through two sets of curtains and the first curtains were so heavy that before they started to open I couldn't hear the music. Missing the first cue unnerved me. I went on with the show, but I was not comfortable, although the response was warm and wonderful as it always has been for me in England.

I was in New York the day the president was shot. We were rehearsing a Garry Moore show for CBS, and the first announcement from Dallas came on CBS. We couldn't hear it, however, because the monitor reflected the cameras focused on our rehearsal, not the network news. I was leaving New York that night for Los Angeles, so my maid at the Plaza was packing for me when I called from the studio to ask if she could come over with a black dress I would need for the show.

She said, "There was something just come over on television. I was ironing and watching television when Walter Cronkite came on and said something about the president in Dallas. They broke into the show. Did you hear anything about that?"

I hadn't, but I asked a cameraman with a talk-back if he would ask the booth to punch into the network to see what it was all about.

They did, and we all caught the next announcement which chronicled the gravity of the situation and the seriousness of the president's injuries. I remember one of the cameraman was an Irishman who used to tease me about the fact that "our people" were in the White House now and everything was right with the world. We were all just sort of standing around in shock. This cameraman came over to me, took off his head-set and very gently said, in a soft voice, "He's strong. He'll make it."

I didn't talk. In about twenty minutes the producer made the announcement. "There's no way we're going to have a show tonight. You're all dismissed."

Where would I go? I'd lost my appetite for planes, and I really didn't want to go back to Los Angeles now anyway. I remembered that Joe was in Philadelphia doing a show—*The Girl Who Came to Supper*, which was a musical version of *The Sleeping Prince* that Larry and Vivien had done together in England.

Hiring a limousine with a chauffeur, I drove to Philadelphia. In isolation, without the radio on, I studied the faces of people in passing cars and on the streets of the small towns along the way. Their faces were set in expressions of astonishment and disbelief—and the hollow look of grief.

I went to Joe's hotel. He was working on something to do with his play since the performance had been canceled that night due to the death of the president. I think that Joe was moved by the fact that the president had been assassinated, but I don't think he was feeling it as deeply as I was. I sensed some impatience on his part with my feelings—just a hint of disap-proval of my behavior and demeanor. Maybe it was because my association with the Kennedys came about while he and I were separated. He didn't like that too much and wasn't quite sure that it was just that—a friendly association—which is all it was.

I sensed this in his attitude and I resented it. I resented his lack of total grief. It was just another of those many things that kept eroding our attempts to give our marriage a second chance. One thing is certain—I had more compassion for the Kennedy family that day than for the Ferrers.

CHAPTER XIV

A Lover and a Divorce

So much happened to me—the really traumatic and devastating events—in those years after 1960 when my last child was born.

I suppose Rafi was about a year old when things between Joe and me were really getting tough. I suspected he was seeing other women, but I didn't know the specifics.

My sister knew something was going on. Betty knew everything. Always. I don't know how mother felt about Joe at this point, but she was feeding me a lot of information, a little bit at a time, about his activities, and that fueled any decisions that I was going to make about ending our marriage.

I returned from a European visit with the resolve that I would ask Joe to leave. I couldn't very well leave myself; it's not easy to pick up five children and move someplace else, and I didn't intend to.

Joe had returned and was home when I arrived. After talking to my mother I went into the living room where Joe was meeting with some people. Joe always had to have people around, and in order not to disturb them with our problems I said to him, "I'd like to talk to you. Can you come upstairs?"

We went upstairs to the bedroom and I said, "I want a divorce."

He had no idea—at least I don't think he did—that I was going to ask for a divorce. He didn't want it, ever, and he fought it vigorously all the way down the line. But right then he said nothing—just let me finish what I had to say.

I told him the things I felt were wrong in our marriage. I didn't see the problem as being me. I saw it in what I believed were Joe's various alliances with other women which were gradually chipping away at the kind of security I needed in a marriage. I told him I thought I'd done a good job of ignoring that for many years, but that it was getting worse and I didn't see any change in the future.

There was shock in Joe's face, but he said nothing and by the end of the day he had packed some things in a suitcase and moved out to a hotel off the Sunset Strip. I was so determined to follow through that I called moving men and had everything that he owned in the house crated and sent to various places. It had taken so much nerve for me to start this break that I had to make sure I didn't falter. I followed through to the end—right down to the last tie tack and toothbrush.

Once all these things started arriving at his hotel, at his lawyer's and other places, I think Joe realized it wasn't just a notion I had; that I was serious. That's when he started a full-time campaign to change my mind and come back home, but I said, "No!" I received telephone calls and letters from him and from friends he had asked to get in touch with me, but the one thing he never took into consideration was the time I had spent thinking about it and the strength of my resolve.

Aware that Joe's lawyer in New York would hire the best legal services in the world to fight me, I did what I thought was a very sensible thing—I went to Jerry Giesler, one of the most famous divorce attorneys in Beverly Hills, or the world for that matter.

The idea of having to go to court was very distasteful to me; I'd always hated that when it happened to my friends. But I filed suit for divorce—charging mental cruelty, the California catchall—and a legal battle was inevitable.

Judge Edward Brand was sitting on the bench in the Santa Monica Superior Court and heard our case. Joe resisted all the way. Every time Judge Brand saw Joe in court, Joe would go into one of his long speeches about how he just wanted to get back together with me and preserve the family and all of that. Assuming from Joe's attitude that there was a possibility we might get back together, Judge Brand urged us to try just that.

I was totally against it, but I refused to go into any of the details of the humiliations alleged in my complaint. It was almost as painful to talk about as it had been to experience. I didn't want anything for myself, just the divorce and that the children be properly taken care of, because, as I explained earlier, at that time I was making an awful lot of money.

Of course, that "awful lot of money" was just that—money. Everything I made, from the day of our marriage on, went into keeping up the house. My earnings were dropping some, so there was a lot of hassling about salaries and child support, but I was determined to just stick with what I believed was fair for everybody, if it took until eternity.

It didn't take that long. Joe, his lawyer or somebody found out about another man and me. He was a famous musician whom I admired and perhaps loved. And he too was married. Somehow Joe's lawyer got the point across to Lewis that if I persisted, his name would be brought up in the case. I didn't ever want that to happen, so I said to Lewis, "Settle it any way it can be done, but I can't have this happen."

Ultimately we settled out of court and Joe was ordered to pay $300 per month child support for each of our five children —a total of $1500 a month. That was only the first of several court appearances.

In between that time and our final divorce, we would reconcile for three years, break up, get a divorce again and once again try to settle our financial differences. When I went to court the last time, in December 1968, after my breakdown, I asked for and got alimony for the first time.

As a brief postscript, I was once doing a special at Marine Land of the Pacific when Louella Parsons caught up with me on the phone. She'd received a call from my lover's wife and said, "Rosemary, she was very distraught. She was crying and on the verge of hysteria. Now what I'd like to know from you is how much truth is there in this thing you and her husband are supposed to be having?"

I said very frankly, "Louella, it's true. I'm seeing him and I've been seeing him, but I wish because of his children and my five children you'd not print anything about it right now because nothing is really set between us for the future."

Louella, always compassionate and understanding said, "Okay," and she did not use the item in her column.

There were a number of times in my life when Louella Parsons had her story exactly right and I leveled with her and asked her not to print it and she did not print it. I was not the only person she befriended that way—there were many others. Louella had a sense of honor and a respect for confidences.

In 1962 I was in Houston on my birthday—May 23. My friend's birthday was June 1 and we used to celebrate them together, so I would be going on from Houston to meet him in New York. But in the meantime Joe stopped by Houston and brought me a perfectly beautiful purse made of antique coins. I tried to be friendly with him, but did not succeed too well. I don't really do that Noel Coward thing too easily. I can't do drawing-room comedies in real life. Truthfully, I was happy when he left.

My lover met me in New York and we stayed at the Plaza, went out to dinner and had a lovely time. When we returned there was a message from his wife—a birthday message—and I saw that he felt good about that. Then it happened.

Perhaps the expression on his face as he read the message said something to me, but something seemed to possess me. I felt at the time as if I were outside my own body watching myself do something that I knew was destructive. It was the same feeling I had before I mentally crashed later on. I started, very quietly and calmly, talking to him about the reasons why we shouldn't see each other again. Rosemary was talking and Rosemary was standing outside her body just shaking her head in bewilderment at what she was hearing.

I discussed every reason I could think of for our not seeing each other again, and I watched as he began to wonder about it and then slowly saw him becoming more and more convinced that I was right. The following day he took me to the airport. I remember sitting on a barstool as we had a goodbye drink together before the plane left. It was in a little bar next to the departure gate.

I said, "We shouldn't see each other when we get to California either. So this really should be the last time we are together."

He didn't say a lot, merely nodded assent. Finally he said, "All right. If that's what you think."

When I got back to California and knew he had also returned, I tried to reestablish the relationship. But I had gone too far. I had convinced him that it would be the wrong thing to do, and we never saw each other again as lovers.

I think, despite my misgivings, that ending the affair was what I'd unconsciously sought; that a part of me was saying, "Rosemary, you've been a bad girl. You're involved with a man who is married and you should be punished." I know I felt like two people—one doing this thing she wanted to do, and the other demanding punishment for the deed done.

I was very lonely after the breakup. Working all the time.

Seeing no one. Maybe it was the logical thing to do, maybe it was something else—I don't know—but I found this an opportune time to accept one of Joe's constant proposals for us to go back together. I think one day I just said, "Yes. All right, Joe," and that was it. As a woman I may have opted for a safe haven for my emotions. If I had to be uncomfortable with myself, it was easier to do with Joe than alone. Sounds crazy, but women almost always seek security, however temporary.

I was now getting deeper and deeper into sleeping pills. They became my panacea. Working very hard, I learned to depend on my nightly pills more than I did on anybody or anything. I didn't care much about work, and my career started to go downhill. So did everything else in my life except my children. The joy of work was gone. Really gone. I wanted something for myself that had nothing to do with Rosemary Clooney the singer.

Joe and I ceased to communicate on almost all levels. I would do almost anything to avoid a direct confrontation with him.

It was in 1966, toward the end of my time with Joe, that I was in New York, playing at the Americana. I opened their fall season. Joe was already in New York when I arrived, doing a play, so he simply moved over to the hotel with me.

One night my drummer missed a performance and I came up to our suite afterward and said to Joe, "I'm damned upset about that." I always made my performances and I expected my musicians to do the same.

Joe said, "I wish you could work with a drummer I worked with in San Diego. He's just a great drummer."

I nodded. "I'll go for that. Let's bring him to New York and see what happens."

Joe found him and brought him east—and that's how I met Jay.

I don't think I was operating on any stable level emotionally at the time, except for those moments with my children. I keep going back to that because there must be some significance in the fact that I could always communicate with them.

Clearly, Joe and I were at the end of a very lousy second

run of a play that hadn't been all that good in the first place. We just did not make good co-stars in marriage.

But I owe Joe for introducing me to Jay—and for two years in which I would have the happiest times I could ever remember having with a man.

When Jay came to New York, my conductor, Paul Moer, rehearsed with him because I was performing every night and had no time to rehearse with the band. He was so good; he went to work that night and played the set beautifully. I was delighted with him. That was the first time I saw him—during the first show. Later that night he came up to my suite after the show and I said, simply, "Very good."

It was his first trip to New York and he was wide-eyed that night as he stared out the fortieth-floor window, looking down on Broadway. Everything was quite beautiful from that lofty perch, and I found his enthusiasm very engaging. I was reminded of myself—those years when I had first started in New York, that whole joy of life and discovery, being in a big city for the first time. There is a lot of truth in the old saying that "if you make it in New York, you can make it anywhere."

It was only a few months later that Joe and I split for the last time.

Jay and I did not start romancing right away—it might have been a year later when that started—but we spent time together and enjoyed each other's company. We just kept getting closer and closer together. I learned to love him very much. I believe it was that deep love on my part that brought me up with such a shock when he ended it. You know the rest.

CHAPTER XV

The Road Back

I went to work all too soon after coming out of Mount Sinai. About six months later, somewhere right around Christmas. (It seems like so many traumatic things have happened in my life just before Christmas.)

Being so deeply involved in analysis at the time, I resented having to be away from it so soon, but I had to eat and I had a lot of people depending on me, so I opened at the Tropicana in Las Vegas. Of all places to start my professional life all over again, Las Vegas was the last place I should have begun. I wasn't singing well at all—just doing it by rote, almost automatically. Also, my weight was now starting to gradually increase so that I was getting very fat. I didn't look anything like myself, which pleased me because I could hide inside that fat lady. I was still hiding, not nearly ready to come out but having to work in order to live. That's what I was used to doing, so nothing had changed there.

Every song was executed well, but there was nothing behind it. It was totally mechanical. If there was a computer that could get a tone that was in tune, that was me. Programmed to do it correctly, I always showed up on time. No problems there. But that sort of precision did not delight my employers—nor the audiences, who were not satisfied with my performances. Consequently I didn't do very good business. The spark—the joy of singing—the joy of entertaining—any kind of joy in music was gone.

I knew I wasn't doing well. After a show I'd rush off the stage and back to my dressing room where I had a list of the shows I had to do pasted on my mirror. After each show I'd cross that performance off and count how many I had left to do. Now that isn't exactly enthusiasm for one's work.

It started then and went on for quite a few years after I got out of the hospital. Not pills—I never took any except those Dr. Monke gave me as a part of my treatment—just total indifference to my singing career. I would get up in front of a microphone, recite my litany more or less and collect my paychecks. Word gets around just as quickly when you don't give a damn as it does when you're falling down on the floor from booze or drugs, and word got around that Rosie wasn't what she used to be—and I wasn't.

In 1972 I went to Denmark to play Tivoli Gardens in Copenhagen. I was at one of those plateaus in my analysis (by now in a group), where it was almost imperceptible that I was making any progress. Sometimes you cannot see where you're going and you don't see the end of it, but when you look backward and see where you came from, then you see the strides you've made.

Whatever my state was at the time, it was exactly right for bursting out of the kind of underwater performances I'd been giving. Copenhagen is a delightfully refreshing city, like a fairyland really. It was summertime and it was warm and stayed light until all hours of the night. Tivoli itself has a million tiny white lights outlining every building and is the most beautifully designed park. The music pavilion is extraordinary, the orchestra was marvelous, and I suddenly discovered that I was getting back that kind of spark, the joy of performing. The audience was feeling it, too. For me, it was like coming out-doors after being locked in for a long, long time.

Those two weeks were revolutionary and I almost couldn't handle it. The joy was so great that it frightened me. I first thought perhaps I was slipping back into that manic state that used to precede my depressions—there was that much happi-ness. I hadn't felt that much for so long. I only hoped it was real happiness and not the hallucinating variety.

When I finished that engagement I went to Paris with my daughter Monsita. Paris was just as beautiful and I was just as happy. I loved it, staying at the Raphael Hotel where Joe and I had stayed so many times—familiar settings. Joe was there, and he and Monsita went off traveling and I came back home. The first thing I did was call Dr. Monke.

"Something's happened," I told him when we met in his office. "Something has broken through as far as my work is concerned. I'm feeling very happy and exhilarated and I'm a little bit scared."

"Tell you what let's do," he said. "Why don't we just drop all the medication? See what happens."

I'd been taking medication all along, and after all those years of being addicted to barbiturates and then replacing them with mood elevators as a part of my treatment, I was a little bit frightened of going cold turkey. I'd been so close to pills of one kind or another all my life, relating to a pill bottle a lot faster than I could a person. But I felt so good about the trip and the way my work had gone that I said, "All right. We'll forget the medication. Just cut it all out, if you think that's the right thing."

He smiled. "They're always there if you need them, you know. If it turns out that you need more medication, it will be available. But let's try."

I felt so close to that man and so grateful to him. I was

elated. It was very exciting. I had permission from my doctor— I could live again. That was very important to me.

Taking Dr. Monke's advice, I also started taking charge of my own life, and almost immediately the weight started to peel away. Amazing! No dieting—nothing. Food simply ceased to be an all-consuming passion.

My mother had moved back to Cincinnati and I was alone with the kids, but it felt very good. It wasn't easy. It was very, very hard to get jobs after my performances of the past years. First there had been the flare-up in Reno, which made the rounds fast—and was never explained. Nobody knew I'd had a mental breakdown. They whispered, "Drugs," or "Liquor." People would ask, "Is she still drinking?" Club owners leaned toward that question.

My manager, Bill Loeb, proved his loyalty to me during this period in my life. He was terrifically helpful and genuinely tried to get work for me, but it was not an easy matter for him to convince the club owners that I was a good risk. I can't thank Bill enough for the effort he put forth all the time I was sick. He didn't run away; he didn't leave me, which would have been the best thing to do on some occasions I think. I will be eternally grateful to him for staying.

While I'm crediting those who really understood and helped, there is another man I will never forget. Whether it was my weight gain that tipped him off to the fact that I was in trouble, or whether he had heard weird stories about my behavior in a Reno nightclub—whatever it was, Merv Griffin came to me with a friendship that started years and years ago in New York City when the two of us were there, and he stayed my friend all the time. Always supportive, Merv even let me be on his show, not just once but several times. It didn't matter to him if I was huge and introverted and all those negative things—he allowed me to be on his show and got me through ninety minutes each time without mishap.

When I started coming back a little bit, all of those appearances on Merv's show started to pay off because people could see the gradual change in me. I was starting to sing well—very well—again, and audiences seemed to comprehend what was happening and empathized with my situation.

Even when I wasn't on the show, Merv would talk to other guests about me. I'd be watching his show from someplace and suddenly he'd bring up my name to somebody—always in a favorable light. God bless him.

Wanting to work and knowing I could do the job, but having no job to go to, was very frustrating to me. It was a situation I'd never been faced with before in my life, but lots of people helped me along the way.

My brother Nicky had a variety show—an hour a day in Cincinnati—and when his budget could afford it he would fly me in to Cincinnati and I would do a week with him. Nicky would prod me into conversations that were personal and get amusing reactions from me—family anecdotes that were interesting to people and also showed me that I could do other things besides sing. Nicky gave me courage. He once told somebody something about me that really gave me a lift: "She's the one that went out and slew the dragons for the rest of the family."

Nicky is also a good writer; he knows how to use words to get the best out of them. My brother—I love him desperately and deeply. More than any other person he is responsible for giving me confidence in my ability on the road back from the bedlam I had found myself in. He was family and I could be at ease with him, so it was a good place for me to begin. Later I was able to say to myself, "If you can do it with Nicky, then you can take the next step." And that's pretty much how it went. He gave me faith in myself—something I had lacked for such a long time.

My comeback to normal activity was very gradual, so of course the resumption of income was also gradual. While Bill Loeb was trying to find me work, Dr. Monke allowed me to make only minimal payments on my (by this time) enormous bill. He was very good about that. His was a dedication to medicine, not money, and he saw the progress I was making.

To me he is a giant in his understanding of the human predicament, especially when it becomes too much for an individual to cope with alone.

Dinah Shore is another good friend who has always been there to help. I've done her show a great many times and it is like visiting a dear friend at home in spite of the audience out front. That's the way she makes you feel. I remember last summer on one of her shows Dinah leaned over and whispered something in my ear during a commercial break. I'm sure many in the audience wondered what deep, dark secret she was passing on to me. What she said was, "How's your corn doing this year? Mine isn't nearly as big as it should be by now. You think the drought has something to do with that?"

Dinah, like me, is an avid gardener.

One of the great conflicts in my life ended in December of 1973. My mother died. Funny, but the only way I can remember when she passed away is to go ahead to my father's death, which was in August of 1974, and count back. Maybe I don't want to remember her death. I don't know.

I was really just getting on my feet when I got a call one day from my sister Gail. Mother was in the hospital—again. Mother had been in the hospital so many times that it seemed to be part of her life. During the nineteen years she lived with me she was in the hospital three or four times a year when her emphysema would act up, so it didn't overly alarm me that she was hospitalized now. Mother was just taking a rest.

Gail called back again. Mother was dead.

I didn't feel much right away. In fact, my first thoughts centered on how to get back for the funeral. I didn't have much money and it would be hard for me to get enough together to take all the children back to Cincinnati, but I thought it was important that they go because they were so close to her.

I called Joe. After all, I wasn't asking anything for myself, just for the children. I asked if he would give me the money for their fares and he said no. His reason was that he didn't think it was important to go to the funeral. I felt it *was* important for the children, in large part because the process of grieving starts with the funeral, and grieving helps one come to terms with the loss of someone very close. But the children went. My various relatives, God bless them all, got the money together and we all went back as a family.

My mother's death did not fill me with remorse or regrets. There was only the normal sadness one feels at the loss of a parent. I think I felt good that I'd grown strong enough to reconcile myself to my mother's feelings about me and to assert my rights as an individual to run my own life. I now had more understanding of her than she did of me; but on the other hand, I had a lot more help than my mother had. I guess if you crack up, people pay more attention to your problems.

My sense of deep loss came when I returned to Los Angeles. Though I was by then in group therapy, when mother died I did the same thing I'd done after Tivoli. I had a talk with Dr. Monke, who assured me that I was okay and that my feelings were normal. I needed to hear that from him.

Feeling better after that session with Dr. Monke, I was on my way home, driving down Santa Monica Boulevard in Beverly Hills. It was a couple of days after Christmas. Having sorted out some of my feelings, I was looking forward to fixing a nice dinner for my kids that night. I had a scarf around my head and some old blue jeans on. I was stopped for a red traffic light at Santa Monica and Canon Drive, just sitting there lost in my own thoughts when out of the corner of my eye I was aware of a car pulling up beside me on the right and I heard somebody say, "Hello!"

It was a man's voice. I turned briefly, said hello without looking at him and I promptly looked straight ahead again.

Then the man said, "*Rosella*."

Nobody had called me that in twenty years. Dante Di Paolo had given me a Saint Christopher's medal with that engraved on it when we were both at Paramount. I still have that medal.

I knew the split second when I turned back to look at him that it had to be Dante. Twenty years had gone by, I had brought up five children who were now almost adults—so much had transpired—and here was the man who had loved me a great deal and I wished I didn't have the scarf around my head, that I'd worn different clothes and that I wasn't caught without makeup. I was feeling a helluva lot like a girl wanting to look nice for a guy all of a sudden.

That my joy at this encounter could override the grief I'd just been feeling was an enormous plus for my psyche. I really was alive. Yet, I didn't want to see him this way. I didn't want to be twenty years older. I didn't want all these things to have transpired. I didn't want my life to have been the way it was. I wanted to go back and pick up where we had left off—and at the same time, more than anything else, I wanted that damned light to change so I could get the hell out of there. It all happened in such a short moment.

He said, "How are you?"

"Fine."

"I'd like to see you."

"Call me."

"I don't have your phone number."

"Two-seven-six . . ." (You didn't seriously think I was going to publish the rest of it, did you?)

With that the light changed and I sped off. Once again I was giving myself little tests. I said to myself, "If he remembers the number and if he calls me after hearing it once, then he really will have wanted to." At least I'd given him an excuse in case he didn't really want to call. Maybe he was involved with someone else. I didn't know. It had been twenty years.

He has since told me that he never would have remembered the number in a million years, but fortunately his dashboard was dusty and he just wrote it there in the dust with his finger.

I heard from him an hour later and invited him to dinner in a couple of days. I had so many misgivings about that. What would he think of me? Would I look older? Would he like my chlidren? All the things a girl thinks of when she thinks of a man in a way that hints of something more than hello and goodbye.

I shouldn't have worried, though, because when he walked into my home he walked back into my life and he's been there ever since. It's just as though nothing had changed.

Dante was just what I needed. The missing element in my life. If I had ever doubted the existence of a higher plan for everything, this would have completely dispelled that doubt, because the joy of rediscovering that kind of relationship, timed to fill the need that I had, had to be planned by God.

There is a gentleness about Dante. This gentleness and his way of treating me sometimes, as though I were all of eleven years old, fills needs that I didn't know I had. Helping me on this gentle level really eliminated any need on my part to make adjustments for all the years we didn't see each other. He is astoundingly sensitive to the needs of other people. I can watch him quietly sizing up a situation with my children, seeing their needs—the things they're not saying. He knows what they want almost by instinct. He's remarkable that way. He does the same thing with me.

My son Miguel was a part of my act, playing drums behind me, before Dante came back into my life. Dante, a fantastic singer and dancer—always so poised and sure of himself—was a natural to join up with us on the road. He complements me in everything I do. We work in great harmony together.

One night after we'd finished a job somewhere, the three of us had a couple of drinks and were sitting around a table just sort of baring our souls when Miguel spoke seriously to Dante: "You know, if you decided that you were not going to see mama anymore, you would still be my good friend all my life."

I knew that I was on the right track. All my kids feel that way about Dante, and yet he has never infringed in any way on Joe's position as their father. Joe loves his children and wants them to have friends where there is a good relationship, and there is just that with Dante.

In 1974 I was doing a Merv Griffin show, and after I'd sung a song Merv brought me back to the little dais where he seats his guests and we started talking. He said, "You know, you're different now."

I said, "In what way?"

"You're singing so well. Were you in therapy?"

Merv has a way of getting totally honest answers from me because I trust any question he asks. So I didn't bat an eyelash. "Yes," I said. "I've terminated analysis after three years and now I've been in group therapy for three years. Things were tough, but they're better now."

A writer by the name of Alan Ebert heard that show and suddenly got the idea that there was a magazine article in it, so he called my manager and finally got on the phone to me and we talked. He, too, had been through analysis and come out of it very well. We had a lot in common, and he said he would like to do a piece on me for *Ladies Home Journal*. I agreed and we spent two or three sessions together.

At our last meeting we were just tying up some loose ends when the phone rang. It was my stepsister, Brigette, telling me that my father had died.

I wept a lot more easily for my father than I had for my mother. I felt that a great part of his life was a waste because of his long involvement with the bottle. In effect he had been anesthetized for a great part of his life and a lot of good in him was never developed—his marvelous mind and sense of humor. I find it amazing how people all want to live long lives, yet while they're here they throw away three-fourths of it on either booze, pills or something else to hide from the actual experience of living. I'm so glad I don't do that anymore. People think they're escaping the bad things with these anesthetics, but at the same time a lot of the good is going down the drain, too.

I called Betty that day and said, "Betty, daddy just died."

She felt the same way I did, and she said, "Poor old man." Then she added, "Don't *you* die on me."

We both cried together, neither of us knowing that it would be she who left me—and all too suddenly.

CHAPTER XVI

Bing and Me

Bing Crosby is very special to me and has had a very special meaning in my life. It is only fitting that he should have a special place in my remembrances of that life.

My first meeting with Bing was almost a disaster. After the tremendous success of "Come On-a My House," I was booked into the Thunderbird Hotel in Las Vegas. Milt Lewis, who was in charge of talent at Paramount Pictures, came up to Las Vegas and it was arranged for me to come to Hollywood for a screen test. I came down and met with Edith Head and met a lot of people who would eventually become very much involved in my film career.

Bing, Bob Hope and Dorothy Lamour were making *Road to Bali* at Paramount where they were all under contract for so many years. Milt and I were walking down one of the streets on the way to the talent department when Bing came along on a bicycle. I have a penchant for noticing the color of people's eyes, especially if they match what they're wearing, and the first thing I noticed about Bing (and whether it was by design or accident I don't know) was that his eyes exactly matched his shirt.

It was staggering to see him in person. With all the films he did year after year, he did not make personal appearances so I don't think many people outside his family and close friends ever saw him in person except those who worked with him. There was no place you could go and purchase a ticket to see him except at the movies. I don't think he ever did personal appearances from the time he started with Paul Whiteman's orchestra until 1976, when he appeared at a benefit at the Dorothy Chandler Pavilion in Los Angeles celebrating his fiftieth anniversary in show business.

I was terribly in awe of the man just because of his being the superstar that he was. In my early years I used to hear his voice when my father listened to him on the family radio, and later on when I was a Frank Sinatra fan there would be Crosby-Sinatra contests with different disk jockeys. It seemed like Bing Crosby was almost as much a part of my life as the fact that my name was Rosemary Clooney.

In any event, Milt stopped him and introduced us, and Bing said, "I think you're a very good singer."

I thanked him.

"And I understand we're going to work together," he continued, referring to the fact that we were scheduled to do some Kraft Music Hall radio shows together. "When is that?" he asked, apparently having forgotten just when we were to do the shows.

"Oh, sometime in the twenties." What I was trying to say was that it would be sometime late in the month, but the way it came out made no sense at all, and after a slight pause he nodded, excused himself and pedaled away on his bike.

It was a terribly dumb thing to say and I was mentally kicking myself quite soundly for it. I was so bothered by it that after I finished some of the things I had to do that day I went to his dressing room and knocked on the door. Bing answered.

I said, "Look, I want to explain to you that I don't make stupid statements. I was so surprised and really delighted at meeting you that I wasn't thinking of what I was saying. 'Sometime in the twenties' didn't come out right. I meant toward the end of the month. I want to apologize for that. I'm not dumb and I promise you I'll try not to think of you as Bing Crosby and therefore I won't make those stupid remarks anymore."

He laughed and asked me in for a drink. The ice was broken. Incidentally, I never called him Mr. Crosby—not ever. I didn't call him anything until I got to know him well enough to call him Bing.

Over the years Bing and I have done movies together, recordings, radio, television—the whole entertainment circle. At one point we must have done something like twelve or thirteen consecutive shows together. We were always around each other and became great friends from the time I worked at Paramount with him. When he has his annual golf tournament at Pebble Beach he always has someone come up and entertain at his "clambakes." I did that a couple of times, and what great fun that was!

Joe really admired Bing, but he was never relaxed with him. Joe can be charming and personable and easy to be with, but I don't think he was ever easy for Bing to be with because he was never Joe. He was always very nervous about making a good impression on Bing, so he was pressing too hard. I thought what a shame it was that they never really got together as two men, because they would have liked each other. Joe couldn't do it, and therefore Bing couldn't either.

The best way to get along with Bing is to forget first of all that he is Bing Crosby. It's not always easy. I know that every now and then something would strike me when we were working together—the tilt of his pipe or the set of his hat—the Crosby image—and I'd say to myself, "What the hell am I doing singing here with Bing Crosby?"

Joe always envied the fact that I could be so relaxed with

Bing. It was one of the things that he could never understand—the ease of that friendship. He really wanted to have that kind of friendship with Bing.

When Joe was in college he had a dance band called The Pied Pipers. The band wasn't bad, and Joe still had one record they had made. One side had a boy singer doing a number called "Love Comes but Once," a song that Joe wrote. (The boy singer was a neighbor of mine now, Jimmy Stewart.) On the flip side was Joe Ferrer singing "Sweet Georgia Brown," and it was an exact imitation of the way Bing Crosby sang it.

One day I took the record in for Bing to hear. I said, "Bing, I want to play this for you and see if you recognize the singer on the 'Sweet Georgia Brown' side."

I played it for him and he listened. "Not bad," he said. "I would say he listened to a lot of my records."

I said, "Well, that's perfectly true. That's Joe Ferrer."

Bing's quick rejoinder was, "Oh—I've seen him act!"

Bing has a brilliant mind and an original wit. That casual delivery combined with an unexpectedly wide vocabulary. It is a great device for comedy—and also an effective way of communicating with an audience or with a person.

When I signed with Paramount it was a foregone conclusion that I would be appearing in *White Christmas* with Bing. Originally Fred Astaire was slated for that film because of the tremendous success the two had made of *Holiday Inn* several years earlier when "White Christmas" was first introduced as a song. Something happened and Fred wasn't signed for the picture. Then Donald O'Connor was up for the role, but he got very sick and was unable to do it. Danny Kaye came in because Danny, too, had been working on the lot doing other things and I guess was available.

We started production in the fall of 1953 and completed the film just before Christmas. There was a lot of pre-production preparation—especially for me because I had absolutely no talent as a dancer. I had the "Sisters" number with Vera Ellen, who was an absolutely fantastic dancer, and I had to work like mad to be up for it. Bob Alton, the choreographer was just sensational. He was a pro, having done a lot of Broadway shows and having also been under contract at Metro for years. He did wonders with me and we became very close friends.

Michael Curtiz was the director, and his accent is legend. He used to call Bing "Binkie," and it was hilarious to hear him call out, "Binkie, give me one more take."

He said to me one time—I was sitting on a windowsill in a scene—"Could you give me a little off from balance?" I was thinking, Boy-oh-boy, we'll need a translator to get through this picture. Curtiz was responsible for the title of David Niven's second best-selling book. He was shooting a scene with horses and called out, "Bring on the empty horses"—meaning, of course, riderless horses.

On the day we were shooting the finale of the picture the king and queen of Greece were coming to visit the set. It so happened that we shot the scene in the morning. It had taken two stages because it was a big production number. We were not even going to be on those stages in the afternoon, but the royal couple would be there right after lunch so Curtiz made his announcement: "We're coming back to this set and Binkie and Damny [his version of Danny], Vera and Rosemary—you will come back and you will do the finale again. We will not film it, but we will pretend to film it for their majesties, the king and queen of Greece."

Bing groaned and lowered his voice to me. "Cover for me. I'm not going to be here."

"Where are you going?" I asked.

"I'm going over the wall. I'm not going through all that again without film."

Well, it was very funny to most of us. Vera and I were trying to pretend that Bing wasn't supposed to appear in the finale, but here we're all singing "White Christmas" to the playback and Bing's voice is coming out of my mouth. Just a falling-down-funny situation. I kept hoping the king and queen wouldn't notice—but I suspect they did.

Curtiz was just flabbergasted that "Binkie" wasn't there, but you don't make an issue with Bing and so that was that.

One night during the *White Christmas* filming, Bing and I went to dinner at Bobby Dolan's house. Bobby was better known as a conductor of Broadway shows, but he was also the producer of *White Christmas*. Bogart was also a guest that night and as we entered the door Bogey called out, "Here comes Miss *Clowney* and Mr. Crosby." So right away you know Bogey is up to his usual mischief.

Bing never discusses his politics, but everybody knew that he was quite a conservative and it was assumed that he was a staunch member of the Republican party. So Bogey picked up on something I said and made a big to-do about it, hoping to get Bing to bite.

I asked Bogey, "Where's Betty tonight?"

"Oh, Miss Bacall is on the road with *Adlai Stevenson*," and he went into quite a speech about Mr. Stevenson for Bing's benefit. "We think *Stevenson's* doing very well. What do *you* think, Rosie? Don't you think *Stevenson's* doing pretty good?"

It was just Bogart's way of causing a little stir—hoping that Bing would say something on behalf of Mr. Eisenhower. But Bing didn't bite. Completely ignored the remarks. With no reaction, Bogey gave up. People usually didn't let Bogart pass that easily, but Bing did.

Bing was never much of a partygoer, but he did come to my house—he was really nice about that—and I would have dinner at his house quite often. Bing and I both enjoyed prizefights, so if I was in town alone I used to go over there and we'd eat in the library on a low table and watch the fights while we ate.

I remember one night he invited me to dinner with Grace Kelly. His four older sons were there also, at the house he had on Mapleton. This was some time before he married Kathryn. As a matter of fact, I think Grace may have wondered why I was there. But Bing and I were just friends—always. Nothing else. Just great friends. His boys were also my friends.

Bing did a radio show with me which was recorded in my

living room. I remember when I was in the hospital giving birth to Miguel, Bing was also in Saint John's recovering from a very painful kidney operation. When he heard I was there too, he sent his nurse down to the delivery room to find out before anybody else whether I had a boy or a girl. When Miguel was born the delivery-room nurse turned to Bing's nurse and said, "Boy." She went right up to Bing's room and said, "She just had a boy." Later, Bing delighted in reminding me that he knew I'd had a boy before Joe did.

He came down in a wheelchair to see me the day after Miguel was born. Although his operation was a very serious one, Bing has always evidenced remarkable recuperative powers, because he is very single-minded about getting well. He's almost Spartan about it.

When he saw me he asked me. "How was it?"

"Not as bad as I thought," I answered.

He said, "I understand the pains I had were a little like child-birth, except I gave birth to a handful of ground glass."

Whether we were recording or just singing together, Bing and I have been comfortable. The best thing about singing with Bing is that our ranges are so compatible; we've never had a problem selecting a key for the two of us that's comfortable. You'll probably be surprised to learn that neither Bing nor I can read music. We manage to phrase well together anyway, using our own system. What we always have is a setup that allows us to look at each other, because each of us can tell from the way the other takes a breath what the phrasing is going to be. That is the closest contact that we have, and it has worked out very well for us. I still do it onstage, angling myself so that I can see him when we are dueting.

The tours I've been doing in the past couple of years with Bing didn't start out, from my point of reference, to be tours. Bing, of course, is a very wealthy man and certainly doesn't need to work—particularly under the kind of stress involved with traveling all over the world doing concerts. The costs of doing these public concerts are skeletal and the profits go to nonprofit organizations that Bing believes in.

But beyond the pleasure he derives from helping these causes, I think he likes to do these shows because after all these years he's discovered the joy of personal appearances. There is a kind of marvelous thing I see in his face when he's taking a bow at the end of a show: his attitude toward the audience— and their outpouring of love for him. It is a kind of adulation he's receiving from fans all over the world, which he has never been overtly responsive to. Bing has a tremendous personal dignity and reserve that is not easy to penetrate. I think people have finally touched him in a way that perhaps he couldn't be touched before. All those people on their feet, with one voice, roaring their approval, standing in the aisles, on their seats—on tables. I think he is finding the audiences just as entertaining and warm as they find him.

I was at a party one night just before Christmas of 1975 and Bing was there. He was talking with me about a party that was going to be held in Kentucky by a friend who was a big racehorse owner, and he wanted to know if I was going to be able to go to it. As an aside he said, "I'm doing a benefit on March seventeenth. Would you like to join us?" To both of us that meant Saint Patrick's Day. A benefit. I saw a lot of stars coming out and singing a song or two and that would be that. I figured it would be a one-night stand and that would be the end of it.

Nobody told me that it was the kick-off of Bing's fiftieth year in show business. He treated it so casually. So I said, "Of coure, I'll be glad to appear," and I promptly forgot it.

While on a cruise, halfway through the Panama Canal, I got word from a fellow passenger that the *Los Angeles Times* had carried a big announcement of the forthcoming Bing Crosby Concert at the Dorothy Chandler Pavilion—and that they were sold out. When I got home and tried to obtain tickets for my kids I got my first clue that I was to be a part of something astronomical in the business.

I immediately developed a bad case of nerves—stage fright— call it whatever you will. I was frightened of the challenge, I think, and entertained some thoughts of backing out of my commitment. All of a sudden I had these pangs of the sick Rosemary I had been: Could I handle such a major event? Maybe I should just ignore it and it would go away, or maybe I could develop some throat trouble. . . .

As the date grew closer, though, I sat down and had a little one-on-one talk with myself. "Rosemary," I said, "you either do it or you'll be right back where you were in nineteen sixty-eight. You've come too far to blow it now."

I was terrified when I walked out on the stage that night, but the reviews were fantastic for me. The analysis, all the work I'd been doing handling my own problems, were now a solid base for me. I could do anything I wanted to. I was the old Rosemary Clooney.

The reviews, I'm sure, encouraged Bing to invite me to go on his tour, which I'd known nothing about and which would include the Palladium in London. I accepted. Photographs of Bing and me together were on the wire services all over the world. Rosemary was back, indeed.

All of my children accompanied me to England with the exception of Gabri who was taking some tests at school and couldn't get away. The rest of us had a lovely time. When I introduced Miguel, who was my drummer, from the stage of the Palladium, I took great joy in telling my audience that the first time I'd played the Palladium I was a proud new mother —Miguel had been three months old and had spent the summer outside of London and missed most of my shows; now he was an integral part of them. The audience loved it.

It was during this tour with Bing that I discovered the real difference between my first success and my new successes. I no longer have that burning ambition to reach the top of anything. My burning ambition now is to do as well as I can. I don't seek or anticipate some unseen vistas to conquer. I don't need any kind of merry-go-round success. I had that once and I wouldn't want it again.

While we were at the Palladium we were all invited to Buckingham Palace to a small party before our performance one evening. Prince Philip was involved with a charity that was one of the beneficiaries of our performances and I suppose our invitation was a way of saying thanks.

Prince Philip was wonderful to us, a most charming and amusing man. He said, "It's wonderful that you have your son working here and you have all your children. It's a very good thing to do. We should talk that over in our family."

Kathryn Crosby and I were in the middle of the room, chatting, when suddenly, without any warning, the queen walked in. The only time I'd met the queen was at a royal command performance where introductions were brief. She wasn't even scheduled to attend this party.

I had a sherry in one hand and my purse in the other, and realized I'd have to get rid of the sherry very quickly because she was approaching us and I had to have my hand free. The queen was almost to us when I saw a footman go by with a tray from which he had been dispensing drinks to the guests. I threw the glass on the tray just in time to manage a very unstable, totally unrehearsed curtsy.

She stayed and talked with us for a full twenty minutes and I found her a fascinating woman. It became a case of three women—one of them a reigning monarch, one the wife of a legend and the other an Irish-American singer—reduced to the common denominator of discussing their families and children. I thought it interesting that in the final analysis, when all the titles and positions in life are swept away, we are all really quite basic.

Some things Bing has feeling about but doesn't approach you directly with. He knew how close my sister Betty was to me, but when she died he never spoke to me directly about it—and hasn't to this day. But he cares about it, about my feelings. He called Miguel twice and wanted to know from him about it. "Now tell me, what happened?" he asked. "How did it happen? And how is your mother? How is she taking it?"

Bing cares, but he is the kind of man who doesn't ever intrude on what he feels is something private. He's some kind of gentleman and I'm privileged to have him as a friend and to have had so many wonderful times with him over the years.

CHAPTER XVII

Betty

All things must eventually terminate. This hour, this day, this year, this book—and life. Of all these pages the most difficult remembrance for me is the chapter with which I conclude the story of my life and existence to this point.

My sister Betty, as you must know if you've followed me this far, was like my alter ego. She was always wherever I was, even when we were miles apart. We had a thing between us that only identical twins ordinarily possess. We were as one person. As children we survived together. As young women and singers we blossomed into maturity together. And as mothers and wives we shared the experiences of having and bringing up our families. We had great love for one another.

When I returned from the Continent and the successful tour with Bing, as well as a new album I'd done there, I went to Virginia Beach to honor an engagement at a lovely place, The Moonraker. I opened on August 1, 1976. The owner,

Chester Rodeo, was a nice Italian man with a wonderful warm, giving nature. I'm sure he must have changed his name from something more Italian, but at any rate I loved working for him. He found me an apartment on the beach, only a block from work, and Dante and Miguel were with me. It was a happy time for us.

The night I opened I ran into a friend of long standing, Andy Roberts. Andy had been the boy singer with Skitch Henderson when I was seeing Skitch a long time ago, and Andy used to go out with Betty. He was married now, with three lovely children. I love them all, and one of them—Mary—is especially very close to me.

On the third of August, Mary, Dante and I drove over to Colonial Williamsburg. We spent the day there and had a great time. Dante bought me a gorgeous copper pan. In the afternoon I was getting tired and I wanted to get back to the apartment so I could take a nap before the show that night. It was Thursday.

When we got back to Virginia Beach, Miguel was waiting for me at the apartment. He said, "Mother, Uncle Sherm called you." He always called Phyllis's husband "Uncle Sherm." "He wants you to call him back as soon as you can."

It could mean only one thing—illness in the family. My first thoughts went to Monsita and Maria who were due back that day from a trip to Russia. Something must be wrong with one of them. I called Sherm right away and I could tell by the tone of his voice when he said hello that there was something really wrong.

He said, "Rosemary, Betty's had a stroke."

It just didn't register at first. It was something so far from my mind. I'd never even considered that it might be Betty. Her daughter was getting married the following Saturday. With such a happy occasion coming up, how could anything be wrong with Betty?

Very cautiously I asked, "What does that mean?"

"I don't know what it means right now. She's in the hospital and she's being monitored. I'll have to have more information. But I think it's serious enough for you to think about coming to Las Vegas."

If something was that wrong with Betty, then it was also a critical situation for me. I could feel a weakness sweeping over my entire being. So I asked him again, "Well, how serious *is* it?"

"I just don't know, Rosemary. I'll have to call you back."

After I hung up I phoned my house. Maria and Monsita had just come from the airport and hadn't even put their bags away yet, but of course they said would leave for Las Vegas on the next plane to be with their Aunt Betty. They were very close to Betty, as were all my children.

I couldn't just sit and wait for phone calls, I had to do something, so I started making some calls on my own. I called the hospital. Marsha and Les Kurtzman were there. Marsha was head of my fan club for a long time when she was a kid, and out of that had grown a very deep and lasting friendship. She felt the same way about Betty and had come up for the wedding. She was helping Betty entertain her in-laws who were also there for the wedding. Betty, she said, had been outside talking to them and suddenly looked up to the sky as though something were bothering her in the back of her head. She said, "I have a terrific headache."

She was standing by her pool and she just slid down on the grass. She said, "Where's Carlos?" Carlos is her son. He walked over to his mother, totally unaware of what was happening to her—and shocked, I'm certain, because it was all happening so quickly. Betty looked up and said, "I'm dying. Jesus take care of my children." And she was unconscious.

She had been taken immediately to the hospital and it was felt at that time that she had sustained a cerebral hemorrhage and that it was very serious.

Well, I couldn't work that night. I couldn't even approach it. And I couldn't cry either—not yet. I just stayed on the phone talking to anybody who could give me any information.

Surgery was scheduled for the following morning. There was nothing I could do, but I couldn't leave the phone for a minute. There was no phone in the bedroom, so I slept on the living-room floor by the phone. Dante stayed beside me and just held me through the night. I couldn't imagine facing life without my sister, and I now knew I was not going to have her. I knew she was going to die, and I didn't know if I would ever be able to face it.

My sister Gail phoned early the next morning. Betty was in surgery. She said, "They're going to try to relieve the pressure. I'll call you the minute I know anything else."

After the operation she called back. I could tell she was heartbroken. "There's no point," she said. "They couldn't do much because there were two aneurysms. Betty will probably live another forty-five minutes. That's what they tell me."

My first thoughts were of the time I'd gotten angry with her when she was fifteen years old and we were on our first road trip with Tony Pastor. I threw a bottle of green ink at her. I'd been busy writing a marvelously passionate love letter to some boy and I thought that green ink was just about the sharpest thing going so I was writing it in green ink and she did something or other just once too often and I let her have it. Then I was totally shocked by the fact that she was covered with green ink from head to foot and I stuffed her in the bath-tub and tried to get it all off her.

And I thought about the time when she was having difficulty in her marriage and had brought her children to my home, along with her dogs—and the problems all those dogs were in the backyard with all my dogs.

I was realizing that I had forty-five minutes or so left with her in the same world and that I couldn't do anything for her. All too soon those minutes ticked away and I flinched when the phone rang with Gail's message. Betty was gone. My daughters were there and had been with her to the end. I was glad for that.

Dante arranged for me to get on the next plane. My brother Nicky was already airborne from Cincinnati. He didn't know she was gone until he landed in Las Vegas.

I had several drinks on the plane. I wanted desperately to get drunk, to escape this horrible thing that had happened in my life, but there was no escaping. I couldn't drink my way out of reality. It was like watching a newsreel of our life together—all the memories flashed by and then the screen was blank. It was that kind of trip. That desperate feeling. That awful feeling of having her dead was so fresh that it was almost impossible to bear.

Nicky met me at the airport and we just looked at each other. Oh, God, how I loved him at that moment. I found myself suddenly remembering things about him, too—when he was a blond-haired baby and the fattest baby I'd ever seen. Fat, fat little boy. In fact, I don't think he even walked until he was about two because he was so chubby. But, oh, so cute. I adored him. And so did Betty. Betty and I were living with my grandmother at that point in our lives and we didn't get to see Nicky very often since mother always kept him with her.

But he was a marvelous little boy, with a vivid imagination. By the time he was ten he was a voracious reader. Just a terribly bright boy. I remembered that as we walked to the car together.

I also remembered when he lived in Indian Hills with my Grandmother Guilfoyle. He used to ride a bicycle to school, which was a long way, and his little hands used to get so cold because he either didn't have gloves or wouldn't put them on.

And when we were on the road Nicky came to visit us when mother brought him back from California with her. We were singing with Tony and traveling a lot and Nicky came to spend one summer with us and I remember his greatest joy was to buy gum and mints for everybody on the bus. He'd buy them with his own money and go right down the line giving them to each of the guys. I think he must have developed nocturnal habits at that point because Nicky used to stay up a lot at night and read and write. He used to write a lot. He wrote me a letter after Betty's funeral that is a treasure to my heart.

I sat in the back of the car and suddenly realized that we were all that was left of a family—and how much I loved him. But we never spoke until we started driving down the Las Vegas Strip with all the activity and all the shows and excitement. It all seemed so incongruous to our mission. Nicky turned to me and said, "What a ridiculous place to die."

I was too deep in shock this time to wonder if my old problems would come back to plague me. Those feelings came later. The pain was just too deep. It was a grief that I never before evidenced with anybody. Not my mother. Not my father. It was almost as though I were grieving for every loss in my life.

When I walked into the funeral home and saw her, it didn't look like Betty. That stone-stillness. Betty was the most alive person I've ever known. Always in motion. Her face—her expressions changed fifty times in a minute. Her little hands—oh, how she hated her thumbs. She used to say, "My thumbs look like toes," and she would hide them in her palms. I suddenly wished somebody would hide her thumbs.

The funeral was on Saturday and I had to leave in the middle of it because I had two shows that night and a plane to catch. Chester had been so good about letting me off on Thursday and Friday, I just couldn't let him lose the Saturday-night business. It wouldn't be right. Betty would have wanted me to go on with the show, but that's not what I was thinking about. It was just something I had to do. It would be my first step toward a normal life without Betty—although it would never be the same without her.

Once again all those years with Dr. Monke came through for me. There was never a moment when I tried to fantasize about Betty as I had when Bobby Kennedy was killed. Her death was a reality. I knew she was dead and I accepted it. But, oh, God, it was hard.

I got a direct flight to Norfolk, Virginia, and on that flight my faith in God was renewed once again. The pilot came back to where I was sitting and said, "I've got to tell you something. I've never been able to write you a letter about this, but when you and your sister opened with Tony Pastor at the Palladium in Hollywood back in the Forties, I had a summer job with a couple of my buddies cleaning out the ballroom there. One night when all the people and the orchestra were gone, I noticed your dressing-room door was open and a light was on. It was about four in the morning and there were two plaid taffeta dresses hanging up in your dressing room. One of my buddies and I put on those two dresses and went out and broke up all the rest of the kids with our imitation of you two. I just wanted to let you know about that."

The two plaid taffeta dresses that our Grandmother Guilfoyle had made for us to take on the road with us. Things had truly come full circle.

I looked up at this big man with tears of gratitude in my eyes. I thought to myself, Betty must have told him to tell me that story or arranged it so we would be on the same flight. She wanted me to see some humor in all of this grief. God and Betty were letting me know that everything would be all right. That it was right with Betty. I really loved him for telling me that story. It brought me up a little from the lowest point of my life. I hope somebody tells him that—for me.

The show that night was very difficult for me, but I hung in there. When Dante got to a part in "You and Me Against the World" where he sang the phrase ". . . and when one of us is gone and one is left alone to carry on," our eyes filled with tears.

God and Betty had stayed with me throughout all my problems. I still had God—I still had my kids—I still had Dante. I still had a lot of things. Most importantly, I had my sanity. I knew I'd make it.

Epilog

This fall I'll be going out with Bing Crosby again, and I'll also have achieved a great deal of personal satisfaction in the release of my autobiography. Writing it was almost the equivalent of going through a period of mini-therapy again—not always easy, but an immensely rewarding experience.

My present and my future are tied up in knots of happiness with those whom I love and who are a part of me. I want to share with you some of the things that are a part of my future —the people who really count, who are with me always:

Miguel will be going in February to Fordham University. Miguel, as I've said, looks exactly like his father. He has a gentleness that is very moving to me. Miguel is the only one of my children in whom I can still see all the phases of his growing up. I can look into his eyes and see the same eyes that I looked at when he was a little baby. He loves music, and we have exactly the same sense of humor. We have so many things in common that it's almost unfair for anybody else to be in the room or in the world with us because we also talk shorthand to each other.

My daughter Maria Providencia will be starting Catholic University in Washington this fall and will probably have her own apartment in the same building where my Aunt Chris lives. That makes me feel good. There's a feeling I have with Maria—I think she's the loveliest thing I've ever seen. She also has an ability that I envy tremendously: She can take care of almost any situation. It's as though she were born full-grown, she is so mature. Yet, like me, she has a sense of fantasy. The two of us can discuss the most ridiculously far-out things and laugh over them. We react the same way to other people's words. But she has another quality—her expressions change so many times in a minute. I watch those expressions change and I see that there's a bit of Betty there, too.

Gabriel will be going to Pepperdine College in the fall, so he will be living at home. I cannot tell you what satisfaction that gives me. I've never asked Gabriel to do anything he hasn't done. I suppose of all people in the world, Gabri has been the nicest to me. I'm very proud of him . . . and I love him very much!

Monsita Teresa will be starting Skidmore this year. and looking at Monsita is like looking at myself. She looks exactly like me. It's like looking back twenty years through a mirror, except she's freer—more in charge of her own life and much more able to show love or to show whatever she is feeling. So it is like looking at what I might have been. Monsita is loving —and very funny.

Rafael is a senior at Beverly Hills High School and I still have him at home. There's never been a doubt in my mind that he would be an actor. He's been acting all his life. He has my coloring—blond and blue-eyed—but speaks perfect Spanish, so he is kind of a happy combination of the two of us—Joe and me. As I've told you, Rafi has great drive—he's a very purposeful young man—and I can almost hear the other four chiming in my ear, "...and he's your baby!"

Yes, it's true. Because he's the last, I'm enjoying him in a very special way.

And then, there is Dante. Always there. Always supportive. Always loving. Always showing me another side. If I have a problem he can make me laugh, getting me through the most difficult situations with very little obvious effort.

I don't really think of my children as ever leaving home. We may not live in the same place, but we will always be just as close-knit as Betty, Nicky, Gail and I always have been. I think my children have one advantage we didn't have. They have a home to come back to. I look forward to having them come home and to having grandchildren in "this ole house."